A Confederate
in Congress

A Confederate in Congress

The Civil War Treason Trial of Benjamin Gwinn Harris

Joshua E. Kastenberg

McFarland & Company, Inc., Publishers
Jefferson, North Carolina

LIBRARY OF CONGRESS CATALOGUING-IN-PUBLICATION DATA

Names: Kastenberg, Joshua E., 1967– author.
Title: A confederate in congress : the Civil War treason trial of
    Benjamin Gwinn Harris / Joshua E. Kastenberg.
Description: Jefferson, North Carolina : McFarland & Company, Inc.,
    Publishers, 2016. | Includes bibliographical references and index.
Identifiers: LCCN 2016039860 | ISBN 9781476664897 (softcover :
    acid free paper) ∞
Subjects: LCSH: Harris, Benjamin G. (Benjamin Gwinn), 1806–1895—
    Trials, litigation, etc. | Trials (Treason)—Washington (D.C.) | Military courts—Washington (D.C.) | Slavery—Law and legislation—
    Maryland, Southern—History. | Secession—Maryland—History. |
    United States—History—Civil War, 1861–1865. | United States—
    Politics and government—Civil War, 1861–1865. | United States.
    Congress—Officials and employees—Biography.
Classification: LCC KF223.H376 K37 2016 | DDC 345.73/0231—dc23
LC record available at https://lccn.loc.gov/2016039860

ISBN (print) 978-1-4766-6489-7
ISBN (ebook) 978-1-4766-2655-0

BRITISH LIBRARY CATALOGUING DATA ARE AVAILABLE

© 2016 Joshua E. Kastenberg. All rights reserved

*No part of this book may be reproduced or transmitted in any form
or by any means, electronic or mechanical, including photocopying
or recording, or by any information storage and retrieval system,
without permission in writing from the publisher.*

Front cover: Benjamin Gwinn Harris in his last years (Saint Mary's
Historical Society)

Printed in the United States of America

*McFarland & Company, Inc., Publishers
    Box 611, Jefferson, North Carolina 28640
        www.mcfarlandpub.com*

To my fellow judge advocates

Table of Contents

Preface   1

Introduction   4

1. The Origins of a Maryland Secessionist   17
2. Harris and Secession, 1861–1863   40
3. Congress and the War   63
4. "A damning speech," the Roots of a Trial   84
5. The Democratic Party Convention of 1864   106
6. The Military Prosecution of a Congressman   125
7. Aftermath of the Trial, 1865–1892   147

Conclusion   166

Chapter Notes   171

Bibliography   187

Index   197

Preface

Benjamin Gwinn Harris first entered my knowledge in 2005 when I researched a biography of the Army officer who prosecuted him in a military trial. That officer, Colonel William Winthrop, had many admirable traits, including the belief that the color of one's skin should not be a basis for inequality before the law. Harris, a congressman and a slave owner from Maryland, deeply held an opposite belief and until his death in 1895 he worked to prevent African Americans from becoming participants in the political and economic life of his state if not the country. Harris was not very well liked by many of his contemporaries in Congress, but hundreds of his constituents in the southern counties of Maryland supported him. I tried to write an article on Harris in tandem with my book on Winthrop. The Winthrop biography was published in 2009, but the article on Harris was never completed. Harris' personal collections, now housed at the Maryland Historical Society, are small in comparison to those of the nation's legislative giants of the Civil War era such as Thaddeus Stevens, Benjamin Wade, or Schuyler Colfax. This made an article, let alone a book, on Harris difficult. But because Harris was an outspoken opponent of Lincoln and had been prosecuted in a military trial, I worked on hunches and searched the historic collections of his contemporaries. In this regard, I would like to acknowledge the Saint Mary's Historical Society as well as the Maryland Historical Society, and, of course, the archivists in the Library of Congress Manuscript Division.

Harris advocated a belief system that is antithetical to modern justice, and of course he was hardly alone in this. He was an ally to the Copperheads in Congress, though he was overshadowed by anti–Lincoln congressmen such as George Pendleton and Fernando Wood. Yet he does deserve a biography for several reasons, though this book is not simply a biography of Harris, and certainly not a laudatory biography. I have attempted to dispassionately analyze the willingness of his supporters to embrace the twin institutions of slavery and racism that are so noxious to humanity. The slavery and bigotry which Harris espoused were not his creation. These institutions originated long before his birth and the racism he championed lasted generations after his death. The reason for a dispassionate approach is two-fold. A historian is supposed to approach a topic in this manner, and Harris was a lawyer. He, and his peers, insisted that slavery and racial codes were constitutionally sound and therefore required in the law. Indeed, the legal codes which subjugated African Americans were, to these men, necessary to preserve a natural order. This statement about the law, slavery, and racism is hardly an original thought of mine. That said, a study of Harris should add to the weight of historic evidence that the Civil War was indeed fought over slavery, that racial barriers in the south were not enacted because of a widespread animus to Reconstruction but rather because of a deeply held need to preserve a white hierarchy, and that the studies of the Civil War, Reconstruction, and even the pre–Civil War are not yet complete. For instance, Democrats in Maryland's southern counties repeatedly tried to convince him to run for Congress from the time he left Congress in 1867 until his death in 1895, and given that his primary focus was on disenfranchising African American males and having the federal government compensate his state's former slave owners for the loss of their "property," the men who encouraged Harris to run for office either embraced his arguments or tolerated his racism.

And yet there were aspects of Harris which could be considered "on the right side" of the Constitution. He fought against the attempts of the American Party—known as the Know-Nothings—to restrict religious liberty and spread intolerance of Catholic and Jewish immigrants. He also argued that restrictions on freedom of speech and freedom of the press were a vast step toward tyranny. Yet his argument was not unblemished. Like many pro-slavery men, before the war, he tried to restrict the mails in Maryland against abolitionist literature. Nonetheless, he pointed out a critical challenge that confronts us in the present. How far can a president, whether or not Congress acquiesces, direct federal agencies to intrude on the privacy of citizens during crisis times? This is an important question not withstanding that in the Civil War there was a real "enemy from within," and Harris championed this enemy.

By the time this book is in print, I will be a retired Air Force officer. My last duty was as a military judge where I tried to ensure the fairness of more than two hundred courts-martial, and protect the due process rights of service-members while recognizing the government's interest and authority to prosecute persons alleged to have committed crimes. Before my judicial tenure, I was assigned to the headquarters of the Air Force Judge Advocate General's Corps where I assisted in the repeal of 10 U.S.C. 652, better known as "Don't ask, don't tell." This was a fascinating duty as some politicians and retired senior military leaders insisted that permitting openly gay service-members would destroy military efficiency. They wrongly feared that "the natural order" would be upended. But no discernible impact resulting from the repeal in either society or the military can truly be discovered. Before this duty, I was on a one-year tour of duty in Iraq. This was my second time stationed there (the first was in 2006). I have also served as an advisor on international law matters, national security law and the protection of the Department of Defense's cyberspace. And I prosecuted and defended service-members in courts-martial. This is a brief synopsis of a twenty-year career, with one exception. After the September 11 attacks, I also advised, from a relatively junior level, the law and regulations governing the use of the military to fight terrorism. I witnessed some very bright judge advocates, including general officers, urge restraint against the zeal of political appointees who espoused a unitary executive theory in concluding that a president while serving as commander in chief had the authority to unilaterally act with little regard to legal constraints, particularly in regard to international laws and norms. While the law today is far more voluminous than in Lincoln's time, the tensions which existed during the Civil War had an analog to our time. For the record, I join with the senior officers in condemning torture and was appalled at the belief that the law of war was a "suggestive nicety." Mostly, I was impressed by my peers who believed that neither due process nor individual and civil rights protections are as malleable as the adherents of the unitary executive theory have made these rights out to be. These uniformed lawyers are unique. They could have left the military and increased their salaries, but they decided to serve a cause much larger than themselves and their bank accounts. I will miss them. It is for this reason that I dedicate this book to the judge advocates, civilian attorneys, and paralegals in the United States Air Force that I had the privilege to work alongside of for more two decades.

Introduction

On May 2, 1865, the Army prosecuted Benjamin Gwinn Harris, a United States citizen and resident of Maryland, in a military trial. Called a "military commission," the trial mirrored a court-martial in almost all its aspects. Military authorities accused Harris of aiding and abetting the Confederacy and charged him with "harboring and protecting" two paroled Confederate prisoners of war, providing them money, and encouraging them to continue fighting against the United States. The two specific offenses the War Department alleged Harris violated were enumerated under the Articles of War, rather than the civil laws or even the Constitutional offense of treason, and they were purely military in nature. Even if Harris were guilty of these offenses, in 1807 Congress enacted the Articles of War to only apply to soldiers. But, by 1865 and without an express congressional mandate, the jurisdiction of the Articles of War had expanded to civilians. Like a number of citizens during the Civil War, Harris, once accused of treasonous activity, was swept into a military trial, despite the existence of fully functioning civil courts which would have provided him with full Constitutional protections under a rubric of due process. What set Harris' trial apart from almost all of the other military prosecutions of civilians was his status. He was a sitting United States congressman, overwhelmingly re-elected to a second term by his district.[1]

Most of the nation's major newspapers and many of its smaller newspapers reported on Harris' arrest and trial. Nationally, he was not a sympathetic figure, and in our times, he would likely be a considered an unelectable politician with a belief system despicable to all but the most ardent bigot. In his own time, a majority of congressional Republicans and many pro-war Democrats approved of his arrest and trial. Likewise, anti-war Democrats outside of his district did not rally to his defense, though there were two main reasons for their lack of support. With the Union's victory in 1865, there were few anti-war political leaders who believed they could support Harris without incurring a similar fate. And, many congressional Democrats were fighting for their livelihoods after being swept from office in the 1864 election. Secondly, because of Harris' often vitriolic conduct in the House of Representatives, he made a number of enemies in his own party. While several anti-war congressmen called President Abraham Lincoln a tyrant and warned the populace that he intended to subvert freedom of speech, Harris went further in openly proclaiming the justness of the south's cause. At one point, he accused presidential candidate General George B. McClellan of treason to the Constitution. In 1864, he supported another congressman facing expulsion from the House of Representatives after that congressman expressed his desire to see an end to the bloodshed by giving the south its independence. When Lincoln was assassinated, Harris showed no public remorse or sorrow. Indeed, he compared John Wilkes Booth's act favorably against the actions of John Brown some five years earlier. To Harris, Booth was a patriot and Brown a villain.[2]

Prior to 1865, Harris' most unlawful act appears to have been permitting Marylanders who fought in the Confederate Army to quietly stay at his house during their journeys through Union lines. He also, on one occasion, clandestinely let a Confederate official stay at his house. Unlike the majority of so-called "Copperheads" and "Peace Democrats" who were both virulently racist and anti-war, Harris was an unabashed supporter of the Confederacy, an outspoken proponent of slavery and racial superiority, and he voted against every bill to increase the size of the Army, raise revenue, or in any way boost the chances of a Union victory. He was, in short, the only "Confederate" serving in the federal government.[3]

Yet Harris was also not, at the time, a hero to the Confederacy. Although he was a champion of the Kentucky and Virginia "Resolutions"— the two documents written by Thomas Jefferson and James Madison which articulated the right of state secession—he did not act on his beliefs as fully as did some of his brethren. A number of Marylanders left the Union and served in the southern armies. He remained in Congress, protected his investments in slaves, and looked out for his other economic interests. He did not, at any time, fund the southern war effort or ever threaten to leave the Union. He did, however, during the five years of conflict, publicly argue for permitting the southern states to secede as a matter of law and claimed that slavery had a moral and biblical basis. So while Harris was emotionally "a Confederate," he did not take up arms against the Union.

The "great political trials" of alleged reactionaries, revolutionaries, or treasonous actors in American history such as Fernando Nicola Sacco and Bartolomeo Vanzetti, Thomas Mooney, and Julius and Ethel Rosenberg were all accompanied by far-reaching news-media coverage and enormous public interest. After the trials and sentences of these individuals, wide sections of the population rallied against what they considered an injustice. For instance, in the 1920s, future Supreme Court justice Felix Frankfurter argued that the Sacco and Vanzetti and Mooney trials were farces. Members of Britain's Parliament, the Vatican, and noted scientist Albert Einstein also protested this trial. Much of the literature on the Rosenberg trial espouses that the prosecution was in error and the trial unfair. Added to this mix are the opinions of Supreme Court justices Hugo Black, William O. Douglas, and Frankfurter which show that high-placed government officials were willing to argue that the Rosenbergs did not receive a fair trial. Of course, federal judges serve with a qualified life-tenure and the three justices may have been more willing to articulate an opinion than would a congressman who faced elections. But Harris' trial was different. No figure of prominence rallied to Harris.[4]

Harris' trial did not occur in a vacuum. The war was a life or death struggle for the nation's survival, and Lincoln, as well as many congressional Republicans, approached the war as such, to the consternation of conservative politicians and their supporters. In early 1861, Lincoln contemplated arresting the Maryland state legislature to prevent a state vote on secession. In September of that year, the Army arrested several state legislators who intended to press the secession vote forward. Anti-war Democrats and others were arrested throughout the war for their perceived support to the Confederacy. The 1863 New York Draft Riots were roundly believed to have been fomented by pro–Confederate agents. Other attempts at draft enforcement often resulted in a violent public response followed by the War Department's imposing a *de facto* martial law. Events such as arson in New York and Chicago were thought to have been caused by an "enemy from within." Even a prominent Union general with democratic political leanings was prosecuted after being accused of intentionally failing to follow orders and costing the Union a horrific defeat at the Second Battle of Manassas. The underlying reason for the general's court-martial was that the secretary of war and other ranking Union officials believed the general was sympathetic to the Confederacy. By 1864 the Union Army was used not only to defeat the Confederacy but also to "police" the nation.[5]

Introduction

Military Arrests and Trials in the Civil War

In spite of his status as a congressman and the extensive newspaper coverage at the time, Harris' trial was not the most controversial or publicized military trial or military arrest of the war. At least five other military arrests are far more embedded in studies of the nation's legal history than Harris'. However, four of these trials influenced Harris' trial as well as his political legacy.

Early in the war, Union soldiers seized John Merryman in Baltimore for the purpose of prosecuting him in a military trial. While acting under the orders of Maryland's governor Thomas H. Hicks, he oversaw the destruction of railroad bridges to prevent Pennsylvania militia troops from entering Baltimore. These acts led to him being accused of treason. As a result of a martial law decree, Lincoln believed Merryman lacked any judicial recourse to challenge his military detention. Merryman appealed under a writ of *habeas* to Chief Justice Roger Baldwin Taney, who in turn issued a writ ordering the military to hand over Merryman to the federal court. Lincoln ignored Taney's order, and Army officials kept Merryman in military custody. For Lincoln this was an easy decision because Taney had acted in his capacity as a circuit judge, and the Supreme Court itself had not issued a decision. After Taney's order, Attorney General Edward Bates went so far as to issue a formal legal opinion stating that, as the nation's commander in chief, Lincoln possessed the authority to hold citizens deemed dangerous to the Union in custody. The government never prosecuted Merryman and he was eventually released, but Lincoln's actions were a clear statement as to his belief in the Executive Branch's sweeping wartime powers.[6]

Two years after the arrest of Merryman, Clement Vallandigham, a former congressman and an outspoken critic of Lincoln's administration, was arrested and prosecuted in a military court. Vallandigham believed that secession and slavery were neither unconstitutional nor immoral. The two-day trial, which took place beginning May 6, 1863, occurred without Lincoln's knowledge, and Vallandigham's conviction caught Lincoln and Secretary of War Edwin Stanton by surprise. Like Harris, Vallandigham did not violate a civil statute. Rather, while in Ohio, he publicly spoke against the war and encouraged his listeners not to take part in it. Vallandigham's speech ran afoul of an order issued by General Ambrose Burnside who was in command of the Union's military forces in Ohio. One of the most important aspects of this episode was that Vallandigham's speech, arrest, and trial occurred in a northern state whose population was largely loyal to the Union and where the civilian criminal courts were fully functioning. The military court sentenced Vallandigham to be confined for the duration of the war. Lincoln and Stanton determined, however, that the trial and sentence were an embarrassment to the presidency and ordered Vallandigham to be conveyed to the Confederacy. Vallandigham would ultimately appeal to the Supreme Court, and although the justices initially determined to listen to his appeal, they also decided that the federal courts had no jurisdiction over a military trial. This decision was an extension of an 1857 decision, *Dynes v. Hoover*, in which the justices determined that the only judicial oversight of military trials that the federal courts possessed was over the question of jurisdiction. Thus, the federal courts could not consider an appeal which alleged that a court-martial was unfair, but the courts could consider a claim that the Army or Navy did not possess jurisdiction over the prosecuted person. In peacetime, this standard of jurisdiction presented an easy question, but not so during the war. That is, had Vallandigham been court-martialed as a civilian during a time of peace, the Court would have overturned the conviction and ordered his release. In 1863 the Court in *Ex Parte Vallandigham* determined that military trials of civilians existed in the same category as courts-martial. This categorization would last until another decision titled *Ex Parte Milligan* was issued in 1866. For reasons later noted, *Ex Parte Vallandigham* was unsurprising.[7]

Civil War era and legal historians are familiar with Vallandigham's case, and law school graduates certainly should be. Historically Vallandigham's prosecution has been proclaimed, depending on one's view of Lincoln, as a case of despotism in which the population's civil rights were trampled, or as evidence of Lincoln's stellar leadership in taking risky but necessary actions against an internal enemy to ensure the Union and the Constitution survived. The administration's actions in the Merryman and Vallandigham cases had a direct relevancy to Harris' conduct and arrest. Harris publicly stated that both trials proved that Lincoln sought to become a dictator, and the administration's conduct provided him with the fodder he believed he needed to justify his continual efforts at obstructing the war effort. At the same time, the Army's judge advocate general, Joseph Holt, concluded that *Vallandigham* legitimized Harris' arrest and trial. Holt was to become Harris' prosecutor from afar in 1865, and Harris had come to his attention as early as 1862.

The military trial of the Lincoln assassination conspirators was politically controversial at its time, and it has remained so for a number of reasons. Stanton and Holt were pilloried for their role in the military commission. During the trial, Holt unknowingly used perjured evidence, and both Stanton and Holt zealously sought to avoid a criminal trial in federal court with a civilian jury. Instead, the two men demanded a military trial by arguing that the assassination of a wartime president was a crime under the laws of war. Some of the trial was conducted in secrecy and there were other unique aspects to it. Holt tried to couple Mary Surratt and the other conspirators to a greater conspiracy originating with Jefferson Davis, Confederate secretary of war Judah Benjamin, and other leading Confederate government officers. Harris' name was brought forth in witness testimony in an effort to link other witnesses to overt southern sympathizers. This "grand conspiracy" was an untenable stretch, and although there was a Canadian-based connection to the assassination in the sense that Surratt's son had been a Confederate courier who conveyed messages to Confederate officials in Canada, there was no proof that the conspiracy extended beyond John Wilkes Booth, Surratt's son, and the others on trial. Initially, much of the public's criticism of the trial was centered on Mary Surratt's execution. She was a woman and a Catholic, and her execution gave rise to a dual issue of Victorian morality and charges of anti–Catholicism. Additionally, the fact that some of the military "jurors" in her case sought clemency later led to a fight between President Andrew Johnson on one side and Holt and Stanton on the other. Johnson claimed that Holt hid the fact that some of the officers had voted for a recommendation of clemency and Holt countered that Johnson knew of the recommendation but willingly ignored it. Surratt appealed to a federal judge prior to her execution on the basis that the military did not possess jurisdiction over her. However, her attempts at being freed from military custody were unsuccessful. Indeed, in what was almost a replay of *Merryman*, a United States district court judge named Andrew Wylie ordered the Army to produce Surratt and Johnson responded by suspending the writ of *habeas corpus*. The commanding general of the capitol, Winfield Scott Hancock, then refused to obey Wylie's order. Harris would later note that while Hancock was a Democrat, he would refuse to support his presidential candidacy.[8]

The military trial of Henry Wirz, the commandant of Andersonville Prison, was less controversial than that of the conspirators, and it has remained, with some exceptions, accepted by legal scholars as a justified result. During the war, thousands of captured Union soldiers housed at the Confederate prison died of injuries and maltreatment. Wirz's trial became a well-studied event. As in the trial of Mary Surratt and her fellow conspirators, there were allegations of the use of perjured testimony.

Another criticism had to do with the *ex post facto* nature of some of the charges. However, beginning in the twentieth century, a number of the world's foremost international law scholars concluded that Wirz's trial was an instrumental legal marker in establishing the doctrine of "command responsibility" into the modern law of war. Wirz's trial served as a basis for the post–World War II trials of Nazis at Nuremburg and Japanese war criminals in Tokyo, and was considered an important precedent in the Vietnam War court-martial and appeals of Lieutenant William Laws Calley.[9]

Following the war, the Supreme Court issued *Ex Parte Milligan*, which has since curtailed military authority over civilians, and more than one justice has viewed the decision as a critical guarantor of individual rights. Indeed, across the jurisprudential spectrum from the conservative Chief Justice William H. Rehnquist to his ideological opposite Justice William O. Douglas, *Milligan* has been considered as one of the more important rulings for individual rights in the Court's history. The path that Lambdin Milligan and his cohorts' appeals took to the Supreme Court is not only important in contextualizing why the War Department arrested and prosecuted Harris in a military trial, but also in illustrating the passions of both the ardent Unionists and pro-slavery and pro-secessionist northerners during the Civil War.[10]

On August 16, 1864, Union agents raided an Indianapolis business office. There, they discovered evidence of a plan led by one Harrison H. Dodd, an Indiana native, to free Confederate prisoners of war and cause havoc in Indiana. Dodd was already well known to the Lincoln Administration as a leader of the Sons of Liberty, a pro-southern organization. He planned for an uprising to occur contemporaneously with the 1864 Democrat Party Convention in Chicago. Prior to the war, Dodd was also a prominent member in the state Democrat party, and his political beliefs aligned with Harris.[11]

Dodd's cohorts included Indiana men of local importance such as Milligan, William A. Bowles, Stephen Horsey, Andrew Humphreys, James Wilson, and Horace Heffren. None of these men were adept at keeping their plans secretive. Like Harris, they publicly espoused the principles of the Kentucky and Virginia Resolves of 1789. (Wilson and Heffren were later released as defendants in exchange for testimony against the others.) Three decades prior to the Civil War, Milligan tested for the bar in Ohio and the state's supreme court graded him above Edwin Stanton. In 1864 Milligan unsuccessfully ran for governor in the Democrat primary but lost to James McDonald, who in turn lost to Oliver Morton, the Republican incumbent.

On September 17, 1864, General Alvin Hovey, the commander of the District of Indiana, convened a complex military commission to prosecute Dodd and his followers. In actuality, there were two commissions, one against Dodd and one formed to prosecute the others, but Dodd escaped to Canada and evaded his trial. The charges against Dodd, Milligan, Bowles, and Horsey included conspiracy, plotting rebellion, and violations of the laws of war. It is also worth noting that before the war, Hovey was the chief judge of the Supreme Court of Indiana and a staunch Unionist. The records of the military trials show that all of the defendants objected to the jurisdiction of the military to convene such trials against civilians in the state of Indiana. The government's attorney, a judge advocate named Major Henry Burnett who later assisted Holt in the prosecution of Surratt and other conspirators, countered that the trial was permissible as the nation was in a war for its survival and the battlefield extended into the Union state of Indiana as a result of the defendants' anti–Union actions. Burnett cited *Vallandigham* as proof of this point. One reality of the military trial was that, unlike in a civil trial, it was doubtful that any of the officers sitting in judgment would have a hidden sympathy for the Confederacy.[12]

This point was not lost on Chief Justice Rehnquist who, in 1998, noted that the only practical means to secure a conviction in Indiana was in a military court. At any rate, the military commission sentenced Dodd, *in absentia*, and Milligan, along with Bowles and Horsey, to death. None of the men would ultimately be killed, and by 1868 all were free. Indeed, Milligan would not only re-establish a successful law practice, he would ironically become a Republican and tutor Thomas Marshall who would later become vice president under Woodrow Wilson. This is because in 1866 the Supreme Court, in *Milligan*, determined that as long as the civil courts functioned, the government could not prosecute citizens in military trials. In 1871, Milligan successfully sued Hovey for false imprisonment, thereby creating a precedent for citizens to sue the government on the basis of a claim of unlawful arrest.[13]

In April 1865, Harris, as a sitting congressman, was more important to Stanton or Holt than Dodd or Milligan, despite what would later occur in *Milligan* to reverse this importance. For reasons later noted, if the Judge Advocate General's Department could prosecute Harris in a military trial, then the War Department's leadership believed it could prosecute Jefferson Davis and the Confederacy's other prominent civilian leaders. Indeed, both Stanton and Holt believed that by removing persons they considered traitors they could prevent a resumption of war and enable the Union to permanently survive. Harris, and others, would vehemently and sincerely proclaim that the War Department with Congress' acquiescence violated the Constitution. With equally forceful argument and sincerity Harris' prosecutors argued the constitutionality and necessity of their actions.

Benjamin Gwinn Harris in American History

In addition to serving as a political, social, and legal history, an examination of Harris' life is helpful to understanding several paradoxes of American history. He was a slave-owner who championed the rights of religious minorities and decried a large federal government as a subjugator of individual rights. He claimed to oppose limits on freedom of speech, but prior to the war, he took part in efforts to prohibit abolitionists from using the mails to reach audiences in Maryland. After the war, and indeed, until he died on the eve of the twentieth century, he sought to use the Constitution as a basis for having Congress and the courts recompense former slave-owners for the loss of their "property." He also tried repeatedly to have his home state of Maryland disenfranchise African Americans from any influence in the politics of the state, but then argued for former Confederate soldiers to have their rights to vote and hold political office quickly restored. Although he had been convicted in a well-reported military trial, he retained his political influence not only in Maryland but also was considered for further public service. Finally, perhaps, his absence from historical works has contributed to the abilities of a few revisionist writers who are motivated by reasons other than dispassionate historic accuracy to claim that the Civil War was not fought over slavery or that Reconstruction caused southern politicians and voters to enact "Jim Crow" laws and terrorize African Americans after Reconstruction came to an end.

Historian William Marvel, a scholar of the Civil War and prodigious writer who recently authored a detailed though unflattering biography of Secretary of War Stanton, earlier observed that modern scholars "find it irresistible to condemn the Southern advocates of secession because of the obnoxious institution that underlay their impulse." Marvel goes on to question whether, in 1861, secession was unconstitutional, and if so, whether Lincoln, his cabinet, and the War Department—the civilian administration which oversaw the Union Army—had the right to combat secession with "equally unconstitutional measures." These are interesting questions, and although this book is study of Harris, the mindset of

Maryland's slave-owners, and the nature of both bigotry and dissent, this book also addresses Marvel's questions.[14]

Between May 1, 1865, and the end of that month, major national newspapers including the *New York Times, Philadelphia Inquirer, Baltimore Sun, Chicago Tribune*, and even the *San Francisco Chronicle* reported on Harris' trial. Dozens of smaller newspapers reported on the trial as well. Harris' trial is now largely forgotten, in part because he spent less than one month in jail before returning to Congress. Although the military trial found him guilty and sentenced him to three years' imprisonment and prohibited him from government service for life, after significant lobbying from former postmaster general Montgomery Blair, President Andrew Johnson remitted the sentence. Harris returned to Congress when it reconvened, and he left public service on his own accord. He could have challenged the War Department's jurisdiction and run for re-election, and he would have likely won. Even the most ardent proponents of Executive Branch supremacy today who espouse what has come to be known as the "unitary executive doctrine" would likely concede that the Executive Branch does not possess the unilateral power to bar someone from being elected to Congress. Since 1865, the Supreme Court has more than intimated that there is a limit to the authority of the Executive Branch to dictate the membership of the Legislative Branch.[15]

A greater reason Harris' trial eludes scholarly legal and historical analysis has to do with the fact that the trial of the "Lincoln assassination conspirators" consumed much of the public's attention in the summer of 1865. After all, Harris had not killed anyone, and to much of the public he was merely an obnoxious outspoken critic of Lincoln and the Republicans. The greatest reason of all for Harris' current obscurity, however, was that by freeing Harris, President Johnson avoided the spectacle of a congressman imprisoned by the military appealing to the Supreme Court, and unlike Milligan, Harris did not file suit against the Executive Branch. Thus, the world would not see an *Ex Parte Harris* or *Harris v. Stanton*, alongside *Ex Parte Milligan*.

In the major historic works on the Civil War and American legal history, in spite of vast analysis on treason trials, Copperheads, and Reconstruction, the Harris trial is hardly ever mentioned. For instance, Frank Klement, the prior generation's historian who pioneered studies on dissent in the Civil War and argued Lincoln conflated the threat northern dissenters posed, did not note the fact that the military prosecuted a sitting congressman. Jessica Weber, in her recent study *Copperheads*—which effectively serves as a counterweight to Klement's conclusions—does not mention Harris. Nor does Joanna Cowden, in her treatise *Heaven Will Frown on Such a Cause as This: Six Democrats Who Opposed Lincoln's War*, highlight Harris. Harris' name comes up in Jack Waugh's study on the election of 1864, *Reelecting Lincoln: The Battle for the 1864 Presidency*, but Waugh presents Harris as nothing more than an obnoxious gadfly at the Chicago Democratic convention. And surprisingly, in Mark Neely's oft-cited exceptional work *The Fate of Liberty: Abraham Lincoln and Civil Liberties*, the Harris trial is not mentioned. Noting the absence of Harris in these books is not intended as a criticism of these scholars. All of these authors significantly contributed to a greater understanding of the history of civil liberties and political development in the United States. But certainly the inclusion of Harris' arrest and trial would have added to their analyses.[16]

That said, despite Harris' obscurity, there are other important reasons for a history of both the man and the trial. The military's prosecution of Harris provides historians, and military and constitutional law scholars, with an insight into the high-water mark of the Executive Branch's assertion of its supremacy through its military authority. It can hardly be disagreed that the willingness of the Executive Branch to prosecute an elected member of the Legislative Branch in a military tribunal placed the Constitution in peril. This type of arrest and trial had occurred in the monarchal and post-revolutionary European states, particularly after 1848. In the last two-hundred and fifty years, dictatorships and resurgent monarchies were often created by arresting elected legislators. In France in 1851, Napoleon III accomplished a forced transition from the Second Republic to an empire in part by arresting French legislators. From the early American Republic's founding, there was a fear of standing armies based on the ability of the nation's executive to compel the other branches of government and erode freedoms. In 1956, noted military historian Walter Millis claimed that by the turn of the twentieth century, public fears of a standing army had dissipated completely, and if the constitutional debates on a standing army were to have occurred after World War II, there would have been little worry over the military's subservience to the civil government. Professor Millis did not note that military trials over civilians were plentiful during the Civil War. Had the military trial of a congressman been permitted to stand, one would have to wonder whether Millis' argument would remain viable.[17]

In addition to the trial and its constitutional import, a study on Harris also provides historians with an analysis of Maryland politics during the Civil War and Reconstruction. Maryland was a critical border state for the Union. A section of its population enthusiastically voted for Harris to represent them in Congress. He promised to protect slavery as well as maintain a legal structure which relegated African Americans to a lower status than whites. He was outspoken against the war and he campaigned against Lincoln and the Union Army which, in his terms, occupied southern Maryland much as a conquering army occupied captured enemy territory. He embodied the political, social, and cultural beliefs of a region's majority population. Reconstruction did not apply to Maryland in the same manner it did to the southern states, but emancipation affected the state's economy and social hierarchy. After leaving Congress, Harris would take part in the exclusion of African Americans from the political process and thereby secure the state's economic prosperity for whites only.

Finally, a study of Harris adds to the political history of both the federal government and the local political history of Maryland. The list of politicians who interacted with him included presidents Abraham Lincoln, Andrew Johnson and James A. Garfield, presidential aspirant Winfield Scott Hancock, governors Augustus Bradford and Thomas Pratt, former postmaster general Montgomery Blair, and congressmen Alexander Long, Fernando Wood, George Pendleton, and Samuel Cox. He was also acquainted with noted pro-southern journalist Manton Marble and a host of other newspapermen.

Thus, this book is not simply a biography of Congressman Benjamin Gwinn Harris, nor is it solely about a single trial. It is also not relegated to a study of the due process deficits in Civil War military tribunals. It is a legal history bridging the Civil War and what followed, and it is a cultural and social history of a part of a state whose white residents overtly supported a champion of slavery and racism. That is, it is a holistic legal history with the understanding that legal history is not simply a recitation of when laws are enacted, modified, and rescinded. Nor is legal history a relegated to itemizing and analyzing court decisions. As one of the leading scholars of American legal history observed, it is a study of personalities, social forces, and laws.[18]

Conclusion

It is often said that the fairness of criminal justice can be measured by the trials of unpopular and repugnant defendants. Put another way, as Frankfurter once explained to fellow Supreme Court justice Sherman Minton, "it is a fair summary of history to say that the great safeguards of human liberty have most frequently been forged in controversies involving not very nice people." If the prosecution arm of government adheres to the letter of due process, or at least does not depart from normal procedure, then society as a whole can have some degree of confidence that the system of criminal justice is fair. Yet a trial can be fair where the prosecution ethically adheres to the letter of the procedural law and still be of questionable legality. Harris could not complain that his trial was deprived of the due process required of military trials at the time. He could, of course, challenge the jurisdiction of the military over him.[19]

The roots of this trial begin in antebellum Maryland, with the signing of the Constitution in 1789 in which the nation's founders compromised on the twin issues of slavery and equality. Just as slavery was the constant burning political issue after 1820, it was Harris' foremost concern. He supported the "peculiar institution," as his nemesis Lincoln coined it, and until his death in 1893, he believed that whites had wrongly been deprived of their property. In order to understand Harris, his political stature, and the Union's response to him, one has to first know something of southern Maryland and its place in national politics before, during, and after that conflict. Although residing in a border state, Harris and his supporters fit into a pro-slavery deep-south Democrat model of championing specified rights of white slave-owners, while limiting the right of free speech as it applied to slavery's opponents, ignoring the principle of a truly representative government of one vote per man, and disparaging the concept of universal freedom.[20]

In January 1868, a group of Maryland attorneys lobbied the state legislature to appoint Harris as a senator in an effort to provide a vote against the impeachment of Andrew Johnson. One of the attorneys, Jonathan Norris, informed his son in Nebraska that Harris, "a straight out repudiationist," was "their best hope" and then penned "the infamous nigger worshippers of New England who will come after us will not curse their infiledic revels in debauchery, may God arrest their wicked deeds." Harris would use similar language throughout his political career and after. This study on Harris, as distasteful as he is in our time, attempts to dispassionately explain why he and his supporters acted in their defiant manner by analyzing how they perceived the events of their time and how their belief systems were challenged by the other participants in those events.[21]

1

The Origins of a Maryland Secessionist

"If the black republicans should gain ascendancy, we are a doomed people and war will be inevitable."
—Martha Harris, diary entry for Tuesday, November 6, 1860

In 1858, Benjamin Gwinn Harris joined a group of southern Maryland slave owners who petitioned the state legislature to re-enslave the state's freedmen. By that time, Maryland's freedmen and slaves were almost equal in number. That is, there were roughly 80,000 freedmen and 80,000 slaves in the state. Harris and his fellow petitioners believed that the rising population of freedmen, particularly in the southern and coastal areas of the state, would invariably result in their slaves running away or an increase in slave rebellions such as Nat Turner's in 1831 in Virginia. As a well-known orator, Harris became a spokesman for the petitioning slave-owners and argued to the legislature that the state's freedmen either had to be forced northward, deported to Liberia, or re-enslaved within two years. He reminded the legislature that in 1845 over one hundred slaves left their plantations in southern Maryland and marched toward the Pennsylvania border where they intended to gain their freedom. Led by slaves named William Wheeler and Mark Caesar, the group came close to the Pennsylvania border, and they were armed with farm implements and a pistol. State militia forces stopped them and killed over a dozen of the freedom seekers near Rockville, Maryland. Wheeler was prosecuted in Charles County and sentenced to be executed. His attorney, John M.S. Causin, had served as one of Saint Mary's County's representatives in the House of Delegates, and then was elected as a congressman in 1843 as a Whig. However, his political career ended after the trial and he moved to Chicago. Caesar's trial ended in an acquittal, and in an action which can only be described as a blatant violation of the common law prohibition against double jeopardy, another jury convicted him and sentenced him to forty years in prison. The prosecution in Caesar's first trial charged that he was a slave involved in an insurrection, but at the second trial they captioned him as a freedman who unlawfully stoked an insurrection.[1]

None of Harris' slaves escaped, but there were over twenty in Saint Mary's County who joined Wheeler and Caesar. Unsurprisingly, the trials of the survivors and executions were quick and efforts were made to publicize the "crime" of seeking freedom. Although the re-enslavement movement might have had a large receptive audience in the immediate aftermath of either Nat Turner's Rebellion or the 1845 exodus, by 1858 it stood little chance of succeeding in Maryland. That said, the idea of viewing freedman as a menace to the state's social and economic order was not new. As Christopher Phillips points out in his study on Baltimore, *Freedom's Port: The African American Community of Baltimore, 1790–1860*, in 1827, Nicholas Brice, the chief judge of the Criminal Court of Baltimore, warned the governor that freedmen encouraged acts of insubordination amongst slaves.[2]

At the time of the 1858 re-enslavement movement, in Baltimore there were over 25,000 freedmen and less than 3,000 slaves. These freedmen worked as laborers and artisans and they significantly contributed to the city's economy in a manner which slaves could not do. Historian William W. Freehling, in his acclaimed *The Road to Disunion: Vol. II, Secessionists Triumphant*, noted that Baltimore's white residents had no interest in the re-enslavement movement. This was not the only reason for the failure of the movement to re-enslave freedmen. Non slave-owners, particularly in the western part of the state, already suspected that slave owners would gain further political power in the state, much as had occurred in Virginia where slaves were counted for voting apportionment purposes.[3]

In 1859, the re-enslavement movement held a convention in Baltimore in the hopes of generating further support for their cause. They argued that the creation of 80,000 new slaves would not make the rich slave-owners richer, but make slave-owners out of more whites. They also claimed that the failure to re-enslave freedmen would result in Maryland becoming a "free state," and then having to economically compete with their northern neighbors. The re-enslavers failed to address what their most ardent foe, Senator James Pearce, pointed out. The only means to re-enslave freedmen would be to rewrite the state laws governing manumission, thereby depriving the original owners the right to determine the status of their former slaves. Although abolitionists were hardly politically powerful, the majority of Marylanders would simply not tolerate the radical concept of re-enslavement.[4]

For a politician who would later decry Lincoln's wartime policies for "quashing the nation's freedoms," it might appear inexplicable that Harris was willing to break the manumission determinations of his fellow slave owners. Harris' own explanations, given after the Civil War, provide some answer for his adamancy to the point of disregarding the wishes of his fellow slave-owners. Certainly, Harris placed the status of African Americans, free or slave, at such a low position, that he would have never recognized freedmen as sharing in the same individual rights as the white population. However, in 1866 he urged that for the "greater good of the state" the manumission decisions of his fellow white slave-owners could no longer fully be respected because of changed political conditions in the two years before the war.

The Education and Development of a Maryland Slave-Owner

One of the earliest British settlements in the "New World" was in Saint Mary's County. The Maryland Colony was first settled in 1634, for the first fifty years of the its existence, the colonial government operated from Saint Mary's City, a small town within the county. From the time of its sanction by the British Crown through the independence of the colonies, a few families came to dominate the county, and their names resonated through Maryland's history. George Calvert's son Leonard established the colonial government, and from that time through the middle of the nineteenth century the Calvert family expanded through southern Maryland. Likewise, the Key family whose progeny included Philip Key, the speaker of the Maryland House of Delegates from 1790 to 1796, Philip Barton Key, an early American congressman and federal judge, and Francis Scott Key, the author of the national anthem during the War of 1812, resided in the county. The extended Key family would be involved in Maryland's state government through the twentieth century.

The Calverts and Keys were not, however, the only prominent political families. From 1790 until the beginning of the twentieth century, the names of Saint Mary's elected officials in the House of Delegates and Senate evidenced that early plantation owners and their progeny formed the county's power elite. In 1790, the first of Saint Mary's post–Constitution representatives included Thomas Bond, Henry James Carroll, George

Plater, Jr., and Philip Key who was elected as speaker of the House of Delegates, a position akin to the speaker of the United States House of Representatives. All of these men were slave owners, and all had fought in the war with Britain. One distinguishing feature about them had to do with their approach to religious tolerance. For instance, Carroll, a Catholic who owned over one hundred and fifty slaves, had married a Protestant from Virginia and this marriage was acceptable to the electorate. As for the others, Plater was a Federalist who supported President Washington, served as one of Maryland's early governors, and inherited a plantation from his grandfather that had begun construction in 1691. Plater's son, John Rousby Plater, served in the House of Delegates at various intervals from 1805 to 1819 only to be replaced by his son George Plater in 1820. In 1831 Charles J. Carroll, the grandson of Henry James Carroll, was elected to the House of Delegates. He also inherited twelve slaves from his father. Thomas H. Bond, the great grandson of Thomas Bond, represented Saint Mary's in Maryland's lower house as a Democrat after the Civil War. At one point the Bonds owned over one hundred slaves.[5]

Other Saint Mary's family names, including Abell, Neale, Greenwell, Gardiner, Blakistone, Stonestreet, Sothoron, and Maddox, are found in positions of government and economic power from 1634 through the end of the nineteenth century. Most of these families prospered, in large part, because of their land-holdings and slaves. The first mention of Maryland's slaves in a recoded court decision arose in Saint Mary's County. In 1696, the Maryland Court of Appeals determined it possessed the jurisdiction to decide whether a man named "Jeoffrey a Malatta" was a slave owned by Elizabeth Blakistone or a freed servant, but because Jeoffrey had fled, the issue could not be solved. Because of their desire to maintain their economic and political status, the majority of these families would support Lincoln's opponents during the war.[6]

Benjamin Gwinn Harris' southern Maryland roots were both deep and wide, not only because his predecessors could be counted as part of Maryland's "First Families," but also because his predecessors established themselves as politically and economically powerful planters in the state. He was able to trace his lineage to the fourteenth century court of the English king, Edward III. His father, Joseph Harris, was born in 1773 in Charles County, Maryland, and died in 1855. His mother, Susannah Reeder, was born in Saint Mary's County in 1782 and died in 1827 at the age of forty-four. In 1802 Susannah gave birth to their first child, Anne Elizabeth Harris, who moved to Charles County after her marriage to Nicholas Stonestreet, an attorney who later practiced law with Benjamin.

Anne Elizabeth died in 1879. Two years later Susannah gave birth to another girl named Maria Louisa. In 1825, Maria Louisa married Henry Greenfield Southron Key, a nephew of Francis Scott Key. Both of the men that the two Harris sisters married possessed the honorific title of colonel. Born in 1806, Benjamin Gwinn Harris was the third child of Joseph and Susannah, but he was not the last. Four sisters and a brother followed his birth. In 1809 Susannah gave birth to a daughter named Mary Eleanor, two years later she gave birth to a daughter named Martha, and two years later another daughter, Jane Harris, was born. Mary Eleanor married George Forbes, a prominent southern Maryland attorney, and their grandchild who also had the name of George Forbes was instrumental in discovering and preserving the Harris family lineage. In 1815, Susannah gave birth to another boy named Henry Reeder. Finally, in 1817, Susannah gave birth to a daughter named Josephine. All of the children, except Martha Harris and Jane Harris, survived past 1850, and all remained in southern Maryland. As of 1827 Joseph and Susannah Harris owned fourteen slaves.[7]

Joseph Harris' father, Thomas Harris, was born in Charles County in 1741 and fought in the Revolution against Great Britain, attaining the rank of colonel of militia. On his death in 1815, his will divided his properties among several siblings and children, including twelve slaves. One of his sons was commissioned as a naval officer during the War of 1812, while Joseph Harris was commissioned as a colonel in the state militia during that conflict. Joseph's mother, Anne Gwinn, was likewise born in Charles County in 1741. She gave birth to twelve children including one named Benjamin Gwinn, for whom Benjamin Gwinn Harris was named. Both Thomas Harris' and Anne Gwinn's parents were born in southern Maryland. Susannah Reeder's father, Henry Reeder, was born in Saint Mary's County in 1742 and died in 1784. Like Thomas Harris, Henry Reeder owned slaves. Henry Reeder's wife, Elizabeth Cunningham, was born in Charles County in 1738 and died in 1784. While the Harris lineage originated in England, Elizabeth Cunningham's parents were born in Scotland. By the time of Benjamin Gwinn Harris' birth, the family remained tied to the Protestant faith, but religion did not play a prominent part in his life. As of 1868 he attended an Episcopal church, but not with regularity.[8]

In 1850 Harris' estates, including Ellenborough, were valued at $38,000. This translates into an amount worth over $1,060,000 today. He had over forty-five slaves laboring at Ellenborough and owned several other properties throughout the county. In 1833 he married Martha Elizabeth Harris, his third cousin. In addition to Martha Elizabeth, his daughters Susan Ruth, born in 1839, and Ann Delia, born in 1838, also lived in

Ellenborough. Susan Ruth Harris married George Frederick Maddox, a lawyer who served as a state senator from 1868 to 1871, and championed Harris' positions against rights for African Americans. On the eve of the Civil War, in addition to Harris' family living at Ellenborough, four other Harrises resided there along with a "white insane pauper woman" named Emily Long. According the 1850 census, Ellenborough had a higher value than any other single property in the county to include a hotel.[9]

From its creation as a colony until the 1830s, Maryland was essentially a southern state. Its economy relied on slavery, and at the signing of the Constitution, enslaved African Americans outnumbered freedmen at a proportion of eleven to one. Yet, as a result of the Baltimore and Ohio, the nation's first railway, along with other industrial developments and demographic changes, the state increasingly became a "middle state" which, in addition to its agriculture, developed a vibrant industrial and import economy. By 1850, the slave population was only slightly higher than the population of freedmen. The state's original constitution which was enacted in 1776 created an upper and lower house for the legislative branch and a governor who was elected by the legislature rather than by a direct vote from the people. Under the original state constitution, only Christians were permitted to hold office, though in 1826 the bar against elected office was lifted against Jews. In 1837, the state's electoral districts were reapportioned and representation in the lower house of the state government was determined by the overall population regardless of whether African Americans were free or enslaved. The upper house was apportioned by county, in that each county elected a single state senator. While gradually the state permitted the inclusion of non-propertied white males and non–Christians in its political machinery, slave-owners in the south-eastern shore maintained a disproportionate political power as long as the slave population counted in establishing legislative districts.[10]

If, by 1850, northern and central Maryland evolved toward a more northern or industrial economy, Harris' home as well as those of his fellow slave-owners in Saint Mary's County remained staunchly southern. By 1854 its voters referred to their county as "the Democratic banner of Maryland." Over half of the residents in the county were African American and very few of these were freedmen. The county produced the majority of the state's tobacco and rice, and it contributed to the production of fish and orchard fruits. Wealthier citizens in Saint Mary's County, including Harris, also bred race horses. When one of Harris' race horses named Reliance died in 1858, the *Baltimore Sun* and *New York Times* reported the horse's passing. That Harris came from slave-owning family gave to him a special status mirroring the lesser British aristocracy in the sense that he was able to assert a greater political authority in the state than non-slave owning farmers. In spite of the political and social standing of slave owners, there were risks to themselves as well as the county's residents. In 1817 there was small-scale slave revolt in the county, but the slaves, who were armed with nothing more than farm implements and rocks, were subdued by armed patrols.[11]

Beginning with the ascendancy of Andrew Jackson to the presidency, Maryland's politics became increasingly polarized not only between the regions but also as a result of the growth of Baltimore as a powerful economic center to the state. As John T. Willis and Herbert Smith observed in their *Maryland Politics and Government: Democratic Dominance*, prior to Jackson's presidency, the majority of state leaders came from the "planter class." Almost two thirds of the state legislators came from rural southern Maryland and the Eastern Shore. But in the early 1840s, lawyers from Baltimore and other towns to the west began to enter the state government. The planters then transitioned to the Whig Party as a means for retaining their influence.[12]

In the 1828 election between John Quincy Adams and Jackson, over seventy percent of Maryland's eligible voters participated. In 1840, over eighty-five percent of the state's eligible men voted. Election results for the governor's office were close affairs. Between 1835 and 1850, the margin of victory averaged 745 votes. The Democrats held the governor's office for twelve of these fifteen years, but at the same time, for eleven of these years, Whig politicians held the majority in Maryland General Assembly. Baltimore served as the convention site for the Whig presidential nominations in 1832, 1844, and 1852. In 1860 the city served as the convention site for the Democrats who nominated Stephen A. Douglas, the southern Democrats who nominated John C. Breckenridge, and the Constitutional Union Party which nominated John C. Bell. Only the Republican Party was absent from Baltimore, though for good reason. Although western Marylanders may have opposed slavery, the state as a whole was unlikely to welcome a party dedicated to the demise of that institution.[13]

In the early 1850s, a new political force entered both federal and state politics. A large segment of Maryland's craftsmen viewed the growing numbers of immigrants as a threat to their economic livelihood, and in response, they coalesced into nativist organizations. The ultimate expression of their nativism was found in the creation of the "the American Party." Initially derided as the Know-Nothing Party by its opponents, Maryland's nativists were elected to city councils, the state legislature, and one leader became Baltimore's mayor. The rise of nativism contributed to the demise of the state's Whig Party. Often referred to as "mob town," Baltimore's embrace of the Know-Nothing Party resulted from politicians allying with gangs such as the "Plug Uglies" and "Rip-Raps," and immigrants were coerced into voting for particular candidates or intimidated from voting at all. As Baltimore's Whigs became the Know-Nothing Party, southern Maryland's Whigs affiliated with the Democrats. Since many of Maryland's southern residents were Catholic and the nativists had become vituperative toward both Irish immigrants and the Vatican, Saint Mary's transition from Whig affiliation to the Democrat Party is unsurprising. When, in 1856, the Know-Nothings gained control of the state legislature, Harris became one of their staunchest opponents. To understand how this occurred, some exposition of Harris' life is further required.[14]

By the time Benjamin Harris was born, his father had constructed a large plantation house named Ellenborough, and from Harris' birth in 1806 until his death in 1895 the plantation was his home. At Ellenborough's economic peak in 1840, Joseph Harris owned forty slaves, a large number by Maryland standards. When Benjamin Harris turned eight years old, his father sent him to Charlotte Hall Academy, a school which had already educated Edward Bates, Lincoln's first attorney general, and Robert Bowie and James Thomas, two of Maryland's early governors, as well as Roger Taney. Raphael Semmes, who gained fame as a Confederate naval officer, attended the school two years after Harris.[15]

The Maryland General Assembly established Charlotte Hall, named for Queen Charlotte, in 1774 as "a free school." In 1852, the school began to function as a junior military academy. However, the curriculum in place when Harris was a student had military aspects to it. The students drilled and were instructed in military affairs. Harris was, on graduation, expected to be an officer in the state militia should the need arise. By the time of his adulthood, the most likely need for the militia to be called into uniform by the governor would not have arisen from a foreign invasion, but rather a slave revolt. The school served another purpose. Because of its exclusivity, it enabled the planter class to maintain its political and economic power in the state.[16]

During his first year at Charlotte Hall, his mother gave birth to another son, named Henry. Although Henry, like Benjamin, had shown some promise of becoming a political leader, he remained in Benjamin's shadow. When he died in 1894, the *Port Tobacco Times* published his obituary: "had he been so inclined he might have been a leading star in the public affairs of the state, but his inclination led him in a different channel and he spent his whole life on his farm." As a result of economic difficulties, by 1856, Harris became a trustee over Henry's farm and eighteen slaves.[17]

Little is recorded about Harris' early years and education. After leaving Charlotte Hall, in 1824 he attended Yale, but did not graduate. In 1827, he participated in what became known as the "stomach rebellion," an event in which students residing in a campus dormitory showed their anger at the poor quality of the dormitory's meals by breaking the dormitory's crockery in the streets. Yale's administrators labeled Harris as one of the ringleaders and expelled him along with several other students.[18]

Expulsion from Yale did not affect Harris' rise to local prominence. Nor did it encumber the Harris name. In 1829 Henry Harris attended Yale and graduated four years later. In the fall of 1828, Benjamin Harris matriculated into Harvard's law school and graduated in 1830. There are several ironies to Harris' collegiate education. Yale's future president and staunch abolitionist, Theodore Dwight Woolsey, served as a tutor in the very dormitory that Harris resided in. There is no record that the two men ever discussed any matter of political significance, but there is the likelihood that Woolsey and Harris at least knew of each other. The officer who would later serve as a judge advocate prosecuting Harris in the military trial, Major William Winthrop, was Woolsey's nephew. Winthrop was yet to be born when the "stomach rebellion" occurred, but he too attended Yale and then Harvard for the study of law.[19]

After returning to Ellenborough, Harris gained admission to the local bar and he entered state politics. He married a cousin named Martha Elizabeth in 1826, associated with several of Maryland's influential families, including the Keys, through the marriages of his siblings. His legal practice extended throughout the eastern parts of Maryland and he drafted contracts for renting slave labor from owners to farmers and ship builders in Baltimore and Annapolis as well. He also represented claimants in contested probate actions in Port Tobacco. He was often listed as a court appointed trustee over large farms in which the male owner died. As a result of Maryland's property laws, women were not permitted full economic control over slaves. By 1849 he also represented the interests of Maryland's northern manufacturers in Charles and Saint Mary's counties.[20]

In 1832 Saint Mary's County sent him to the House of Delegates, as a Whig. He served in the legislature for two terms until 1835. Saint Mary's voters also sent William J. Blakiston, Benedict I. Heard, and Richard Thomas to the lower house with him. All four men were prominent slave owners. They were also related through distant marriages and all four would intermittently serve in the legislature in the 1830s, 1840s, and 1850s. Harris left the legislature in 1835 to re-engage his business pursuits, but he won a special election to a one-year term in 1836. He was defeated for re-election the next year and elected once more in 1849 only to lose the next year. In 1856 Saint Mary's voters returned him to the state legislature where he served a single two-year term once more. When Harris first entered the House of Delegates, Saint Mary's County's voters had the ability to elect four representatives to the lower house. However, as a signal for the loss of political power to the growing urban center of Baltimore, by 1856, Saint Mary's representation in the House of Delegates was reduced to two representatives.

During his first term in the state legislature, he campaigned for road construction and the establishment of a state bank. Between 1836 and 1852 Saint Mary's voters preferred the Whig presidential candidate over the Democrat. Even Winfield Scott, who was the last Whig presidential candidate, received over sixty percent of the county's vote. Moreover, Harris served as Scott's campaign manager in southern Maryland. Scott, however, was roundly defeated by Democrat Franklin Pierce, a pro-slavery northerner. It was not until 1856 that Harris ran as a Democrat, but when he did so, he adopted Pierce's position that the "rights of slave-owners over their property were fully enforceable in the northern states." In reality, Harris' transition as a Democrat occurred 1854. That year, he became the Democrat Party chairman for Saint Mary's County. Looking back on his political life in the 1880s, Harris conveyed to congressional historian Charles Lanman that he was, at one point, "a National Republican, and then a staunch Whig who believed Daniel Webster represented the best element in that political party." Harris explained to Lanman that there were two reasons for his transition from the Whig Party to the Democrat.[21]

Although less important than the Whig Party's fracture over slavery, a number of Northern Whigs, including Millard Fillmore, were doctrinally exclusive in their belief as to who should be included in the nation's political machinery. Northern Whigs maintained a Puritan outlook which viewed Catholicism as undermining the social fabric of the nation. Not only did the Whigs attempt to pass temperance laws directed primarily against Catholics, they also sought to limit the growth of Catholic educational institutions. Many of Harris' constituents were Catholic, and he opposed discrimination against Jews or other Christian sects. Indeed, Harris championed the principle of freedom of religion to require the inclusion of non–Judeo Christian faiths in the nation. If a voting district

1. The Origins of a Maryland Secessionist 27

were "to elect a Mohammadean, then so be it," he later argued. In 1848, Harris lauded David Yulee as an example of a patriotic citizen who placed the Constitution above religious belief. Yulee was one of the country's first prominent Jewish politicians and President Jackson appointed him as a territorial representative of Florida. When that territory achieved statehood, Yulee became its first senator. When former Northern Whigs questioned Yulee's fitness to hold office in the Senate because of his faith in1854, Harris spoke in his defense.[22]

Southern Whigs were not generally anti–Catholic. They supported federal government funded infrastructure programs such as building roads, canals, and railways. They also sought to re-establish the national bank which President Jackson had destroyed. Infrastructure expansion and a national bank alike would have helped slave-owners prosper. However, once Daniel Webster, the Whig Party's icon, pronounced the bank an obsolete idea, most Southern Whigs gradually determined that the Democratic Party was more likely to protect slavery than the Whig Party. This belief was particularly evident in the debates over Texas annexation and the war with Mexico in in 1846. While Democrat congressman David Wilmot unsuccessfully sought to prohibit the spread of slavery into territory captured from Mexico, southerners understood that most of the anti-war opposition which was linked to abolition was with the Whig Party's northern men. Many of these men would exit the Whig Party for the Free Soil movement and then the Republican Party. Even though Webster, Robert Charles Winthrop (the one-time speaker of the House of Representatives), and other so-called "Cotton Whigs" tolerated slavery, others such as William Henry Seward and Salmon Chase increasingly became outspoken in their support for abolitionism.[23]

In 1851 Harris lost a re-election bid for the state legislature. He had campaigned on a platform centered on religious toleration, but also promised to limit the numbers of freedmen from entering slave areas. For the first time in his political career, he also urged voters that it was essential to limit the spread of abolitionism, because this movement was a threat to Maryland's social stability. His argument was hardly unique and it reflected an "aristocratic Whig" ideal. He promised that he would introduce a law to prohibit anti-slavery newspapers and pamphlets from entering Maryland because, like many southerners, he was convinced that such material encouraged slave rebellions and escapes and continued to use attacks on abolitionism as the centerpiece of his campaign in 1856.[24]

The American Party proved vexing to southern Maryland's former Whigs. Often referred to as the Know-Nothing Party, its members opposed immigration from Catholics and Jews, and accused southern and central European Catholic immigrants of being part of a "papal plot" against the United States. Given Maryland's demographics, one might assume that this party would not have achieved any success. But it did, and in 1856 the Know-Nothings controlled the state legislature and the Baltimore mayor's office. That year, Thomas Watkins Ligon, the state's governor and a Democrat, in his annual message warned against claims of the existence of secret societies, and in response the Know-Nothing dominated legislature formed a committee of five delegates, three Know-Nothings and two Democrats, to investigate whether papal plots existed in the state. The legislative committee called no witnesses and relied on newspaper reports. When, predictably, the committee determined that such plots existed, Harris took the lead in denouncing its findings.[25]

Championing the Rights of Religious and Ethnic Minorities Under Maryland's New Constitution

The rise of the Know-Nothing Party in the state can also be understood in light of the state's new constitution. In June 1851, Maryland's free white male citizenry accepted a new state constitution by a vote of over sixty percent of those who went to the polls. The new constitution resulted from a push by Democrats who wanted to reform the allocation of state legislators in both the House of Delegates and Senate, and the Whig Party suffered in its representation. Baltimore City, for example, gained two delegate seats, but Saint Mary's County's allocation of delegates was reduced from four to two. One other feature of the new state constitution was the election of judges and magistrates, rather than the old system which mirrored the federal government's appointment process. While this feature reduced patronage, it politicized the state judiciary. Five months later, in the state's first post-constitution election, the Democrats took forty-three of the seventy-four seats in the House of Delegates. Several Whigs left from their party and ran as independents. Slavery, oddly, was absent as a political issue in the new legislative body. Property tax reductions, a ten-hour workday, and the establishment of a state "insane asylum" known as the "House of Refuge" took up much of the delegates and state senate's time in 1853.[26]

With the Know-Nothing Party's emergence, however, new divisive issues dominated the state legislative debates. State aid to religious, or parochial, schools came under attack by Protestants who campaigned on the "dangers" of the Catholic Church. Ironically, while Maryland had been the colony most aligned with the concept of religious freedom, and the state still possessed a sizeable Catholic minority, the idea of tax monies supporting religious schools was staunchly opposed. The debate occurred contemporaneously with the Vatican establishing a new bishopric in Baltimore as a reflection of the influx of Irish and German Catholic immigrants into the city. When, in 1852, a Catholic legislator introduced a bill enabling the state funding of parochial schools, the House of Delegates refused the take it up for debate. When the bill was introduced the next year, Protestant leaders led demonstrations against the Catholic Church. At the same time, a temperance movement formed to oppose Catholic immigration based on the alleged overuse of alcohol by immigrants of that faith. By 1854, with the fall of the Whig Party, the Know-Nothings adopted both the temperance platform and a very anti–Catholic position.[27]

In essence, the emergence of the Know-Nothing Party did not occur as a result of the new state constitution, but the new constitution enabled the party to accrue power. With the exception of a few influential Whigs such as Reverdy Johnson, who had served as attorney general during Zachary Taylor's presidency, many of the state's former Whig elites became the Know-Nothing Party. But so too did many of its Protestant Democrats, particularly in the cities. In 1855, the Know-Nothings took fifty-four of the seventy-four seats in the House of Delegates and eight of twelve seats in the state senate. By this time, Saint Mary's County's voters had fully gone over to the Democrat Party.[28]

One of Harris' criticisms against the state legislature's investigative committee into "secret societies" was that it had met in private and therefore resembled a "star chamber." Equally important was that despite its report concluding subversive plot existed, the committee produced no witnesses substantiating the existence of a "papal plot" against the state government. To Harris, the committee represented what he detested about the Know-Nothing movement itself: it was a party built on fear and rumor-mongering with little substance. In response to the committee's report, Harris delivered a fiery speech to the House of Delegates criticizing the Know-Nothing Party as "an unconstitutional aberration." Although he pointed to certain constitutional rights that the nativists had ignored, he reached back to pre-constitutional history as a prelude for explaining those rights. Hearkening back to the late period of the Roman Republic, he promised a fight with the Know-Nothings "equal to the naval battle of Actium," predicting "the modern Anthony will have succumbed before the superior arms of our Augustus." He next proclaimed that the principle of religious freedom had far more of a constitutional basis than the Know-Nothing legislative majority who he accused of plotting to "setting the fire and the faggot to a dozen Popish Priests."[29]

Harris then accused the Know-Nothings of acting as "blustering bullies" when making accusations and retiring as "skulking cowards" when confronted by the falsity of their charges. Interestingly, he insisted the Know-Nothings were worse than abolitionists. "The Know-Nothings," he claimed, "allowed bigotry to become the captain of Protestantism." He also argued that while abolitionists—"Black Republicans," he called them—sought to liberate slaves, Know-Nothings "would make slaves of white ones." And, as he reached the apex of his long introduction, he stated, "abolitionists may succeed in dividing this Union; [Know-Nothings] would make this Union not worth dividing."[30]

After his fiery introduction, Harris settled into a constitutional and historic analysis of why the committee was unlawful—"If this legislature representing the entire people were to unanimously pass an act which would come into conflict with our Constitution, it is unnecessary for me to say that the act would have no validity"—before claiming that any legislative act as envisioned by the committee constituted "treason" against the people of the state. Harris also used the example of the state's prominent Catholics, and in particular Chief Justice Roger Baldwin Taney, as examples of loyal Catholics.[31]

Like many politicians before the age of television, Harris had a tendency to deliver long speeches and his attack on the committee continued with a lesson in Maryland's recent history. He reminded the state legislators that prior to 1853 neither the Maryland Whig Party nor the Democrats "professed the detestable principles" of the Know-Nothings. Harris also turned the attention of former Whigs to the 1839 Whig Party Convention where nativism was expressly rejected by men such as Daniel Webster, Henry Clay, and William Henry Harrison. He also reminded the House of Delegates that Franklin Pierce had argued for religious tolerance between Catholics and Protestants. Harris finally closed his speech with a number of biblical passages and references to Christian tolerance.[32]

There is a final important element in Harris' speech. He used the example of Aaron Burr as a comparison to the committee's work. Harris professed that Burr was a wrongly maligned man for the same reasons the committee wrongly maligned Catholics. He pointed out that Burr was acquitted of treason before a trial and lived freely until his death, yet many Americans considered him a traitor. Harris reminded his fellow delegates "public opinion drew distinctions which the law cannot draw, and the fair fame [Burr] had previously won in the service of his country, withered before the blight, and his name has been branded with ever-lasting infamy." In essence, Harris argued that the committee's accusations, though having no basis in fact, would tar Catholics in Maryland because of the nature of the public's suspicions against Catholics.[33]

Harris and Maryland's Slave Laws

Harris' conduct both in politics and society cannot be understood without a study, however brief, on the law of slavery in Maryland. He, his fellow slave-owners, and their political allies strengthened and vigorously enforced the state's slavery laws as well as restrictions on freedmen, and they generally prevailed in the state courts. Like most of his fellow lawyers, particularly the elites who were educated in formal law schools, Harris believed that the law represented natural order, and any disturbance to this order threatened society's stability. Unlike Harris, most of the nation's lawyers were not educated in universities, and indeed, the few existing law schools, including those attached to prestigious universities such as Harvard and Yale, were viewed as separate entities from main campus. Yet these schools educated lawyers that the law reflected necessity, and strict adherence to the letter of the law enabled society and individuals to progress to their "natural stations" in life. Under this system, a poor inventor or recent immigrant could obtain wealth, but the government could not take wealth for redistribution. And African Americans were to be confined to the lowest of all status regardless of whether they were free or enslaved. For instance, a white citizen had the right to bring suit against a sheriff for a wrongful arrest, but an African American could not do so, including in instances where the arrest was a result of an unlawful attempt to re-enslave the freedman.[34]

The Supreme Court in a number of decisions enhanced the southern states' control over slavery, but the first and foremost of these, *Prigg v. Pennsylvania*, was one in which Harris plated a minor role. In 1826 Pennsylvania's legislature passed a law forbidding state officers from assisting in the capture or return of fugitive slaves. But the Constitution's framers placed into the nation's foremost document of freedoms and limits on the federal government a clause within Article IV which stated in exact language: "No Person held to Service or Labour in one State, under the Laws thereof, escaping into another, shall, in Consequence of any Law or Regulation therein, be discharged from such Service or Labour, but shall be delivered up on Claim of the Party to whom such Service or Labour may be due." This "Fugitive Slave Clause" did not compel the individual states to spend their resources and time in capturing fugitive slaves, but it was intended to prevent state governments from interceding on behalf of runaway slaves. In 1793, Congress passed the Fugitive Slave Act which enabled slave owners to hire marshals to seize fugitive slaves in free-states and free-territories as long as a federal judge or local magistrate granted a warrant to do so. Persons interfering in the recapture of slaves faced a fine of up to five hundred dollars. One of the oxymoronic features of this law was that it created a federal crime for the benefit slave-owners who championed both limits on federal authority and expansive states' rights. Facially Pennsylvania's law did not, in all matters, conflict with either Constitution or the Fugitive Slave Act of 1793.[35]

In 1832 a Maryland slave named Margaret Morgan fled into Pennsylvania, and five years later, a Pennsylvania law enforcement officer refused to assist Edward Prigg, a hired marshal—a polite term for "slave catcher"—in capturing Morgan. Morgan's original owner had died and his heirs asserted rights of ownership. Prigg and three of his assistants, Nathan S. Bemis, Jacob Forward, and Stephen Lewis, captured Morgan and her children who were considered by Pennsylvania to be wholly free, and brought them back to Maryland. A Pennsylvania grand jury issued indictments against Prigg and his assistants, and Joseph Ritner, the state governor who was elected in 1835 as an anti–Mason, demanded that Maryland extradite the four men to face trial for kidnapping. Under Maryland's slave laws, Morgan's children were slaves regardless of where they were born because the original owner had not manumitted them. Thomas Veazy, Maryland's Whig governor, refused Ritner's demand and submitted the question of extradition to Maryland's legislature. The state legislature, in turn, declared that no Marylander was subject to the laws of another state regarding the return or recapture of slaves. Harris denounced Ritner to the House of Delegates during this vote, but because he was among the majority of delegates who believed that Ritner was in the wrong, his comments were gratuitous. In 1839 Pennsylvania's legislature enacted a law permitting the trial of Prigg and his assistants, but permitted them to post a bond so that they could appeal from a conviction without having to serve time in prison.[36]

It was unsurprising that the Supreme Court would take up an appeal on this issue since the case could, in reality, be titled *Pennsylvania v. Maryland*, and the nation's highest court has original jurisdiction over disputes between the states, even though such disputes typically arose from boundary and riparian rights claims. The justices, in a decision authored by Justice Joseph Story, overturned the convictions and decided that Pennsylvania's law was unconstitutional. But the Court also determined that the Pennsylvania had no responsibility to assist in the enforcement of the Fugitive Slave Act. Story was a Bostonian who generally sided with the interests of slave owners, but he was also a nationalist who supported a stronger federal government. Chief Justice Taney, the Marylander who had owned slaves, concurred with Story that Pennsylvania's law was unconstitutional, but he disagreed with Story that only Congress possessed the authority to legislate over the status of fugitive slaves, and instead argued that the states could pass laws governing the status of fugitive slaves, and that other states were required to adhere to those laws when an owner attempt to reclaim "property."[37]

Maryland's fugitive slaves, like their deep-south brethren, had to travel far north to have a hope for freedom. The New Jersey Supreme Court in an 1836 decision titled *State v. The Sheriff of Burlington* determined that a slave who had fled from his "owner" in 1820 and then married and raised a family at least had the right to a trial by a jury before being returned to an "owner." Moreover, New Jersey's laws determined that the children of runaway slaves who were born in New Jersey were free. The New Jersey decision marks an important point in legal history because the right to a trial by jury denotes a form of membership in humanity, rather than a property clarification. Of course *Prigg v. Pennsylvania* impacted the latitude that northern state magistrates and northern state supreme courts could interpret the Fugitive Slave Act. To Harris and his fellow Maryland slave owners, *Prigg* justified their assertions of slave laws into free states. The growing numbers of northern abolitionists concluded that a minority of slave owners had subverted the federal and state courts to protect an evil.[38]

Taney and his southern-leaning brethren on the Court were not finished with affirming, if not increasing, the power of slave-owners. In 1857 in *Dred Scot v. Sandford*, in all likelihood the most infamous decision ever rendered by the nation's highest court, Taney led a majority of justices to determine that African Americans could never become citizens within any constitutional definition. The Court went further and expressed a fear that freedmen who had obtained citizenship status would also be able to claim rights of assembly, speech, and the bearing of arms. The attorneys on both sides represented the foremost legal minds in the nation. Montgomery Blair, who was the son of one of the founders of the Republican Party and later Lincoln's first postmaster general, and George T. Curtis, the brother of Justice Benjamin Curtis, represented Dred Scott. Senator Henry Johnson of Missouri and Reverdy Johnson, a former attorney general and Maryland senator, represented Sandford. Taney could have simply adhered to Reverdy Johnson's arguments that if the Missouri Supreme Court had determined that Dred Scott, despite his colorable argument that had become a freedman, remained a slave, the Court had to respect the state decision. But Taney went further and issued an expansive decision.[39]

Taney was a generation older than Harris and a Catholic, but the two men had a distant familial connection. Born in 1777 in Calvert County, Maryland, Taney was surrounded by, and benefited from, slavery. His father was a wealthy tobacco farmer, and although he did not inherit his father's estate, he was sent to Dickinson College in Pennsylvania and returned to Maryland to become a prominent attorney and slave owner. He also married Anne Phoebe Charlton Key, Francis Scott Key's sister. Benjamin Harris' sister, Maria Louisa, had married Anne Key's and Francis Scott Key's cousin. Taney served in the Maryland legislature both as a delegate and state senator. He began his career as a Federalist, but transitioned to Democrat Party and by 1824 had become a loyal supporter of Andrew Jackson. In turn Jackson had an affinity for Taney. He unsuccessfully attempted to nominate Taney as secretary of the treasury in 1829, and unsuccessfully attempted to appoint him as an associate justice to the Supreme Court in 1835. However, Jackson successfully placed him as chief justice the following year after John Marshall's death. Taney's opponents in the Senate were mainly Whigs led by Daniel Webster and Henry Clay. Once on the Court, Taney led his fellow justices to undermine federal grants of monopolies to corporations and uphold legislation democratizing the economy. He generally sided with "states' rights" assertions and opposed limitations on personal liberties, except, of course, in regard to African Americans. By 1860 Taney achieved heroic status amongst slaveowners. Like Harris, Taney tried to undermine the Union's war efforts.[40]

An examination of Maryland's slave laws as well as its laws governing freedmen further illustrate how Harris' beliefs were within the parameters of the state's laws and were not extreme among his peers. Whether slave or free, Maryland's African Americans were deemed incompetent to testify in courts against whites, with few limited circumstances such as claims of their own freedom. That is, freedmen, including those who were claimed by whites to still be slaves, occasionally had access to the courts to challenge their enslavement. But these claims were seldom successful, particularly when manumission occurred as part of a will, and the living family members or debt holders challenged the will. In 1752, over two decades before Maryland became a state, the colonial government prohibited manumission clauses in a person's last will and testament. In 1796, the state legislature passed a statute recognizing manumission clauses as legal and enforceable statements, but determined that such clauses could not be drafted contrary to other state laws such as those laws governing the rights of creditors. In *Fenwick v. Chapman*, a white woman's will freed several slaves and also left certain properties to her white children. She also owed certain debts to creditors, but her real property was enough to pay those debts without nullifying the manumission statement in her last will. The creditors and the white inheritor of her property sought to have the manumission clause overtaken by the debt. The state court of appeals determined that the rights of a creditor outweighed a deceased person's manumission statement, even when the rest of the will prioritized the manumission statement above the sale of land properties in the event that her debts remained unpaid. In *Fenwick v. Chapman*, the Supreme Court reversed the Maryland Court of Appeals decision, and favored the rights of a deceased person so long as all debts were paid to creditors.[41]

In 1798, the Maryland Court of Appeals determined that an unmarried white woman could not, on her own, sell slaves that she inherited from her father, even to satisfy a debt. Once married, however, the woman could lawfully sell her slaves. The next year, the same court determined that a slave-owner who leased a slave to a Pennsylvania farmer, and in comporting with the laws of Pennsylvania the farmer freed the slave, the law of Pennsylvania governed the enslaved person's status. In other words, even if the enslaved person were retaken by the "owner," the enslaved person had to be released to his freedom in Pennsylvania. The decision, *Negro David v. Porter*, is very brief, but appears that the judges applied a *caveat emptor*—known as "buyer beware"—doctrine to the decision. That is, the Maryland slave owner should have known the risks of the lease before entering into it and could not then succeed in the courts as a resort. But *Prigg* undermined this decision.[42]

At times, slaves had an economic status less than farm animals. In 1836, the state legislature determined that railroads, an increasing political power in the state, were liable for damages to horses, cows, and other farm animals as well as fires to forests and farmlands resulting from sparks emanating from locomotives and railcars. The legislature did not specifically include slaves in this list, and in *Scaggs v. Baltimore and Western Railroad Company* the Court of Appeals determined that a slave-owner could only sue a railway under a common-law theory to negligence rather than as a statutory violation. However, because the witnesses to the slave's death—he was working alongside of the railroad's track—were other slaves, and since these individuals were not legally competent to testify against the railroad, the slave-owner's lawsuit failed.[43]

In 1817 the Maryland legislature prohibited licensed distillers and alcohol retailers from selling "spirituous liquors" to "persons of color." In 1843, the court of appeals upheld convictions under this law. Maryland had few prohibitory laws regarding alcohol, and the production and sale of alcohol was generally deemed as a commercial right as it applied to white adults. But, as the judges on the state's highest court concluded, providing alcohol to slaves and freedmen alike would not only reduce their workplace productivity, it could also lead to rebellion. A decade and a half later, the appellate court overturned a conviction for a violation of this act. In that case, a white seller was convicted for selling liquor to a slave, but the slave had a note from his "owner" to the seller that the purchase was at the "owner's" behest. The conviction is interesting because even with the letter, a prosecutor and a jury were convinced of the necessity of preventing any "person of color," from even holding liquor for another person who would otherwise be in lawful possession of the liquor. The appellate decision is equally interesting because the judges determined that the plain language of the statute did not prohibit a slave from acting at an owner's direction.[44]

The Saint Mary's County Court records show that between 1835 and 1850 Harris represented over two hundred parties in civil cases, and of these there were at least forty involving the sale of slaves. But Harris also represented clients throughout southern Maryland and the Eastern Shore as well as clients in Baltimore. It would be difficult, given that the majority of the cases Harris took part in resulted in settlements without a published decision, to determine what percentage of his legal practice involved slaves, but there are some existing cases on appeal. In 1847 he represented a slave-owner who leased a slave to another party, and that party sold the slave to a third party creditor. In a legal action to recover the slave—known as a "trover" suit—Harris convinced the Court of Appeals that no matter the indebtedness of the original owner, the owner had unhindered authority to determine how to satisfy his debts.[45]

In another case, Harris convinced a Saint Mary's court to side with him regarding his ownership of a male slave named John Lloyd. Harris' father purchased Lloyd's mother while she was pregnant. However, Susanna Abell had originally owned Lloyd and contested Harris' ownership over Lloyd some seven years after his birth. Harris rested his arguments on the state's statute of limitations and prevailed on this basis. But the Court of Appeals determined that the Saint Mary's trial court erred in not permitting the jury to interpret for themselves when Susanna Abell first made her claims over Lloyd.[46]

Maryland's slave-owners such as Harris had to compete with pressures that were virtually non-existent in the deeper south. Beyond the growing numbers of freedmen whose presence might influence slaves to seek their freedom, Maryland had not entirely prohibited abolitionist literature from being distributed within the state. Moreover, two of the abolitionist movement's most prominent individuals, Frederick Douglass and Harriet Tubman, were originally from Maryland. Finally, while the slave owners held conventions, such as one in 1842 which resulted in the state legislature increasing restrictions on the movement, assemblage, and employment of freedmen, the state did not prohibit abolitionist assemblies. In a representative democracy, including a democracy which was limited in its representation, the law is rarely fixed to a point of inflexibility. On the eve of the Civil War, a subtle change occurred in Maryland's laws regarding freedmen. While in *Dred Scott v. Sandford*, a majority of justices determined that African Americans could never be considered citizens, the Maryland court of appeals in *Hughes v. Jackson* determined that freedmen were citizens of the state with the right to sue other citizens in civil claims. It is notable that *Hughes* was issued after *Dred Scott*. Yet it would appear that there remained an almost insurmountable barrier for a freedman to prevail against a white citizen because African Americans were still deemed incompetent to testify against whites.[47]

Conclusion: The Election of 1860

In 1858 Democrats in Calvert and Charles counties lobbied Harris to run for Congress in the following year's election, but Harris demurred. The next year, the *Saint Mary's Beacon* encouraged Harris to run in the state's special 1861 congressional election. Between 1858 and 1861 both the *Beacon* and the local Democratic Party began referring to Harris as "Colonel Harris." This was an honorific title, though technically he could have been commissioned as such in the state militia. The use of the title evidenced Harris' and his constituents' growing militancy over slavery. In the last year of James Buchanan's administration, Harris publicly spoke on the need for secession should an abolitionist become president.[48]

As the election of 1860 neared, Harris led a group of Saint Mary's Democrats to oppose Stephen A. Douglas, a popular Illinois Democrat who had prevailed over Lincoln when the Illinois state legislature selected him senator in 1858, because Douglas had not fully committed to preserving slavery to their satisfaction. Douglas had, in fact, championed "popular sovereignty" as a means for preserving the Union, and he debated Lincoln over slavery several times. These debates were reported across the nation. Under Douglas' plan, newly admitted states in which the majority of citizens favored slavery would maintain slavery within their borders. In the inverse, newly admitted states in which the majority of citizens opposed slavery would thereafter prohibit slavery. Though "popular sovereignty" was theoretically palatable to Harris, in reality, the experience of "Bleeding Kansas," led Harris to conclude that Douglas' compromise was unworkable. Before Kansas voted on statehood, violence between pro-slavery and abolitionist factions resulted in widely reported killings. Moreover, James Buchanan had disavowed "popular sovereignty" almost from the beginning of his presidency.[49]

On September 4, 1860, Harris conveyed a letter to Douglas warning "the difference existing between the wing of the party represented by yourself and that represented by Mr. Breckenridge seem to be irreconcilable and must lead to the disastrous result we so much fear—the election of Mr. Lincoln." Harris went on to ask Douglas to "retire" from the campaign and assured Douglas that he would ask Breckenridge to do the same so that a third candidate could be selected with the hopes of unifying southern and northern Democrats. He informed Douglas that Chief Justice Roger Baldwin Taney could be a viable candidate because "the full people respect the decision in the Dred Scott case."[50]

Harris attached a resolution of the Saint Mary's Democrats to his letter to Douglas. The resolution began, "when a ruthless and perfidious enemy is assailing from without, the laws of the citadel, it is the height of folly and madness for its defenders to allow dissension and discord to exist within; such a course must give encouragement to its enemies." Like Harris, the citizens who endorsed the resolution asked for both Douglas and Breckenridge to withdraw from the election, so that a third candidacy could be undertaken. Another important feature of this episode was that the Saint Mary's Democratic Party once more elected Harris to be their spokesman, thereby later enabling his election to Congress.[51]

On September 11, 1860, Harris convened a second meeting of Saint

1. The Origins of a Maryland Secessionist 39

Mary's County Democrats to nominate Taney for president with Associate Justice Samuel Nelson as his running mate. Harris' belief that Taney was a viable candidate was overoptimistic. Neither justice was willing to abandon the Supreme Court to run for the Executive Branch. However, that Harris wanted the author of the *Dred Scott* decision as the nation's next president is telling as to conduct and lack of a realistic assessment of the electorate. Once Harris learned that the aged Taney opposed any consideration of his name on a ballot, Harris switched to campaigning for Breckenridge, the most ardent slave advocate running against Lincoln. In all likelihood, this second committee contributed to Harris' ultimate arrest and trial four years later. The *New York Times* reported on the meeting on its front page, as did the *Philadelphia Inquirer*.[52]

Maryland was an unfriendly state for Lincoln. He captured less than three percent of the state's popular vote. Put another way, of the over ninety thousand ballots cast, he won slightly over two thousand. More troubling to Lincoln was that Douglas, the Democrat candidate who had championed popular sovereignty, came in second behind Breckenridge. The difference between Douglas and Breckenridge was stark. Douglas campaigned to maintain slavery in the south, and to permit the territories to determine whether to become free or slave at their statehood. Breckenridge campaigned against the Republican Party with no possibility of a compromise, including respect for prior compromises. Moreover, while Douglas had promised to enforce the fugitive slave laws and derided Lincoln's stance on emancipation, Breckenridge promised to extend slavery into all territories and place demands on the north to liberalize the slave trade. A vote for Breckenridge was nothing short of the assertion of a southern white minority to dictate to a northern majority the political conditions of the country.[53]

None of these differences mattered as the Democratic Party imploded. On election day, Martha Harris entered in her diary, "if the black republicans should gain ascendancy, we are a doomed people and war will be inevitable." Two days later she notated that Lincoln would "enter into the White House in the midst of discord and bloodshed." Whether Martha Harris wanted war to come is unknown, but she predicted that it would come and last for a long time. Her husband, though, appears to have welcomed the possibility of secession even at the cost of war. He began to make speeches in favor of the southern states, and would go so far as to call on Saint Mary's residents to raise a regiment to fight against the federal government.[54]

2

Harris and Secession, 1861–1863

> "But two assurances I can give—that Maryland shall not go out of the Union, and that I have done & shall do nothing tyrannically, wantonly, or unnecessary to the fixed purpose I have in view."
> —General John Adams Dix to a friend, November 1861

On December 20, 1860, the South Carolina legislature, with the endorsement of the state governor and ostensibly the majority of its white male population, voted to secede from the United States. Within two months, Mississippi, Florida, Georgia, Louisiana, and Texas joined with South Carolina. On March 4, 1861, Abraham Lincoln was inaugurated, and state legislatures in the upper south began to vote over secession, particularly after his call for the states to contribute militia forces to the federal army. On April 12, 1861, South Carolina militia bombarded Fort Sumter, a federal fortress in Charleston Harbor, and its commander surrendered the following day. Harris publicly rejoiced in the bombardment, hoping that it would presage Maryland's secession. But he acknowledged to his friends that Lincoln was more decisive than Buchanan, and unlike Buchanan, Lincoln was "bent on the subjugation of southerners" and would "order the occupation of Maryland." Martha Harris added in her diary "much evil may be close and I dread contemplate it."[1]

Within a week of Martha Harris' diary entry, 1,200 soldiers of the Sixth Massachusetts Volunteers under the command of General Benjamin Butler attempted to traverse through Baltimore to get to Washington City, as the capitol was then known. Their transit was briefly halted when an anti–Union mob confronted them. In what became known as the "Pratt Street Riots" civilians tore up streetcar rails and threw bricks at the soldiers. The soldiers, in response, fired their rifles into the crowd. Four soldiers and twelve civilians were killed. Lincoln was convinced that city officials had fomented the riots and ordered the Army to police the city, in effect taking over much the city's governmental functions. To Harris, it was clear that Lincoln was responsible for the "Pratt Street Riots" and that the president's placement of soldiers in Baltimore was direct evidence of a "new tyrannical power."[2]

On April 25, 1861, Lincoln apprised General Winfield Scott, the commanding general of the United States Army, that the Maryland legislature would shortly meet in Annapolis to decide whether to secede from the Union. Lincoln did not order Scott to arrest the legislature. However, he wanted the general to use the Army to watch over it, and, in the event a vote in favor of secession occurred, to take quick action to prevent the state's secession. Although Lincoln recognized that the legislature had a right to peacefully assemble, he hinted that both the suspension of *habeas corpus* and naval a bombardment of Annapolis was within his authority to order. The next day Scott notified Butler that he too had the authority to arrest citizens who were deemed hostile to the United States. However, Scott stressed to Butler that the Army had a duty to ensure the safety and care of any citizens in its custody. While Annapolis was free from military assault throughout the war, *habeas* was another matter.[3]

The Battle Over Habeas Corpus: Maryland in the War's First Year

During the secession crisis and into the summer of 1861, George H. Morgan and Clark J. Durant represented Saint Mary's County in the House of Delegates, while Oscar Miles served in the state senate. All three of these men were Democrats and each sympathized with the southern cause of slavery. Miles was born in 1822 and could trace his roots to Kenelm Cheseldine, one of the original settlers of the Maryland Colony who was instrumental in establishing the state court of appeals as well as the state's county courts. Miles, like Harris, had been a vigorous opponent of the Know-Nothings and at one point he threatened to resign his legislative position because of a bill offered by Governor Thomas Hicks that would, in his estimation, limit the rights of Catholics. In addition to owning a plantation and several slaves, Miles also profited from his business of purchasing, selling, and leasing slaves. Durant and Morgan likewise owned slaves and publicly entertained the idea of Maryland's secession. In September 1861, all three men would be arrested, along with one of Harris' other friends in the legislature, Ross Winans, an inventor of naval equipment and army ordnance. The federal courts would not intervene to assist any of these men, even though, in theory, federal judges had the constitutional authority to order the Executive Branch to free the men or bring them to a public trial.[4]

From the beginning of the nation's history, *Habeas Corpus* was considered as a fundamental guarantor of a free citizenry. That is, the Judicial Branch, beginning with the Supreme Court, possessed the constitutional authority to order the government to produce a citizen it held in captivity in the United States so that the person could argue his rights before a court. But, prior to the Civil War, the Judicial Branch's authority had rarely been challenged. In 1795, the Supreme Court, in *Ex Parte Bollman*, determined that a federal judge had the authority to order the Executive Branch to bring a person into court. Several residents in rural Pennsylvania refused to comply with a federal tax on distilled spirits and engaged in a violent, albeit brief, insurrection against federal agents who attempted to enforce this tax. President George Washington ordered the Army into Pennsylvania's western counties and the insurrection ended. Over a dozen of the insurrection's leaders were arrested and brought to trial for treason, though the federal government only secured two convictions. One of the arrested citizens appealed to a federal judge, but the Executive Branch challenged the judge's authority in an appeal to the Supreme Court.[5]

In *Bollman*, the justices reasoned that without the judicial authority to order the Executive Branch to produce a person, an aggrieved person would be unable to challenge his or her arrest, or assert their other constitutional rights in a federal court. Ironically, Justice James Wilson certified to the Executive Branch that an insurrection existed in Pennsylvania thereby enabling, under the Militia Act of 1792, the government to send the Army into that state. President Washington did not contest *Bollman*. Indeed, he showed a great deal of deference to the Judicial Branch in letting it define the powers of the presidency. During the early part of Thomas Jefferson's presidency the Supreme Court determined that the political branches, that is, the Executive Branch and Legislative Branch, could not supersede the Constitution as the document was determined through federal judicial rulings.[6]

The power to order a writ of *habeas* is fundamentally important for another reason, albeit one related to the protection of individual rights. The Constitution's framers created a Judicial Branch independent of the two elected branches of government. Legal scholars ranging from James Madison to William Howard Taft have consistently stated that while the judiciary was weaker in its powers than the other two branches by design, judges were not impotent in regards to Congress or the president. Federal judges, once confirmed by the Senate, served with life tenure and could only be removed through impeachment. Life tenure was a critical element to maintaining the independence of judges. But so was the authority to order a *habeas* writ. After 1860, southern-leaning citizens and slave owners hoped that federal judges would protect their property and political rights, but for several reasons, this was not to be.[7]

The Civil War resulted in the partial upending of Washington's example of the Executive Branch's deference to the judiciary. From the start of the war, Army officials arrested citizens in the northern states on the basis that such persons had colluded with the Confederacy to undermine the Union's war efforts. During the first year of the conflict, Secretary of State William Henry Seward oversaw much of the Union's efforts to discover treasonous activity. However, by 1862 the War Department assumed the responsibility for the "internal policing" of the Union in regards to citizens accused of undermining the Army. Accusations against persons ranged from authoring or publishing newspaper articles critical of Lincoln's administration, encouraging protests against conscription, or simply publicly speaking against the war. Some northerners actually took up arms against the Union, spied for the Confederacy, or provided material support to the Confederacy, but such persons were in the minority of all individuals detained, arrested, or prosecuted by the Army. By 1862, the Army conducted military trials, called military commissions, against not only citizens accused of supporting the Confederacy, but also against black-marketers and citizens who committed fraud in the sales of goods or other contracting with the War Department. By the end of the war, the Army conducted 4,271 military commissions. Over three hundred such trials occurred in Maryland.[8]

Although rare in American legal practice prior to the Civil War, assertions of military authority over the civil laws were not unheard of. In 1815, General Andrew Jackson declared martial law in New Orleans as a British force approached the city. Two months after his celebrated victory over the British, martial law remained in place because, as he justified, he had not received word of a treaty between the United States and Britain. A French language newspaper criticized his governance of the city, and in response he ordered the author of the offending article arrested and charged with inciting a mutiny and spying. The article's author, Louis Louailler, a Louisiana legislator, appealed for a writ of *habeas* to Dominick Hall, a federal judge. Hall ordered Jackson to bring Louailler into court so that Louailler could challenge the constitutional basis of his detention. Jackson sensed that Hall would order Louailler released and this would, in turn, erode his authority to declare martial law. Instead of complying with Hall's order, Jackson arrested Hall. A court-martial ultimately dismissed charges against Louailler and Jackson released Hall. This did not end the matter. Jackson ordered Louailler's confinement to continue and also ordered Hall to be transported out of New Orleans. However, once Jackson learned that the peace treaty was signed, he released Louailler and permitted Hall to return to New Orleans. After Hall resumed his judicial duties he ordered Jackson to appear before him and, not satisfied with Jackson's explanations for his conduct, he fined the general $1,000 after finding him guilty of contempt. Jackson paid this fine, and in 1842, President John Tyler petitioned Congress to repay Jackson. Two years later Congress voted to do so. Because Jackson never appealed against Hall's finding of contempt and Congress never passed a resolution either condoning or condemning the participants, Jackson's conduct in arresting Hall was never given constitutional sanction.[9]

In response to the "Pratt Street Riots," Lincoln followed Jackson's example and ordered *habeas corpus* suspended between Philadelphia and Washington, D.C. He realized that the foremost impediment to militia forces assembling in the capitol were saboteurs along the rail lines through Maryland, and he certainly believed that the capitol was in danger until sufficient numbers of loyal forces were able to assemble there. But this also meant that the routes between the populated areas of the loyal northern states, particularly New York, Pennsylvania, and Massachusetts, had to be protected. On May 25, 1861, Union officers arrested John Merryman, a member of Maryland's legislature. Merryman had participated in the destruction of railroad tracks and bridges during the riots, and he was a well-known sympathizer to slave owners and secession interests. Shortly after the arrest, Merryman appealed to the United States district court judge for Maryland, William Fell Giles. However, the commander of Fort McHenry informed the judge that since habeas had been suspended, the Army did not have to comply with a judicial order to produce Merryman. On May 26, a lawyer representing Merryman appealed directly to Chief Justice Taney, who in turn traveled to Baltimore to preside over Merryman's appeal. Taney, in actuality, had determined to issue a judicial order corralling Lincoln's abilities to suppress secession in Maryland.[10]

Once in Baltimore, Taney acted as a federal circuit judge instead of as a Supreme Court justice. He ordered General George Cadwalader, the military commander of Fort McHenry, to produce Merryman so that Merryman could challenge his detention. But Cadwalader refused to do so, and asked for a postponement so that he could receive orders from the president. In his request Cadwalader implied that because Lincoln had suspended *habeas*, Taney was without any authority over the Army. In response, on May 28, Taney issued an order, *Ex Parte Merryman*, which eloquently described the Constitution's limits on the president, but which nonetheless, if adhered to, could significantly hamper the Union's ability to preserve Maryland as part of the Union. Indeed, Taney considered the president's "commander in chief authority" as ministerial in nature. That is, according to Taney, the president had the authority to assemble the Army, but unless the Army was transported to fight a foreign enemy, he had to comply with the orders of federal judges in regard to the Army's functions. After Cadwalader refused to comply with Taney's order, the justice traveled back to the capitol. The Supreme Court as a whole neither openly backed Taney nor Lincoln, but Attorney General Edwin Bates issued an opinion informing Lincoln that he had acted in conformance with his authority as the nation's commander in chief. Attorney general opinions have been held to be binding on the Executive Branch in the absence of contrary law and Bates' opinion strengthened Lincoln's resolve. As legal historian Brian McGinty pointed out in his study on the Merryman episode, had Lincoln failed to be resolute in his refutation of Taney, Maryland could have been lost to the Confederacy, and, with it, the Union dissolved.[11]

The Merryman episode received national attention, and throughout Maryland it dominated the news. On May 27, the *Baltimore Sun*, Maryland's largest newspaper, headlined Merryman's arrest. The next day that newspaper headlined Merryman's appeal to Taney as well as Cadwalader's refusal to comply with the chief justice's order. As an attorney and states' rights advocate, Harris was not only innately familiar with the importance of judicial independence, as a result of Lincoln's treatment of Taney, he became irrevocably convinced that Lincoln had tyrannically usurped civil rights by asserting that the presidency in wartime was immune from a *habeas* order.[12]

Another facet of *Merryman* which later affected Harris had to do with the government's treatment of Giles, and the response of both Giles and Taney. Giles concluded that as long as the war continued it would be impossible for any citizen accused of treason to receive a fair trial, so he refused to hold hearings on whether to order *habeas* writs or hold a trial for Merryman. Taney shared Giles' opinion on the inability to conduct trials which fully ensured accused persons' due process. When, in 1865, federal authorities arrested Harris, he may have believed that he had no recourse to appeal to Giles for a *habeas* writ.

Harris, of course, lionized Taney and it did not matter to him that the chief justice had already lost much of his credibility with the Republican administration over the *Dred Scott* decision. Whatever else may be said about Taney's abilities, *Dred Scott* was barely rooted in Constitutional law and Taney went far beyond the issue raised in the appeal in determining that African Americans could not be considered as citizens with the full array of civil liberties guaranteed by the Constitution. Indeed, this issue was not even argued to the Court. To slave-owners and secessionists in Maryland, however, it was Taney's stand on *Dred Scott*, *Merryman*, and *Kentucky v. Dennison*, a decision issued after Lincoln's inauguration in which Taney led the majority of justices to agree that not only was Ohio's governor required to assist in the return of fugitive slaves to Kentucky on the demands of that state's governor, but that Ohio was also required to extradite its citizens who assisted in a slave's act of escaping. In *Dennison*, Taney, at least, recognized that it was one thing to issue an opinion and another to enforce it, and he caustically remarked in the decision that the courts were without the power to compel a state governor to make arrests and extradite individuals.[13]

Taney's recognition on the limits of judicial authority when confronted by a dynamic president was also a reason for Harris' re-entry into politics. Harris reasoned that if the Judicial Branch could not protect the property rights of slave-owners and safeguard a status quo which subordinated African Americans, whether free or slave, into a citizen-less position, then Congress had an obligation to do so. However, several other actions occurred in the summer of 1861 which also led Harris to this conclusion. Namely, within a short time of *Merryman*, federal forces were stationed in Baltimore, Annapolis, and southern Maryland, and Army officers began to arrest citizens.

Soldiers arrested Baltimore's chief of police, George P. Kane, on June 27, 1861, after Army officials determined he aided secessionists to destroy Baltimore and Ohio railway property. The next day, Baltimore's mayor appealed to Postmaster General Montgomery Blair to intercede on Kane's behalf, but Blair remained silent on the matter, and for good cause. Although Blair was not a radical abolitionist, he opposed secession. Throughout the war, while serving in Lincoln's cabinet, Blair clashed with abolitionists such as Secretary of War Edwin Stanton and Secretary of the Treasury Salmon Chase. Although he later aligned with President Andrew

Johnson against the "Radical" Republicans, in 1861, he would have found it distasteful to intervene on behalf of Kane.[14]

Kane was openly sympathetic to the Confederacy and after his arrest he admitted to taking part in the sabotage of bridges connecting Baltimore to other areas. But he claimed that he did not commit treason. Instead, he argued that he merely followed the governor's orders, and insisted that the prevention of Union troops entering Baltimore was only done to prevent another riot. Like Harris, Kane was a "states' rights" Democrat, who had earlier opposed the Know-Nothing Party. Yet some of his initial actions did not indicate treasonous activity. During the first Baltimore riot, on April 19, Kane attempted to be a neutral arbitrator and assisted the Massachusetts regiment's travel through the city. His sons had already departed Maryland to fight for the Confederacy. From that point onward, Kane's actions hardly appeared as neutral as he claimed. Kane was placed in the same prison cell at Fort McHenry with Merryman. Unlike Merryman, who was quickly released, Kane spent seventeen months in a prison cell. He then traveled south and joined the Confederate secret service, operating out of Canada.[15]

In September 1861, Lincoln worried that the Maryland legislature would once more vote for secession. A number of state legislators determined to hold a vote away from its Annapolis capitol with the surrounding federal forces and instead debate secession in Frederick. The vote was scheduled to occur on the seventeenth of that month. After learning of the planned vote, Secretary of War Simon Cameron, with the tacit concurrence of the new commanding general of the Army, George Brinton McClellan, ordered General Nathaniel Banks to arrest suspected members of the legislature. At the same time Cameron ordered General John Adams Dix to arrest suspected secessionists in Baltimore. Several legislators were arrested and confined in military prisons and McClellan lauded Banks and Dix for defeating pro-southern Marylanders' attempt at secession. In an apparent "about face," Governor Hicks also endorsed the arrests. Although Harris was not arrested in Frederick because he had yet to take his seat in the state legislature, his fellow Saint Mary's residents, Clarke J. Durant and George Morgan, were. General Banks transferred Durant and Morgan, along with eighteen other state legislators, to the military prison at Fort Warren in Boston Harbor, but on December 16, 1861, both men took an oath of allegiance to the Union and were freed.[16]

The next month, William Matthew Merrick, a federal judge on the circuit court for the District of Columbia, in Washington, D.C., issued a ruling ordering the release of a minor child from the Army. The minor had voluntarily enlisted, and like many of his peers, he lied about his age in order to join. Lincoln's suspension of *habeas corpus* included the capitol, and from the War Department's vantage point, the federal courts had no jurisdiction to order the release of the minor. Because Merrick had been appointed by Franklin Pierce and had been a slave-owner, he was likely suspected of southern sympathies. In reality, the question of *habeas* was not necessarily pertinent to Merrick's decision, since, under the Articles of War, the Army could have court-martialed the minor for fraudulently enlisting into the Army in the first place, and the Supreme Court in *Dynes v. Hoover*, as noted in the introduction, had already determined that the federal courts possessed no jurisdiction over an appeal of this type. Yet, during the early days of the war, a court-martial resulting from an act of youthful patriotism or a desire for adventure was unlikely to occur. General Andrew Porter, the commanding general over the Union's forces in the city, not only refused to accede to Merrick's order to produce the minor, he also had the lawyer delivering the judge's order arrested. The other federal judges on the circuit court then ordered Porter to appear and explain himself to a full judicial panel, but Lincoln intervened and had his personal secretary John Hay inform the United States marshal that the president forbade the service of the judicial order on Porter. Secretary of State Seward likewise informed the marshal that he was without any authority to serve a summons on the general. Because judges enjoyed the constitutional protection against removal from the bench by any means other than impeachment, Merrick's position as a federal judge, was reasonably assumed to be safe. But Merrick's judicial tenure was not secure. Seward, under Lincoln's orders, placed Merrick under house arrest and had his salary suspended during the arrest. This action ran afoul of the Constitution, which contains in its Third Article "the Judges, both of the supreme and inferior Courts, shall hold their Offices during good Behavior, and shall, at stated Times, receive for their Services a Compensation which shall not be diminished during their Continuance in Office." From the beginning of the nation, judicial rulings when issued in good faith were never believed to constitute a basis for removal, even if the ruling was in gross error. In 1863 Congress abolished the circuit court for the District of Columbia which had the effect of removing Merrick from the federal judiciary. Unlike the suspension of pay, there was nothing unconstitutional about the court's abolishment. However, in 1885, President Grover Cleveland appointed Merrick to the Supreme Court for the District of Columbia, the successor court to the abolished circuit court.[17]

To Harris and his peers, Lincoln's treatment of Merrick again added to their belief that the president intended to "subjugate" Maryland through military force. Merrick was a native of Charles County, Maryland. He began practicing law in Baltimore in 1839, and opened a legal practice in Frederick in 1844. He served as a Frederick County's prosecuting attorney from 1845 to 1850, and in 1854 Franklin Pierce appointed him the federal judgeship in the capitol. Harris had not only known Merrick and respected him, Taney was also one of Merrick's supporters. Thus, to Harris, Merrick's placement under "house arrest" was not only an affront to the constitution's guarantee of an independent judiciary, it was an assault on Taney.[18]

Harris' desires for Maryland to secede were to fail not only because of the state's proximity to the capitol and the loyal northern states, but also because the most influential of the Maryland's political elites did not support secession, even if they opposed emancipation and believed that Lincoln had abridged their constituents' civil rights. On the eve of the war, Maryland's most influential politician was not its governor, but rather one of its senators. Born in 1796 in Annapolis, Reverdy Johnson was admitted to the bar in 1816 after studying law in a judge's office. In 1821 he was elected to the state senate and served until 1829. From 1829 until 1845 Johnson acquired a reputation as one of the state's leading attorneys. That year, the state Whig Party dominating the legislature successfully placed Johnson in the Senate, but he did not serve a full term. When Zachary Taylor became president in 1849, he named Johnson as the nation's attorney general. Johnson served as attorney general through 1850, but with Taylor's death, he resigned his office so that Taylor's successor, Millard Fillmore could appoint his own choice. By the war's outbreak, Johnson was not only an influential Marylander, he was a nationally prominent and important to the Democrat Party.[19]

By 1855 Johnson had not only argued cases before the Supreme Court, he successfully represented clients in London before an international court of arbitration. In 1856 he campaigned for Stephen A. Douglas, believing him a far superior Democrat candidate to James Buchanan, the eventual president. Although Johnson did not own slaves, he believed in the constitutionality of the institution, and it was for this reason that he accepted Dred Scott's owner, John F.A. Sanford, as a client. In 1860 Johnson campaigned for Douglas, once more warning that if the Republicans were elected to the nation's executive office the nation would end. "As sure as Heaven's clouds of fire and tempest carry desolation in their train, so sure is it that this now peaceful and happy land will be shaken to its very foundations, and the Union, the once glorious Union of our noble ancestors, and inheritance to us more precious than was ever conferred on a people, will be tumbled into ruins," he proclaimed. Yet, when war came, he sided with the Union and agreed to serve as a special commissioner in New Orleans when Lincoln asked him to do so.[20]

As a Unionist, Johnson did not sit idle after Lincoln's victory. He insisted, like Douglas, that an election result in and of itself could not be a reason for secession. From the start of the war, Johnson also publicly argued that emancipation could only occur through a constitutional amendment with full compensation made to slave-owners. He took a central role in the 1861 Peace Convention, asking Lincoln to endorse slavery's constitutionality. Yet, in 1864 he proclaimed that "there never was a greater heresy" than secession. If Harris and the other pro-secessionists were to break Maryland, or even Saint Mary's County, away from the Union, they would have to take on Johnson and other long-serving politicians who remained in power.[21]

Among the reasons for Harris' failure to overcome Johnson's influence was that even the residents of Saint Mary's County relied on Johnson to defend their commercial interests beyond protecting slavery. On August 22, 1861, the adjutant general informed General McClellan that Johnson proposed to mediate between the Army and the commercial interests of Saint Mary's County. The Army had closed the ports in southern Maryland to shipping, out of a concern that Confederates were infiltrating the Union. Harris argued in the House of Delegates that the closure was a punitive measure against southern Maryland and not a military necessity. One of the county's sources of income was the export of guano, a material important for fertilizers. Harris linked guano to bread production and he objected to a federal requirement that required the producers and shippers of guano take a loyalty oath to the Union in order to transport it over the roads to Baltimore, let alone ship the substance in bulk on vessels. But he could make no headway with the federal official and Johnson intervened. Johnson insisted to the Lincoln Administration that the Army's action stifled commerce because much of the county's produce was shipped northward from these ports. He eventually obtained General Dix as an ally for this particular cause. Once the ports were reopened, an increase of commerce aided the county's residents. In March 1862 Johnson forcefully confronted Stanton about "outrages" committed by Massachusetts regiments in Montgomery, Maryland. Stanton issued a rare apology and promised compensation for damages caused to private property. As a result, few of the state's citizens could complain that Johnson had become sycophantic to Lincoln.[22]

2. Harris and Secession, 1861–1863

When the war began, Thomas Hicks, a Know-Nothing, was Maryland's governor. A slave-owner, he declared that while the loss of his slaves would prove financially ruinous, he too opposed secession. On January 11, 1861, he promised Winfield Scott that he would do everything in his authority to keep Maryland within the Union. One month earlier he agreed with John J. Crittenden a former attorney general and governor of Kentucky over the unconstitutionality of secession, and he informed Crittenden that under no circumstances should secessionists consider him an ally. This did not mean that he supported Lincoln or any of the Republican Party's positions. He publicly argued that the fugitive slave laws still had to be enforced regardless of whether the nation was in a state of war. In April and May 1861, Hicks may have ordered the burning of bridges to keep federal troops from moving through the state. But he defended his actions that he ordered the transport ways crippled to keep the state from seceding. In August of that year he informed Dix that he intended to use the state militia to sever lines of communication between Maryland's Eastern Shore and Virginia. If Hicks was a tepid Unionist, his successor as governor, August Bradford, proved more resolute in maintaining Maryland in the Union.[23]

Like Hicks, Bradford initially tried to maintain the state's attachment to the Union without antagonizing its southern population. Indeed, when he gave his Inaugural Address in 1862, he was conciliatory toward the state's slave-owners but he adamantly denied the legality of secession. "When South Carolina, thirty years ago, by her nullification ordnance first formally put forth that pernicious dogma of state supremacy, the Legislature of Maryland as soon as it was brought to their attention adopted resolutions clearly showing that we repudiated it ten, not less distinctly than we do today," he reminded the state. Like Johnson and Hicks, Bradford did not champion emancipation and claimed that the war "should be confined to the legitimate purpose of maintaining the Constitution and preserving the Union." In his speech, Bradford recognized that none of the European nations supported slavery and he called for all state officers and militia men to take loyalty oaths to the Union. While the speech was unlikely to mollify slave-owners and their supporters, it infuriated Harris. Bradford did not mention Harris by name, but he chastised the "one dissenting vote made in the legislature against loyalty to the Union." The dissenting vote was, of course, Harris.[24]

Although Bradford remained a Unionist throughout the war, he deplored federal intervention in state political matters, and criticized the War Department for enticing slaves to run away. In 1862, he appointed

Hicks to the United States Senate after James Pearce suddenly died. Like Hicks, Bradford pursued warrants for the arrest of runaway slaves in the federal courts in Maryland, Pennsylvania, and Washington, D.C. On June 18, 1863, he offered $200 from the state's treasury for the capture of "George Tyler, a runaway negro slave from Anne Arundel County." The next year, he obtained an extradition order from the supreme court of the District of Columbia for Henry Smith, "a free negro for aiding and enticing slaves to run away from their lawful owner." Bradford also asked Pennsylvania's governor, Andrew G. Curtin, for help in the capture of runaway slaves. Although he tried to maintain the support of slave-owners, he never once spoke in favor of secession. In 1863, he published a state-wide proclamation calling for ten thousand volunteers to defeat the Confederacy, and on September 24 he attended a "War Governor's Conference" where he agreed to align Maryland with Massachusetts, Iowa, Ohio, and Maine in supporting Lincoln and the emancipation of slaves in the southern states.[25]

One of Bradford's actions that Harris vehemently opposed was the ordering of state militia to protect Baltimore and Annapolis as well as be stationed in Saint Mary's and Charles counties, after the Union defeat at the Second Battle of Manassas on August 30, 1862. Bradford's purpose in calling the state militia into service was to free up federal forces to protect Washington, D.C., as well as to thwart General Robert E. Lee from sending Confederate forces into Eastern and southern Maryland in an effort to coerce the state to seceding. Lee did, in fact, send his Army into Maryland for this purpose, but he did so in western Maryland where the population was both pro–northern and anti-slavery. Moreover, Lee's army was defeated at the Battle of Antietam and it retreated back into Virginia beginning on September 21, 1862. Although Bradford's actions in ordering the state militia into service were to maintain the state in the Union, Harris was able to accuse him of allying with Lincoln to destroy slavery. But this accusation only resonated in the southern counties.[26]

Harris and Saint Mary's County

Even before James Buchanan departed from the White House, Harris argued for the right of Maryland to join with South Carolina and secede from the Union. As early as January 1861, large numbers of Saint Mary's and Charles counties' residents began to publicly express an affinity for South Carolina. The majority of men in both counties had cast their votes

2. Harris and Secession, 1861–1863

for Breckenridge, and Lincoln was recorded as receiving only one vote out of the over one thousand votes counted. On February 26, at a gathering to celebrate George Washington's birthday, Harris spoke on the need to raise taxes in order to fund a larger county militia and "fight against abolitionists." He, along with the other hundred citizens present, also "toasted secession and the south." One of Saint County's more prominent residents, J. Edwin Coad, formed a rifle company called "Riley's Rifles" for the express purpose of repelling any federal forces.[27]

Harris' legal arguments regarding secession centered primarily on two documents known as the Virginia and Kentucky "Resolutions," which were authored shortly after the Constitution came into being. In response to President John Adams and the Alien and Sedition Acts, in 1799, Thomas Jefferson and James Madison anonymously penned two treatises on the rights of a state to secede from the "union of states." Jefferson and his followers accused Adams of crafting laws, such as prohibiting criticism of the sitting president, as an attempt to maintain Federalist power. Jefferson argued that in addition to violating the Constitution's guarantee of freedom of speech, the Alien and Sedition acts also were impermissible under the Tenth Amendment. The text of the two documents were never secreted from Congress or the American public, even though Jefferson, who had presidential ambitions, wanted his role in authoring the resolutions to remain unknown. The documents were specific to Virginia and Kentucky, rather than all of the states, reflecting, perhaps, that the authors knew the limits of their work. Harris' embrace of the resolutions is unsurprising for two reasons. The first is that both documents were convenient for secessionists to adhere to. After all, the authors of the Declaration of Independence and the Constitution had also written the two resolutions. (Madison wrote Virginia's and Jefferson Kentucky's.) The second unsurprising feature of Harris' use of the Resolutions had to do with the status of property rights. From the founding of the nation, personal property was deemed to be a fundamental right, protected by the Constitution and the common law predating it. Indeed, property was held as fundamental right coequal to freedom of speech and the right of assembly as articulated in the First Amendment. The Constitution's Fifth Amendment prohibited the federal government from taking property without due process of law. Thus, as long as "property" included enslaved persons, to Harris, any federal infringement of his property provided a constitutional basis for his state to secede.[28]

Arguably, secessionists such as Harris erred in relying on the two resolutions for several reasons. In 1809 the Supreme Court ordered the state of Pennsylvania to pay a naval officer named Gideon Olmstead "prize money" for the seizure of a British naval vessel during the Revolutionary War. Pennsylvania's Democratic governor tried to assert that he had the right to nullify an unjust federal law or judicial order. But in 1813, he was unable to obtain President Madison's support to this effect. Secondly, when the Virginia state legislature passed its resolution it enunciated a "warm attachment to the United States." Indeed, Virginia's legislature promised to "defend the Constitution of the United States and the Constitution of this State, against every aggression either foreign or domestic." The Kentucky Resolution likewise held the same conclusion, but it contained more forceful language on the matter of state over federal authority. Specifically, Kentucky's resolution determined "that every State has a natural right in cases not within the compact (*casus non fœderis*) to nullify of their own authority all assumptions of power by others within their limits: that without this right, they would be under the dominion, absolute and unlimited, of whosoever might exercise this right of judgment for them." That is, Kentucky could secede if the federal government were to try to topple its state constitution without an alteration of the United States Constitution first.[29]

Ironically, the conduct of pro-slavery forces in the three decades before the war mirrored the very conduct that Jefferson complained John Adams had engaged in, namely, restrictions on speech. Pro-slavery politicians, including Harris, attempted to restrict pro-abolitionist speech not only in Congress, but also in their local communities, and they prevented abolitionist pamphlets and newspapers from using the mails. It is true that Maryland had not gone as far as other southern states in banning abolitionist newspapers, and there were abolitionists in the state, but this did not stop Harris from campaigning on a promise to prohibit the distribution of abolitionist newspapers in Saint Mary's County in 1854. The Constitution's "Speech and Debate Clause," examined further in the next chapter, was designed to protect speech of any kind in congressional debates. Yet pro-slavery forces in Congress successfully imposed a "gag rule," prohibiting congressmen from expressing criticisms of slavery. Another disconnect between pro-slavery men and the work of Jefferson and Madison was that while Virginia's resolution concluded that its citizens had the right to secede from the nation in instances where the federal government overstepped its authority to the detriment of the rights of citizens, the right of slave-ownership was not included in the two resolutions.[30]

Whatever Jefferson and Madison might have meant in authoring the two documents, and regardless of the fact that the two state legislatures had largely adopted the resolutions, other state legislatures did not embrace either document, including southern slave states such as Georgia, South Carolina, and, of course, Maryland. The New Hampshire legislature denounced the resolution as a political threat without lawful constitutional foundation. When in 1832 South Carolina's legislature determined that it had the authority to "nullify" federal law, all of the other state governments sided with President Andrew Jackson. The issue concerning South Carolina had to do with an opposition to a federal tariff rather than directly with the question of slavery, and this fact enabled Harris and his peers to distinguish it from the loss of the "property," through the abolition of slavery, and particularly so after Lincoln's 1862 war measure titled the "Emancipation Proclamation."[31]

The equating of slavery to a fundamental right is concededly a noxious exercise. Yet it was deeply believed in not only by slave-owners, but also by many northerners who benefitted from slavery. To further explore the depth of the pro-slavery beliefs, it is important to understand that even predating the nation's history, there was a common law acceptance that private property was sacrosanct from intrusion by the government. In 1763, the England and Wales High Court, the rough equivalent to a "supreme court," in monarchal Britain determined, in *Entick v. Carrington*, that a British official, including "the Secretary of State for the Northern Department," could not issue a warrant to enter a person's home, unless the official both possessed the lawful authority to issue a warrant and had a lawful purpose for doing so. *Entick v. Carrington* became part of the American legal landscape, and it continues to be cited to the present day.[32]

Harris found the facts underlying *Entick* important enough to cite to in at least two of his court filings. He also cited to *Entick* in one of his early speeches justifying Maryland's secession. However, the facts underlying *Entick* had nothing to do with slavery. Lord Halifax, Britain's secretary of state for the north, suspected John Entick of publishing a seditious newspaper against the Crown. A marshal named Carrington broke into Entick's house and destroyed Entick's personal property while seizing Entick's papers. Entick then sued Carrington for damage to his property. A jury determined that if the warrant was illegal, Entick was entitled to damages. Under British law, the decision on the warrant's legality fell not to a jury, but to Lord Camden, the chief judge of the King's Bench. Lord Camden determined that because Lord Halifax had not been specifically empowered by a statute, he also was not empowered to issue the warrant, even though his position in the government assumed other important powers. There were several important attributes to *Entick*. First and foremost was that no person, regardless of public position, was above the law. Second, Britain's chief judge determined that the common law property rights of citizens could not be trampled by the government, even on the basis of "public necessity" or "government need." Third, as pointed out by one of the Britain's leading contemporary legal scholars, *Entick* was decided in a time of political turmoil in Britain. British Protestants still feared that Catholics would sabotage the government, Britain was at war with France, and this war was fought not only in the English Channel, but in Europe, North America, and even India. The Hanoverian British monarchy suspected the remnants of the Tudors and their supporters, if, for no other reason, than the Hanoverians were not truly British. After all, Tudor descendants of that royal family had plotted to reclaim the throne only forty years earlier. Thus, even in crisis times, according to *Entick*, the government still had to comply with the law. Harris and his peers believed that the Civil War hardly justified significant departures from the law protecting property rights. One other feature of Harris' use of *Entick* was that the decision was issued by a British lord who operated in the absence of a written constitution. The United States Constitution specifically protected the rights were a part of *Entick*. As a result, Harris was able to claim that the very rights he championed were ancient in nature to the point of being irrefutably sacrosanct.[33]

On April 23, 1861, Harris spoke to a large public meeting in Leonardtown, arguing for a resolution which expressed support for secession. He also urged that the voters raise a regiment of Saint Mary's men to serve the Confederacy. He did not, however, take any affirmative steps to do so. Harris, or course, was not alone in speaking against the federal government. Local politicians and slave-owners including Chapman Billingsley, who would serve in the state senate throughout the war joined with Harris. So too did John H. Sothoron and James Blakiston, both of whom had served in the state senate, as well as Oscar Miles, the current state senator. Two days later, the *Saint Mary Beacon* headlined that Harris had led a "committee of public safety" to "procure arms and gunpowder." The newspaper also reported that several young men from county had crossed into Virginia with Bradley Tyler Johnson, an attorney from Frederick in order to fight with the Confederacy. Johnson would go on to become a cavalry general in the Confederate Army.[34]

Because Harris' activities as well as those of his peers were reported not only by the local newspaper but also by the *Baltimore Sun*, it is unsurprising that federal forces quickly entered into the two counties. By the

2. Harris and Secession, 1861–1863

end of May, over two hundred Marines were garrisoned in Leonardtown and various companies of Army units were scattered throughout Charles, Calvert, Saint Mary's, and Westmoreland counties. Shortly after the Union disaster at Bull Run on July 21, 1861, federal forces conducted house to house searches throughout Leonardtown and arrested citizens who were suspected of assisting other Marylanders travel to Virginia to fight for the Confederacy.

Although a number of state legislators remained under custody after the military arrests in Frederick, over two thirds of Maryland's legislators opposed secession and voted to prohibit any future legislative votes or conventions over secession. The House of Delegates also considered enacting a new state crime of treason based on public expressions of support for secession. Unsurprisingly Harris opposed this bill, and publicly decried the diminution of individual rights of expression as well as the continued military presence in Saint Mary's County. Despite resistance to succession in the state legislature, Harris believed he could become its champion on national level and decided to run for Congress.[35]

In April 1861, Governor Hicks called for a special congressional election to determine who would represent Maryland's recently created Sixth Congressional District. Prior to 1853, Saint Mary's County had been in the state's First Congressional District along with its neighboring counties, and the numeric change had to do with the population growth in Baltimore in which much of the city was sectioned off as a congressional district of its own. The election was scheduled for June 1 of the same year. The Sixth District encompassed Anne Arundel, Calvert, Charles, Howard, Montgomery, Prince George's and St. Mary's counties. All of these counties had slave populations and Harris became convinced that if he secured the Democrat nomination, the district's voters would overwhelmingly side with him. He had an easy time gaining the party's nomination, as no other Democratic candidate entered the contest for the election. This enabled Harris to go so far as to proclaim the Civil War "an unholy war against the southern states."[36]

While campaigning, he argued that secession was constitutional, that Maryland should join with the south, and that emancipation would be ruinous to the state's economy. Essentially, he ran for a federal position with the promise to lead Maryland out of the federal government. His opponent, Charles Benedict Calvert, ran as a Unionist. Calvert was a direct descendant of Maryland's earliest colonial governor, Charles Cecil Calvert, and several other powerful Marylanders. In 1861, Maryland's Unionists were hardly Republicans. Many of these men had supported Stephen A.

Douglas and his concept of popular sovereignty. Calvert did not appear to have any Republican leanings. He owned over three hundred slaves. But he was unique in the sense that in 1860 he had avoided siding with either Douglas or Breckenridge; instead, he campaigned for John C. Bell. He possessed a political portfolio to campaign on. He had financially supported inventors such as Samuel Morse and had become a leading botanist. Calvert had also quietly served three terms in the House of Delegates, but there is no evidence that he and Harris had corresponded. The congressional election, as Harris shaped it, centered on secession since both candidates opposed emancipation.[37]

Harris lost the election by less than 1,000 votes, and he became convinced his loss was the result of tampering and coercion by pro-Unionist groups, as well as the presence of Union soldiers near polling stations. He was embittered at losing the election to Calvert for several reasons. Calvert had supported Millard Fillmore in the 1856 presidential election when Fillmore ran as a Know-Nothing. Fillmore had been Zachary Taylor's vice president and ascended to the presidency as a Whig on Taylor's death in 1850. However, with the demise of the Whig Party, Fillmore transitioned to the Know-Nothings. Calvert justified his support for Fillmore as a desire to continue Whig principles but Harris countered that both Calvert and Fillmore had "embraced the devil" of religious intolerance and he could not fathom why any of the Sixth District's Catholic population would cast their votes for him. Harris actually may have won the majority of Catholic votes, and he may have had more overall support than Calvert. The presence of Union soldiers may have deterred some voters. Harris' views on secession were extreme and likely to lead to Army suppression, and undoubtedly he lost some support as a result.[38]

One of the reasons that could circumstantially provide evidence to support Harris' arguments was that Maryland's pro-Unionists did not prevail throughout the whole state in 1861. The Fourth District's voters, an area which included Baltimore, elected Henry May over Henry Winter Davis for Congress. There were more pro-slavery men in the Sixth District than any other voting district in the state. May had served in Congress from 1851 to 1853, and prior to that, he was one of President Pierce's special emissaries to Mexico. He was also pro-slavery, openly advocated for an armistice with the southern states, and visited Richmond in the war's early weeks to see whether an armistice was possible. The Army arrested May after he returned from Richmond, but within two days of the arrest he was released and served out the rest of his term in Congress. The War Department knew of May's attempts to seek an armistice and the secretary of war concluded that May had not committed an actions detrimental to the Union. Nonetheless, the arrest led to a congressional investigation, but this investigation also determined that he had not criminally corresponded with the Confederacy. Still, Harris later used May's arrest as proof that the Army had placed Maryland's voters in fear.[39]

There is no doubt that Harris and his supporters were determined to support secession by confronting Lincoln and the Army at every possibility. But their efforts to do so, particularly their political campaigning and public demonstrations, brought them repeatedly to the War Department's attentions. At the end of 1861, Colonel Lafayette Curry Baker, an Army officer, established an intelligence network in southern Maryland and reported to Postmaster General Blair that the county postmaster in Leonardtown was disloyal to the Union. "He styles himself as a states-rights man, which is but a mild term for secession," Baker warned. "A number of contraband letters were found in his office, but he positively denies knowing the writers, or the parties to whom they are addressed." Shortly after Baker's warning, he characterized the county as "a bed of treason and Confederate sympathy." Baker also began to collect information on Saint Mary's residents, including Harris.[40]

Harris, for his part, began to take actions which members of Lincoln's cabinet would undoubtedly find to be treasonous. In June 1861 Franklin Buchanan, a naval officer who had resigned his commission and went on to become the only full admiral in the Confederate Navy, informed Maryland's senator James Pearce that Harris congratulated him on his defection. Worse than congratulating a Confederate admiral was that from time to time, Harris permitted erstwhile Confederates to use his house as a stopover place for their transit into Baltimore and other northern points, as well as in their return to the Confederacy. On July 9, 1862, Martha Harris recorded in her diary that "friends from Virginia," who had crossed the Potomac, spent time in their house. "I fear they will be arrested, but have escaped this far into our village," she wrote.[41]

Harris' defeat in the congressional election did not end his political aspirations. All along he had the support of the *Saint Mary's Beacon*'s editor who headlined that the leaders of Maryland's new Unionist Party—a party composed of pro–Union Democrats who were either opposed to slavery or tepid toward emancipation, and the few state Republicans—had the goal of "hanging all men" who advocated for peace. During the period that he was out of state office, Harris served as commissioner of the county's school board. On December 22, 1861, Saint Mary's County once more voted Harris to the House of Delegates. He campaigned as an anti–Unionist and decried the state government's cooperation with the president. During the campaign, his supporters claimed that Union agents rigged the special congressional election by denying all voters access to the polls in Leonardtown, and this fact alone was reason enough to return him to the House of Delegates.[42]

There were, in effect, five state elections between 1860 and the end of 1861. In 1860, Saint Mary's voters sent Durant and Morgan to the House of Delegates. In April, a special election returned them once more. This occurred once more in June and again in July with Durant and Morgan being elected as delegates. Both men were steadfast states' rights Democrats, and indeed they ran on a "Peace Convention" platform which called for the state to maintain its neutrality. Oscar Miles remained Saint Mary's senator throughout the special elections as well. It was not until a fourth special election in December 1861, in which Saint Mary's voters sent Harris along with John F. Dent to the House of Delegates. Dent, like Harris, was a vocal proponent of slavery and had been a delegate to Maryland's constitutional convention in 1850. He served as a delegate intermittently from 1850 until 1864. In 1864, the Democrat majority in the House of Delegates elected him speaker. Miles declined to run and was replaced by Chapman Billingsley who ran unopposed as a "Democrat and Slavery" candidate. Billingsley remained in the state senate until 1867 when he was replaced by Harris' son-in-law, G. Frederick Maddox.[43]

Conclusion

The Army's conduct in Maryland is contextually explainable in light of several factors. Lincoln and most of the members of his cabinet including Postmaster General Blair believed that Maryland had to be kept in the Union or the Confederacy would prevail. Political forces within the state had openly aligned with the Confederacy, and this gave rise to the reasonable fear that large numbers of hidden pro-southern sympathizers would undermine the state's ties to the Union. Governor Hicks, despite his vacillating conduct during the secession crises, went so far as to inform Lincoln that Maryland could secede, and that there were plots underway to attempt this.

Second, the first year of the war could hardly be deemed as a success for the Lincoln, particularly in regard to military accomplishments. On July 21, 1861, the Union Army was defeated in the Battle of Bull Run and this battle took place outside of the capitol and close to the Maryland

2. Harris and Secession, 1861–1863   61

border. Following Bull Run, clashes between Union and Confederate forces occurred near the Maryland border with Virginia, most notably at Ball's Bluff on October 21. Again, Union forces were routed. In between these two events, Secretary of War Cameron, with Lincoln's concurrence, appointed George Brinton McClellan to command the Military Department of the Potomac. In turn, McClellan created the Army of the Potomac. While McClellan did not believe that the war should be fought with the aim of emancipating slaves, he was focused on the preservation of the Union, even at a heavy cost. To this end, his command contained a growing network of spies and officers engaged in what could be termed as "intelligence," and he was instrumental in the arrest of Maryland legislators in Frederick in the month before the Ball's Bluff disaster. From this point forward, Harris would view McClellan as a despot equal to Lincoln.

Almost as soon as the war began, increasing numbers of slaves fled from Maryland's plantations. The flight of slaves grew after Congress abolished slavery in the District of Columbia on April 16, 1862. Union generals commanding in Maryland during the first year of the war such as Benjamin Butler not only refused to assist in the recapture of slaves, but they also understandably viewed southern Maryland's slave owners as aiding and abetting the Confederacy. Ironically, Butler initially assured Maryland's citizens that he would enforce the fugitive slave act but then claimed that the "Pratt Street Riots," and other acts of "disobedience" to the Army equated to insurrection and he would not comply with the act as a result. As distinguished historian James Oakes noted, in Maryland the Union Army was omnipresent and disrupted slavery everywhere it went. However, the disruption of slavery was also related to the imposition of military authority over traditional civilian functions such as law enforcement. Citizens could be arrested by the Army for speaking against Lincoln and the war, and they could find themselves under arrest for trying to capture runaway slaves. To Harris and his political allies, this was another aspect of a "military despotism," which consigned white slave owners to a subjugated status.[44]

Harris clashed with one of Butler's subordinates early in the war. A Union vessel docked near Leonardtown for the purpose of transporting escaped slaves who had ventured into Union-held Norfolk to the north. Harris discovered that some of his slaves were missing and attempted to board the vessel. However, a colonel named Swayne tried to prevent Harris from boarding and Harris threatened the colonel. After the vessel's captain convinced Harris to leave the vessel, Harris continued to berate Swayne from the shore. Swayne did not leave the vessel, and Harris left without recovering his slaves. He would later allege that Butler had intentionally ordered the vessel to be docked at Leonardtown for the purpose of convincing slaves to leave their "owners."[45]

On December 13, 1861, Harris introduced a neutrality resolution in the House of Delegates claiming that "many citizens in the state of Maryland are held as prisoners of the government of the United States, having been arrested by the orders of said government upon the plea of necessity, arising out of the peculiar conditions of this country," and therefore the state should refrain from taking part in hostilities. The neutrality resolution was far less egregious than his calls for state secession. While the resolution also did not reflect reality, to Harris, it was as far as a compromise as he was willing to offer. Once the neutrality resolution failed to gain support, he returned to publicly arguing for secession. His arguments kept him at the forefront of the state's news reporting, which, in turn, maintained his viability for to enter national politics once more.[46]

On July 25, 1863, Governor Bradford issued a proclamation asking for Marylanders to rejoice in the Unions twin victories at Gettysburg and Vicksburg. Alexander Randall, the state's future attorney general and an ardent Unionist, penned in his diary that he found it strange many Marylanders "think otherwise." While he did not mention Harris or southern Maryland in this entry, the entry itself provides context to how divided the state had become, and how, despite the presence of large numbers of federal forces, some of the state's citizens were willing to express their support for slavery as well as their dislike of Lincoln and the war.[47]

3

Congress and the War

The House of Representatives that Harris desired to join was, from the start of its formation, a fractious and sectional entity and seldom were its members unified on any matter of national importance. For instance, during the 1812 war with Great Britain, there were several representatives, almost all Federalists, who spoke out against the war. Their Jeffersonian congressional opponents accused them of aiding their nation's adversary. Debates over the national bank, currency reform, relations with the various native peoples, and the federal role in infrastructure development were usually contentious. With the exception of a period during James Monroe's presidency dubbed "the era of good feelings," one would be hard-pressed not find a congressional session in which the threat of a duel or a censure vote against a representative who advocated for limits on slavery did not occur.

A brief understanding of the relationship between the House and slavery in the half century prior to South Carolina's secession is contextually important to highlighting Harris' role as the one truly "Confederate" legislator in Congress and understanding why he was brought to a military trial. The pro-slavery and abolitionist passions which were endemic to the House—albeit reflecting the nation as a whole—were carried into the wartime Congress by Harris, as well as by his opponents such as Thaddeus Stevens, Elihu Washburne, and Schuyler Colfax. In retrospect, when in 1856 President Franklin Pierce branded anti-slavery efforts in Kansas as a "revolution" and called abolitionists' refusals to comply with the pro-slavery government "treason," it was entirely predictable that once in power, anti-slavery congressmen would respond by labeling southern secessionists and their northern allies as "traitors." Likewise, it was unsurprising that a Republican administration, with the backing of ardent radicals in the House, would also proclaim the legality of restricting the mails to their opponents and suppressing free speech in other ways, since the slavery interests had used similar methods in the decades prior to the war. Because the Thirty-Seventh Congress, which convened on March 4, 1861, and ended on March 4, 1863, and its successor, the Thirty-Eighth Congress, which convened on March 4, 1863, and terminated two years later, was dominated by the Republican Party, when Harris stood in the Thirty-Eighth Congress, he did so as a member of a small minority.[1]

Prior to the Civil War, service as a federal legislator was considered a "part-time" job. Congress typically met in session from December until March 4, and on occasion could be convened into special sessions on the request of the president. While congressional committees met more frequently than Congress as a whole, the "part-time" nature of Congress explains why certain legislators such as Henry Clay or Daniel Webster were able to maintain a vibrant private legal practice. This was soon to change. When Lincoln requested Congress convene for a special session in July 1861, the Thirty-Seventh Congress, which was comprised of one-hundred and eight Republicans, forty-four Democrats, and thirty-one congressmen affiliated with minor parties, passed an extraordinary number of bills which Lincoln signed into law over a thirty-day period. In comparison, the first "New Deal" Congress under President Franklin Roosevelt did not accomplish the number of bills passed by the Thirty-Seventh Congress. Within thirty days, bills expanding the size of the militia, appropriations for the Army and Navy, the first income tax in United States history—a progressive tax on incomes over $800 per year—and significant limits on assertions of property rights related to slaves were among the bills passed into law. Some Democrats resisted these bills but they were unable to stop the Republican majority.[2]

When the nation came into existence, the Constitution's framers intended for Congress to be the preeminent governing body, and the House, in particular, embodied the nation's new democratic ideal of a representative government. Evidencing this ideal was the fact that the leader of the House, the "speaker," would constitutionally ascend to the presidency in the event that the president and vice president had died or were otherwise incompetent to serve. While the House had seldom been unified on any significant national issue, even the parties within it tended to be fractured along regional interests. Between 1790 and 1860, the political parties in the House reflected local and sectional interests far more than found in the Senate, where, until the Seventeenth Amendment's passage in 1913, state legislatures selected senators. The names of the parties in the House during this period illustrate not only the national ideologies such as the Federalist, Democratic, Democratic-Republican, Whig, Know-Nothing, and Republican parties, but also local or passing allegiances such as the Anti-Administration Party, the Jacksonian Party, the Anti-Jacksonian Party, the Anti-Masonic Party, the Conservative Party, the Anti-Lecompton Party, the Crawford-Republicans, the States' Rights Party, and the Nullifiers of South Carolina. By the eve of the Civil War, the varying surviving ideologies had coalesced into both the Democratic and Republican parties, but within each party, and in particular the Democratic Party, unity was an illusory goal. Several long-serving northern Democrats believed that secession was a treasonous act and although they also held to the constitutional efficacy of slavery, they agreed to support Lincoln during the war. There were anti-war Democrats who were also, to a man, pro-slavery. And Harris, in particular, appealed to a part of the Democratic Party that had largely already seceded from the Union.[3]

Harris' slave owning predecessors in Congress possessed an angry passion to protect their property by arguing points of constitutional law, presenting property-rights arguments in the courts, enacting laws to stifle abolitionist dissent, having northern pro-slavery allies win elections, encouraging the nation's territorial expansion, and resorting to violence. Yet there were attempts to reach a compromise between slave interests and northerners who opposed the political influence of slavery. The Constitution apportioned congressional districts on the basis of the total free population of a state, but added to this number was a further apportionment based on three-fifths of the slave population. Thus, a state such as Mississippi, or, for that matter, Maryland, would achieve greater representation in the House than a "free state" such as Connecticut. At the time of the Constitution's drafting, this so called "three-fifths compromise" was believed to be essential to preserve a "union" of the states, but over time it proved contentious because it gave to the southern states a power based on a population that the slave interests did not deem to be worthy of basic rights. Within three decades of the Constitution's ratification, the Three-Fifths Clause came under attack. The Constitution placed a restraint on the House by excluding it from the treaty-making and appointment powers vested in the Senate. In 1820, when the northern part of Massachusetts gained enough of a population to achieve statehood, its residents desired a separation from Massachusetts. Almost contemporaneously the residents of the Missouri Territory also desired statehood. Prior to the admission of Maine and Missouri to the Union, the admission of new states occurred so that for every slave state admitted to the Union, a free state would also be admitted. But Maine presented a thorny issue because unlike

Missouri, which had been a territory, Maine was to be carved out of an existing state. Southern slave interests argued that Maine was a fiction. Following Congressman Henry Clay's urging to preserve the Union through a further compromise, Congress ultimately determined that both Maine and Missouri would become states. Additionally, slavery was prohibited north of Missouri's southern boundary in any future states. This measure barely passed both the Senate and House, but it did result in a lull in slavery being the preeminent political issue. However, the Three-Fifths Clause also remained intact.[4]

The United States' westward expansion between the end of the War of 1812 and 1850 resulted in angry debates over Indian policies, the status of religious rights in new territories, and in particular, the spread of slavery. The catalyst for the most significant argument related to slavery was Mexico. From the time of its independence from Spain in 1821, the Mexican government did not enjoy good relations with the United States. Beginning in 1837, the House debated the coupling of the United States' relationship with Mexico and the spread of slavery. The possibility of a massive territorial gain in the southwest also meant that slavery could expand in its scope, and the political power of slave interests would also grow. Thus, the predictable looming conflict with Mexico ultimately resulted in northern accusations that slave interests sought to force slavery on the northern states. As historian Sean Wilentz observed, along with the War of 1812 and the Vietnam conflict, the United States' war with Mexico resulted in higher levels of vocal public dissent than the nation's other conflicts. Perhaps even the post–September 11, 2001, military actions did not generate as much political dissent as did the war with Mexico. The difference between the war against Mexico and the other conflicts, however, was that the war against Mexico was a one-sided affair which ended with an overwhelming military victory. Indeed, Arthur Wellesley, Duke of Wellington, who had reached heroic status for his victory over Napoleon Bonaparte in 1815, proclaimed that General Winfield Scott—the officer who led an American expedition from the coast of Mexico to seize Mexico City—the "greatest living general." This well-reported comment did not assuage the war's opponents.[5]

The Mexican American War, Slavery and the Realignment of Congress

In 1845 President John Tyler introduced a resolution to the House in which the Executive Branch would have the authority to annex the

3. Congress and the War

Republic of Texas, if the people of Texas voted for annexation. By "people" of Texas, Tyler meant the hundreds of Anglo-American and European settlers who had earlier come to Texas at the invitation of the outgoing Spanish government. For over two decades groups of Americans, as well as European immigrants, had settled in Mexico, but in the 1830s, the Mexican government applied strict religious laws and enacted other restraints which led to some of the settlers and a smaller number of Mexican nations rebelling against that government. In 1830, the Mexican government restricted immigration from the United States. Initially, the rebelling settlers had little inclination to join the United States. Rather, they intended to create their own republic, but they also realized that they had more in common with the United States than Mexico, and their survival would, in some measure, rely on support from the United States. Most of the individuals who took up arms against the Mexican government either owned slaves or were pro-slavery. On March 1, 1836, the settlers, known as "Empresarios," declared independence. This led to a war which resulted in Texas as an independent republic. One year after the declaration of Texas' independence, President Andrew Jackson recognized Texas as an independent nation. By 1840 the governments of France, Belgium, the Netherlands, and Russia likewise recognized Texas' status as nation.[6]

In spite of Texas' independent status, in both the Republic of Texas and the United States, there was a desire to see Texas incorporated—or "annexed"—into the United States as a state. As long as Texas remained as an independent state, Mexico could threaten to retake it. Although Democrat president Martin Van Buren had opposed annexation, his successors Whig president William Henry Harrison and nominal Whig John Tyler supported annexation. But there was resistance to annexing Texas in the House. Northern anti-slavery congressmen feared that the addition of Texas would not only spread the institution of slavery into new territories, it would also make the political power of that institution all the more difficult to curtail. For instance, toward the end of his life, John Quincy Adams, while serving in Congress, warned that the annexation of Texas would "secure and rivet" the "undue ascendancy of the slave-holding power in the government." When Tyler left the White House after his defeat to Democrat James Polk, Texas remained an independent country because the Senate voted against a proposed treaty with Texas. But this was soon to change.[7]

As noted earlier, the House is not vested with the authority to approve treaties, or vote on federal judicial nominations or nominations to ambassadorships and cabinet positions. But its representatives vote on the appropriation of monies as well as the laws governing new territories and federal obligations. The House also votes on the admission of new states to the Union. Thus, while the House had no constitutional role in the negotiations with the government of Texas regarding the terms of annexation, it did have a role in authorizing the president, through a joint resolution with the Senate, to have Texas join the United States. This is a critical point. When the joint resolution came before the House on February 28, 1845, one hundred and thirty-two representatives voted for annexation while seventy-six voted against. The majority of representatives who voted against annexation were northerners.[8]

In early 1846, Polk ordered military forces into Texas to secure its status as a state, but the movement of forces was also intended to provoke the Mexican government. On April 25 of that year, a small American detachment was attacked by a large Mexican force and an almost two-year war between the two nations broke out. The war was a one-sided affair in which the United States Army occupied Mexico City and also resulted in Mexico's loss of territory which now comprises New Mexico, Arizona, and California. Yet, in spite of the overwhelming victory, the war itself resulted in further divisions in Congress. Although the House voted to authorize Polk to commit the Army to a war with Mexico by a vote of one hundred and seventy-four to fourteen, the fourteen dissenters included John Quincy Adams and all were Northern Whigs who accused the president of seeking to extend slavery. Because Polk was a North Carolinian and slave-owner, Adams' accusations resonated in the northern states.[9]

On August 8, 1846, David Wilmot, a Pennsylvania Democrat, with the backing of a small number of other northern Democrats, introduced a measure, titled a "proviso," to Congress that would prohibit the spread of slavery into territories taken from Mexico. The House approved Wilmot's addition to an appropriations measure by a vote of eighty-five to eighty, but the Senate was able to make Wilmot's efforts a non-entity. Southern Democrats came to believe that Wilmot's efforts were part of a new scheme to outlaw slavery. Although many northerners opposed Wilmot, for the first time the Democratic Party was divided over the issue of slavery. Most of the proviso's supporters, however, did not embrace the abolition of slavery. Rather, they believed that the southern states had already exercised political influence far beyond their population at the expense of northern interests. A similar split occurred in the Whig Party in the northern states where anti-slavery Whigs, dubbed]"Conscience Whigs," clashed with Whig merchants and industrialists who at times promoted the legality of slavery and at other times professed neutrality about the institution. Often called "Cotton Whigs," the men in this wing of the party had financially benefitted from slavery.[10]

Four years after the demise of the Federalist Party in 1816, the Democrats who followed Thomas Jefferson and James Madison saw their candidate James Monroe run virtually unopposed for the presidential election in 1820. The led to Monroe's second term with a Congress largely supportive of his policies. In 1824 four men competed for the presidency under the Democratic-Republican banner and although John Quincy Adams won, he only did so with the assistance of Henry Clay. Four years later, Andrew Jackson—who had more votes than Adams in 1824—became president and he held the presidency for eight years. The 1828 election resulted in a contest between Adams who ran as a "National Republican" and Jackson who ran as a Democrat and claimed to be the inheritor of Jeffersonian ideals. Clay attempted to challenge Jackson in 1832 as a National Republican, but like Adams, he did not effectively distinguish himself from his past Democratic-Republican positions by establishing a holistic opposition to Jackson. In 1836, four men challenged Martin Van Buren—Jackson's vice president—under the Whig Party banner. The Whig Party formed from the efforts of the nation's political giants who had opposed Jackson. These men included Henry Clay, Daniel Webster, Robert Charles Winthrop, William Henry Harrison, William Magnum, and eventually John Quincy Adams. Their initial ideology centered on a strong federal government ensuring the nation's industrial growth, economic expansion, and the re-establishment of a national bank. Clay articulated that the government had to impose tariffs and duties on foreign trade to ensure growth, even if these actions had a negative effect on other segments of the American economy. Ironically, southerners usually suffered under his plan and he was from Kentucky.[11]

By the end of the war with Mexico, the United States was in a political crisis over slavery once more. Not only had Texas been admitted to the Union, but California, Kansas, and Nebraska were soon to be as well. As in the case of 1820, the leading proponent of compromise was Henry Clay. Clay had matured into an influential national force. Between 1820 and 1850, he had served as secretary of state, twice run for the presidency, and was, at the time of the compromise, a senator from Kentucky. Clay proposed to have California admitted as a "free state," the voters in both the Utah and New Mexico territories decide whether to be organized as "slave" or "free," Texas to recognize that the New Mexico Territory was not a part of that state, abolish the slave trade in the District of Columbia, and strengthen the Fugitive Slave Act. Although for differing reasons, pro-slavery congressmen and future Republicans such as William Henry Seward were angry with the proposed compromise, each of Clay's measures passed through both houses of Congress in some form. The so-called Compromise of 1850 succeeded in delaying secession by a decade, but it may have accomplished this success partly because the three presidents prior to Lincoln assured the southern states that they too supported the institution of slavery, even though each of them were northerners.[12]

In spite of the 1850 Compromise, both pro-slavery and anti-slavery men in Congress remained caustic toward each other. The most notorious instance of the anger of pro-slavery men resorting to violence in Congress occurred in 1856 with South Carolinian Preston Brooks assaulting Senator Charles Sumner with his cane. Sumner was unaware that Brooks intended to attack him and was unable to defend himself. Although the attack had occurred without warning and violated a social code of honor, and although Sumner was hospitalized with a fracture to his skull, Brooks was lauded throughout the south as a patriot. Southerners defended Brooks on the grounds that Sumner, one of the leading abolitionists in Congress, had insulted the south in a speech. Harris would later laud Brooks as a model of a manly politician. There were other threats and violent acts toward anti-slavery politicians. In 1858, Congressman Albert Rust, an Arkansas Democrat, proclaimed that all Republicans were "treasonable." William McKee Dunn, an Indiana Republican who later became judge advocate general of the Army, rebuked him. Rust demanded "satisfaction" and challenged Dunn to a duel, which Dunn accepted. The duel never occurred, in part, because a number of Presbyterian ministers intervened and the two men exchanged apologies instead. Additionally, Rust did not seem to know that at the time of the challenge, Dunn was an accomplished shot, and found out this fact during a meeting with one of the ministers.[13]

Three men successively took the lead in the 1852 Democratic Convention in Baltimore, Lewis Cass, Stephen A. Douglas, and James Buchanan. Forty-nine roll-call votes resulted in none of the three men receiving the two-thirds required to gain a nomination. Cass had been a military officer during the 1812 War against Great Britain, and then after the war served as the governor of the Michigan Territory. He had also served as secretary of war under Andrew Jackson, minster to France, and in the Senate. In 1848, he ran for the presidency against Zachary Taylor. Although Cass was committed to preserving slavery in the south, he articulated enough doubts about its spread into new territories that southerners in his own party opposed him. Douglas was more palatable to southerners but even among them his stance on popular sovereignty was worrisome because it did not protect slavery enough. After all, northern abolitionists could also immigrate into the new territories and in greater number than southerners. And, unlike the Constitution, Douglas only based popular sovereignty on the voting white population. In short, he did not adopt the Three-Fifths Clause into his doctrine. Buchanan was acceptable to the south, but for this reason, he fell short in the northern votes. In the end, the Convention nominated Franklin Pierce, a former congressman and senator from New Hampshire. Pierce claimed to personally oppose slavery, but he also detested abolitionism. He had supported the "gag rule," and argued that slavery was based in the Constitution's property rights. He was also a brigadier general in the Army during the war with Mexico which became an important point because Winfield Scott was his Whig Party opponent.[14]

If Clay and the signatories to the 1850 Compromise's various provisions believed that peace was at hand, they were soon disabused of this belief. In 1854 Congress passed the Kansas-Nebraska Act which divided the territory covered by the act into two regions for possible statehood. In 1853, the House passed the first version of the act by a vote of one hundred and seven against forty-nine, with southerners constituting the bulk of the votes against the measure. Because the act did not mention slavery, if enacted into law, slavery would have been prohibited from the new territory north of the Missouri Compromise boundary. The actual act as passed into law embraced popular sovereignty in Kansas. Following the passage of the act, settlers began to pour into Kansas and violence ensued as pro-slavery and anti-slavery forces tried to gain control of the territorial legislature. Although in 1855, a congressional investigative committee concluded that anti-slavery votes would have exceeded pro-slavery votes if threats, intimidation, violence and vote fraud had not occurred, the territorial legislature remained pro-slavery. However, even the congressional investigation was divided in its findings between northern and southern legislators. By the summer of 1856, the continuation of violence between anti-slavery men led by John Brown and the pro-slavery forces led to Pierce ordering over five hundred soldiers to be stationed in Kansas. Most of the pro-slavery men in the House and certainly the southern pro-slavery congressmen argued that the violence of the pro-slavery forces was justified on constitutional grounds. Certainly Harris would have joined in this position had he been in Congress at the time. On the eve of the Civil War, Kansas was slated to become a slave state, but because of the war, when it entered to the Union, slavery was no longer permitted in its territory.[15]

In 1856, the national electorate voted James Buchanan over John Fremont, the first Republican candidate, and Millard Fillmore, a former Whig president who represented the nativists. The first three years of Buchanan's administration were marked by a shallow internal peace as the nation turned its attentions to matters such as the Mormon Church's migration into the Utah Territory and an Army expedition to suppress them, an economic downturn which resulted in unemployment and labor upheaval in the north eastern cities, and, of course, debates between abolitionism and pro-slavery factions, the most notable of these being the Lincoln-Douglas debates of 1858. Then too came news that John Brown had tried to lead a slave revolt in northern Virginia with the hope of creating a national insurrection. In spite of Brown, abolitionists did not dwindle in number and several of them were elected to the House. In contrast, following the secession of southern states, Southern Democrats in the House began to defect from Congress. What remained was a leaderless Democratic minority in the House and Senate.

Peace Democrats and Copperheads

By the end of the first year of the war, the Democratic Party's representatives in Congress could be divided into two basic categories: "Peace Democrats" and "War Democrats." The latter group outnumbered the former throughout the war, and although the two factions shared similar positions on the constitutionality of slavery, the desire for popular sovereignty, a weak federal government, and a dislike of Lincoln and the Republicans, they were divided on the war itself. The peace faction desired what their very name implied. That is, they sought peace even if this meant that there would be an independent southern nation founded on slavery. While most of the peace faction wanted reconciliation with the southern states and reunion, they wanted reconciliation based on the legal status of the country prior to the Missouri Compromise of 1820. The war faction favored continuation of the war until the southern states surrendered and were readmitted to the Union as slave states. Some of the men in this faction would have accepted prohibiting the spread of slavery into any future territories and a permanent repeal of the Fugitive Slave Act as well as a modification of the Constitution to repeal the Three-Fifths Clause and base congressional apportionment on the white population only. But almost all of the war faction supported slavery.[16]

In 1862, there were between ten and fifteen Democrats serving in the

House of Representatives who could be classified as Peace Democrats. All, or almost all, of these men were virulently racist even in comparison to their peers and they falsely claimed that Lincoln favored miscegenation, that is, the marriage of African Americans and whites. Among these men were James Brooks, a New York Democrat who first served in Congress in 1835 as a Whig. Brooks argued that slavery was a constitutional right and its emancipation could never be lawfully achieved by either a vote or force of arms. He was joined by Walter Ellis Niblack of Indiana who had been a judge prior to his congressional service which began in 1857. Niblack claimed that because the abolition of slavery violated constitutional rights secession was lawful. Likewise, Charles Eldredge, a Wisconsin Democrat, urged that even if the southern states did not have a right to secede, a war to prevent secession was an unconstitutional undertaking. Daniel Voorhees, an Indiana Democrat who joined the House in 1861 and who had established a loose-knit militia in 1861 to deter a perceived attack from pro-war Indianans, may have exemplified these second tier congressmen. Throughout the war, Voorhees voted against most appropriations bills. However, not all Peace Democrats remained wedded to the argument that secession was constitutionally justifiable or the war illegal. Samuel Jackson Randall was a relative newcomer to Congress, having been elected from his Pennsylvania district in 1862, but as he had campaigned on an anti-war platform, the electorate from his district knew that he supported peace at the price of secession. Ironically, he also served in the Union Army at various intervals, and by the end of the war, he accepted the demise of slavery as a necessity.[17]

The three congressmen most closely associated as being anti–Lincoln, anti-war, and pro-slavery were George Pendleton, Clement Vallandigham, and Fernando Wood. Although in the first year of the war, the anti-war Democrats were outnumbered by their brethren who favored continuation of the war, they shared a common political philosophy that originated in the Jacksonian period. They uniformly distrusted centralized power in the federal government and believed that democracy was best preserved and protected at the county and state level. Most, but not all, Democrats also believed that slavery remained constitutionally feasible, and several pro-war Democrats who gradually became willing to sacrifice slavery to defeat the south and preserve the Union switched to the Republican and new Unionist parties. In spite of being outnumbered even in their own party, however, the anti-war or Peace Democrats were able to focus their party to try to resist the federal government's encroachments on individual liberties.[18]

George Pendleton was younger than many of his anti-war peers. He was born in 1825 in Cincinnati, Ohio, and educated at Cincinnati College—the forerunner to the modern University of Cincinnati—as well as at the University of Heidelberg in Germany. Pendleton was admitted to the bar in 1847 and married into the Key family. Later, when Harris considered Pendleton a friend and political ally, Pendleton's martial connection to the Key family may have formed the basis for Harris' opinion. During his time in Ohio he not only developed a dislike of abolitionists, he also came to distrust both Secretary of War Edwin Stanton and Secretary of the Treasury Salmon Chase. Like Pendleton, Stanton was a Democrat, but he had been outspokenly anti-slavery. After 1861 Stanton was, for practical purposes, a Republican. Chase too had been consistently anti-slavery before the war, and had been one of the early Free Soil Party members. In a sense, Pendleton's opposition to Stanton and Chase had evolved from an intrastate to a national fight. Pendleton served in Congress from 1857 until his defeat in 1864. Although the title "House minority leader" did not exist in the nineteenth century, Pendleton served in a capacity similar to the modern House minority leader. One of the aspects of Pendleton that Harris would find inspiring was that Pendleton argued that the Constitution could not be amended to end slavery without destroying the document in its entirety, since emancipation meant the destruction of property rights.[19]

In 1861 Pendleton spoke to the House and demanded that Lincoln cease the suspension of *habeas corpus* in Maryland and the other borderstates. He accused Lincoln of violating rights that predated the Constitution and indeed stretched back to the Magna Carta of 1215 in which King John of England was forced to recognize that even the British monarchy was subject to the laws of realm and had to respect the rights of Britons. Pendleton then reminded the House that these rights were incorporated into the Constitution. "It is an impeachment of the founders' honesty or their good sense to say that their work was designed to be operative during the quiet days of prosperous peace, and to be superseded whenever strife or commotion should afford both opportunity and temptation as a usurper," he argued. Whether Harris read Pendleton's speech is now unknown but he certainly would have approved of its contents as well as the risk Pendleton took in making it.[20]

Clement Vallandigham was born in Ohio in 1820. His father was a Presbyterian minister and as a result he grew up in a "strict Calvinist" home. He studied at Jefferson College and eventually entered the practice of law. In 1852, 1854, and 1856 he unsuccessfully ran as a Democrat for

Congress, but each election was a narrow loss. However, in the final election, his supporters claimed that voting fraud had enabled his opponent to prevail, and the House Committee on Elections investigated the claim. This resulted in a reversal of the election result and Vallandigham entered into Congress in May 1857. From 1857 until the outbreak of the war Vallandigham supported Douglas' "popular sovereignty" position, but with the war he became stridently pro-slavery. When, following South Carolina's secession, Lincoln called for the states to contribute 75,000 militia soldiers to the Army, Vallandigham countered that the president's actions were unconstitutional. In 1862 he urged the House to force the president to compromise with the southern states and promise to preserve slavery. Like Pendleton, during the war, Vallandigham became a constant critic of the administration. However, unlike Pendleton, his public speeches included encouraging men not to comply with their conscription orders. In 1863 he was defeated in his re-election campaign. Despite his defeat, Vallandigham was a vocal critic of Lincoln and he infuriated Republicans and War Democrats through his caustic speeches.[21]

Born in 1812, in Philadelphia, Fernando Wood moved to New York to begin a business in shipping and international trade. He became prosperous enough to successfully run for Congress in 1840 and served until 1843. In 1854, New York's electorate placed him in the mayor's office where he attempted to reform the city's police force, but in doing so he created another force based on political loyalty. In 1856, the state legislature created a second competing police force and a battle between the two police forces left the city without any effective law enforcement. By the time Wood left office in 1858, the city's poorer areas were dominated by gangs. The city's voters elected Wood to another term as mayor in 1860, and during the secession crisis he was heard to comment that New York City should secede as well. Wood's support for slavery had to do with not only his prejudice against African Americans, but also the source of his personal wealth. As a shipping merchant, he had made much of his income from cotton. In 1862, he was elected to Congress once more where he joined with Pendleton in opposing funding for the War Department and Lincoln's attempts to end slavery. Wood's younger brother, Benjamin Wood, was elected to the Thirty-Seventh Congress and shared Fernando's political ideology. The younger Wood had been a newspaper editor, but the government refused to permit his newspaper, the *New York Daily News*, from being sent in the mails.[22]

Notwithstanding the leadership of Pendleton, Vallandigham, and Wood, the anti-war Democrats were a minority in Congress, and although they often convinced other Democrats to join in their voting efforts, they failed to convince a majority of Democrats to recognize an independent Confederate States of America. However, they were willing to join with their Democratic peers in seeking a restoration of the Union based on traditional pre-war Democrat principles such as popular sovereignty and a firm statement from Lincoln and the Republican Congress that slavery would thereafter be constitutionally protected through vigorous enforcement of the Fugitive Slave Act and the repeal of the various laws and orders emancipating slaves in the Confederate states. The Peace Democrats appear to have believed that the longer and bloodier the war became, the greater their chances of succeeding in the preservation of slavery or the recognition of an independent Confederate States of America through negotiation. However, unlike Harris, who would later publicly express his hope for an actual Confederate victory through the force of arms, these men wanted to achieve their goals through a democratic process after convincing their peers and the population that the war could not be won without further mass bloodshed, if at all.

Republicans and Radical Republicans in Congress

When the Whig Party disintegrated after the 1852 elections, its members switched to the American—or Know-Nothing—Party, as well as to the Democratic Party, but there was no alternative party which had embraced abolition as a central tenet. A decade beforehand, a brief political movement lasting less than four years had coalesced into the Free Soil Party. This party lasted from 1848 until 1852 and its members nominated former president Martin Van Buren for the presidency in the 1848 elections. But Van Buren came in a distant third behind the Whig candidate and eventual president Zachary Taylor and the Democrat Lewis Cass. Moreover, Van Buren obtained no electoral votes and garnered only ten percent of the popular vote. In 1852, its candidate, Senator John P. Hale, fared even worse. The Free Soil Party managed to place nine men in the House. Following the Kansas-Nebraska Act, a fusion of anti-slavery Democrats, disaffected Know-Nothings, and holdover Free Soil aspirants met in Wisconsin to form a new party which became known as the Republican Party. While the abolition of slavery was the party's central tenet, its leaders also tried to mute nativism from its national platform and they formed a protectionist foreign and trade policy reminiscent of Clay's earlier economic plans. The Republican economic policy served its members well after 1856, following a devastating recession. In 1854 twelve men of the new party were elected to the House. In 1858, the Republicans numbered ninety-two men in the House, and while they were outnumbered by the one hundred and twenty-seven Democrats, their rise to prominence presented a challenge to not only pro-slavery forces, but in a larger sense the legal foundation of the nation. Prior to the Republican Party's rise, the abolition of slavery had been a theoretical idea based on Christian and other moral arguments, and abolitionism's adherents' best hope to terminate slavery was by local fiat. But from 1854 the Republicans argued that slavery could be ended through amending the Constitution. The election of 1860 which resulted in Lincoln's election, also resulted in a Republican majority in both the House and Senate.[23]

In 1861, the Republican majority elected Aaron Galusha Grow, a Pennsylvanian, as speaker of the House. Grow had originally been a Democrat, but like David Wilmot, he detested slavery and switched allegiances to the Republican Party during Bleeding Kansas. In 1858, Grow took part in a melee on the floor of the House with several Southern Democrats after he denounced slavery. When the Thirty-Seventh Congress convened, longtime abolitionist Thaddeus Stevens nominated him as speaker, and he had a quick victory over Francis Preston Blair, Jr., for the position. Although Grow was only thirty-seven years old at the time of his ascension to the speakership, Stevens and his supporters found Grow's staunch abolitionism and commanding oratory appealing. When Grow accepted the nomination, he exclaimed, "no flag alien to the sources of the Mississippi will ever float permanently over its mouths till its waters are crimsoned in human gore and not one foot of American soil can ever be wrenched from the jurisdiction of the Constitution of the United States until it is baptized in fire and blood." Although he aligned with the Radicals, and Stevens campaigned for him, in November 1862 he lost his congressional seat to William Henry Miller, a Democrat. Among Grow's accomplishments were several revenue bills quickly passed into law as well as the Homestead Act and the Suspension of *Habeas Corpus* Act in which Congress provided its approval Lincoln's wartime assertion of Executive Branch authority.[24]

Perhaps Grow's most important action as Speaker was his involvement in the creation of a congressional committee to investigate the War Department's war efforts. Titled as the Joint Committee on the Conduct of the War, Grow appointed Republicans George W. Julian of Indiana, John Covode of Pennsylvania, and Daniel Gooch of Massachusetts, and a pro-war Democrat, Moses Fowler Odell of New York. These men were joined by Republican Senators Benjamin Wade and Zechariah Chandler, and pro-war Democrat Andrew Johnson of Tennessee. All of these men not only supported Lincoln, they each were abolitionists of varying degrees. For instance, Odell, the sole Democrat from the House, adopted Stephen Douglas' arguments that secession equated to treason and if the defeat of the Confederacy required the outlawry of slavery, then so be it. While the committee was formed to investigate the War Department, in a short time its members went as far as to accuse Union generals such as Charles Stone of intentionally losing battles because of alleged pro-southern sympathies. Instead of moderating after the setback of the 1862 election, the committee became further entrenched in investigating "subversion" in the Army. Although the committee's members were likely sincere in their beliefs, their frequent investigations into senior officers evidenced how radically Republican a large portion of the House and Senate had become. When in 1917 Democratic and Republican Senators advanced a proposal to recreate the committee to "assist" President Wilson, senior officers including generals Hugh Scott, John J. Pershing, and Leonard Wood joined with Secretary of War Newton Baker in urging Wilson to veto any bill for such a committee because they believed it had a deleterious effect on the Union's war efforts.[25]

In 1863, the Thirty-Eighth Congress elected Schuyler Colfax as speaker of the House. Like Grow, Colfax was a relative newcomer to Congress, and he was staunchly abolitionist. Colfax was born in 1823 in New York City. His grandfather had been a general in George Washington's Continental Army, and his father fought in the War of 1812. In 1841, Colfax moved with his parents to South Bend, Indiana, where he became an attorney and the editor of the *Saint Joseph Valley Register*, pro–Whig newspaper. He spoke against the United States annexing Texas and going to war against Mexico claiming, like Wilmot, that the war would result in the expansion of slavery. During the election of 1852, he supported Winfield Scott, but used the *Register* to denounce slavery. He wrote, "the Negro is either a brute or a man and should be treated as one or the other. We ask you to treat them with humanity," indicating that he would champion equal treatment under the law. Colfax was first elected to Congress in 1856 as an anti-slavery Republican who promised that he would introduce laws to prevent the Army from being used to enforce the Fugitive Slave Act in the territories. Interestingly, he only won re-election in 1862 by a margin of 229 votes, but this did not prevent his ascension to the speakership. Yet, Colfax was not a forceful leader and he deferred to Stevens and others to argue against slavery and funding for the war.[26]

3. Congress and the War 79

Although Grow and Colfax could be considered the third most important men in the Union, in the sense that the speaker of the house is second in line to the presidency in the event that both the president and vice president die in office, neither man was as powerful as Thaddeus Stevens. Indeed, both men owed their position to Stevens, and it was Stevens who insisted on the membership of the Joint Committee on the Conduct of the War. Stevens spoke against the 1850 Compromise advanced by Clay and his supporters. Among its many "obnoxious features," he argued, was that it required his anti-slavery constituents in Pennsylvania to assist in the capture of runaway slaves. "No law that tyranny can ever pass will ever induce them to join the hue and cry after the trembling wretch who has escaped from unjust bondage," he challenged. Stevens personified the furthest reach of Republican aims in the war. In December 1861 he defended the stationing of large numbers of soldiers throughout Maryland. "I have no doubt that if our Army were to be withdrawn from Maryland, she would be thrown into secession in a week. I do not believe anything about the loyalty of the Maryland people," he claimed. More than moderate Republicans, Stevens wanted to destroy the institution of slavery and then ensure that African Americans were accorded equal treatment under the law. He also pushed for the education of freedmen as an instrument to ensure that slavery could never again occur in the United States. His hatred of slavery and southern institutions was perhaps only equaled in its passion by Harris' hatred of abolitionism. Prior to the war, southerners and pro-slavery northerners could openly deride Stevens as a crank. But once the nation was at war, Stevens became the most formidable force against the Peace Democrats in Congress. He also attacked Lincoln for not attacking slavery hard enough.[27]

By the time Lincoln became president, Stevens was an old man who had fought in most of the nation's political battles over slavery. He was born in 1792 in Vermont and when he was a young child his father abandoned his family. After several years of being absent his father was killed in the War of 1812. Stevens graduated from Dartmouth, but other than his intellect and passion he had little in common politically—other than a Whig affiliation—with that college's most illustrious graduate, Daniel Webster. In addition to the fact that Webster accepted slavery as constitutionally sound, he also tolerated the death penalty as well as the accumulation of wealth without restraint. Stevens disliked both of these other positions. Stevens moved to New York and then Pennsylvania to open a law practice. He campaigned against the death penalty, championed the rights of the poor, allied with John Quincy Adams—who Harris considered the worst president in the nation's existence—and became an anti-slavery Whig. At one time Stevens was also a member of the anti–Masonic Party. In 1836 he tried to shape the new Whig Party to accept the abolition of slavery as one of its tenets. Stevens first entered the House in 1849 where he quickly chastised fellow representatives for voting in favor of war with Mexico and the strengthening of the Fugitive Slave Act. By the time the war occurred, he had entered the seventh decade of his life and his health was deteriorating. Nonetheless, throughout the war he assailed Democrats and at times directed his anger at Lincoln for being too tepid on emancipation. As the chairman of the Ways and Means Committee, he had the authority to dispense with bills and appoint congressmen to other committees. As long as the Republican Party remained in the majority, Stevens had the ability to lead the House to "table" Democratic Party bills. At no time would Harris directly confront Stevens, but undoubtedly, Stevens symbolized all that Harris hated.[28]

Stevens influenced an array of Republicans to not only oppose most of the Democrats' efforts to moderate the war into a conflict for reunion only. He was also able to influence the House to have young representatives assume important positions. This included John Bingham who in 1861 argued to the House "some may think compromise is best, that conciliation is best, and that the surrender to principle, to some extent is best. I am constrained to differ with them, to dissent, totally dissent, from all such opinions." Although Bingham lost in the 1862 elections, he became a judge advocate who assisted in the prosecution of Mary Surratt and the others implicated in the conspiracy to assassinate Lincoln before returning to Congress where he authored the Fourteenth Amendment. In December 1863 Congressman James Ashley, an obscure Radical from Toledo, Ohio, who was elected to the House in 1858 introduced a resolution to end slavery for all time through the Constitution's amendatory process. Ashley had earlier proven his abolitionism by accompanying John Brown's widow to his burial site. He would, during the war, become the manager of the Thirteenth Amendment, and was instrumental in its passage. But it was Stevens who appointed Ashley to manage the amendment through the House.[29]

Stevens could also lead Republicans who sought abolition, but could hardly be called radical. For instance, he pushed Amasa Walker to argue to the House that no concessions on slavery could be made to the seceding states for their readmission to the Union. Stevens convinced Congressman William "Pig Iron" Kelley, who had left the Democratic Party over the war in Mexico and the expansion of slavery, to likewise proclaim that no concessions could be made with slave owners in both the south and the border states. Walker had been a long-time abolitionist, but did not approve of Lincoln's suspension of habeas and he had his doubts on the constitutionality of conscription. At the war's beginning, Walker was willing to compromise with the southern states to protect slavery in the south but prohibit it elsewhere. Like Walker, Kelley believed slavery to be an evil but he initially thought that restitution to slave owners was constitutionally required. Stevens disabused him of this idea. Stevens, in short, had a forceful personality and power base to unify Republicans on his most important aim, the permanent destruction of slavery and the establishment of equal treatment under the law.[30]

Perhaps because of the Emancipation Proclamation, historians have concluded that Lincoln was the first leader to apply the law of war to the goal of terminating slavery. Lincoln's act of ordering the emancipation of slaves in the southern states not yet occupied by the Army was, in fact, a move which comported with the laws of war at the time, and the nation's founders recognized a limited application of the law of war. A generation before Lincoln, John Quincy Adams argued that a president could accomplish emancipation through the law of war during a national crisis, though Adams' arguments were notional. But even before Lincoln issued the Proclamation, Stevens had advanced the very basis of it. According to historian William Blair, Stevens invoked the law of war as an instrument of abolition, even while recognizing that the Constitution, as drafted, protected slavery as a matter of property. Once Stevens made this argument, while advocating for what became the First Confiscation Act, other Republicans joined him. For instance, George Julian, a Radical from Indiana, claimed that Lincoln had the authority to order emancipation in all southern states. In addition to Stevens' contributions in the passage of the Thirteenth Amendment, his role in the shaping of the law of war, a recognized subset of international law, resulted in Congress approving laws which narrowed, and then destroyed, slavery for all time. With Stevens' commanding presence in the House, the Congress that Harris tried to enter was overseen by a gifted legal expert with a forceful presence that Harris would have had difficulty confronting even if he had the full backing of his own party. And at no time would Harris directly confront Stevens.[31]

Conclusion

There are three final aspects of the House that are critical to note. The first is that as long as the House was under the control of a Republican majority, the Democrats were limited to voting on bills. The Democrats could not determine the scheduling of votes, and to the extent that a Democrat introduced a bill, its scheduling occurred at the decision of the speaker or Stevens. In addition to the bills noted earlier, Congress also passed the Homestead Act, the Pacific Railway Act, which resulted in the transcontinental railroad, the National Banking Act, which established a basic federal standardization scheme for banks under a new position called comptroller of the currency, and federal laws punishing frauds against the government. No prior Congress had come close to centralizing authority in the federal government to the extent that the Thirty-Seventh and its successor Congress accomplished. While the majority of these laws had little directly to do with the policing of the general public, each had a relationship to the war and to some extent contributed to a powerful federal government. And each enabled an empowered Executive Branch to vigorously prosecute the war.

Related to this aspect of the House is that with secession and the rapid departure and diminishment of the Democratic Party from the House, those congressmen who remained behind were not only initially leaderless but were placed in a position of either having to support the war and quietly remain attached to Democratic policies or denouncing the war. Very few men initially took the second possibility in the war's earliest days. Their numbers and voices grew as time went on. But no congressman could initially argue that secession was justified and the south had a right to take up arms. Again, a few men later would espouse this position, but the overwhelming majority of the war's opponents in the north claimed, like Chief Justice Roger Taney, that although secession was unconstitutional, so too was a war to preserve the Union. In contrast, in 1917, fifty congressmen including the House majority leader Claude Kitchin, a North Carolina Democrat, voted against going to war against Germany. During the Thirty-Seventh Congress, no representative possessed as much vigor against the administration as would Kitchin and a host of others such as Senator Robert LaFollette. Harris possessed not only the vigor of Kitchin and LaFollette, but unlike those men who believed the nation's involvement in the First World War would enrich the wealthy at the expense of the many, Harris believed that slavery—that is, the property of the wealthy—was the supreme constitutional right.

The third aspect of the House was that as the war continued with a succession of Union defeats and stalemates at battles such as Second Manassas, Fredericksburg, and Chancellorsville, the Radicals, led by Stevens, increased their efforts at uprooting the "enemy from within" and pushing for the full emancipation slaves through Constitutional amendment. Although Lincoln would have likely issued the Emancipation Proclamation without any prodding from Stevens and the Radicals, and apparently Lincoln did not take cognizance of the Radicals' legal arguments, to the Democrats it appeared that Lincoln and Stevens were aligned with each other. This too resulted in a hardening of the Peace Democrats opposition to almost all of the war measures pending in Congress. Inevitably a nationally-reported clash would occur, though it could not have been expected that two new Democrats would be the source of the clash.[32]

4

"A damning speech," the Roots of a Trial

"Abraham Lincoln has proved himself not to be trusted for an hour."
—Benjamin G. Harris, April 9, 1864

Because he steadfastly remained convinced that the Army caused his loss to Calvert, Harris determined to run for Congress in Maryland's Congressional 1863 elections. As a result of redistricting, Maryland's Sixth Congressional District was folded back into the Fifth District. The state had yet to align its elections with the two-year election cycle in November during even numbered years, which most of the northern states adhered to. Interestingly, this alignment would occur in 1864, and so Maryland's congressmen who were elected in 1863 would serve an abbreviated term. In addition to his conviction that Lincoln had become a dictator, Harris and his supporters had specific grievances against the federal government, and it was on these grievances Harris forcefully campaigned. On April 15, 1863, Army officers arrested J.S. Downs, the editor of the *Saint Mary's Beacon*. The *Beacon* had printed an article accusing General Robert Schenck of subjugating Maryland's women. Although Schenck had removed the *Beacon*'s editor-in-chief, he was fully unable to suppress it. On October 3, 1863, its owners renamed it the *Saint Mary's Gazette* and the renamed newspaper remained dedicated to the county's pro-slavery cause. In addition to the military arrests and trials of citizens in southern Maryland, the local slave-based economy had deteriorated. The flight of slaves to freedom had become commonplace and with the absence of farm workers, the owners of large plantations, many of whom were in debt to banks, were at risk of defaulting on loans. In turn, the residents of small farms as well as merchants began to forfeit their properties in "sheriff's sales." Harris would have an easy opportunity to run a campaign based on the fear and anger of the district's voters.¹

Harris publicly voiced fears that Schenck would use the soldiers under his command to suppress pro–Democrat voters. In a rare, albeit brief, alliance with Harris, Governor August Bradford excoriated Schenck after the general issued a military order that began with the admonition that because "disloyal persons" were likely to disrupt voting in the state, the Army could arrest "such persons hanging around or approaching any poll or place of election." On November 3, 1863, Bradford wrote to Lincoln that he objected to the presence of soldiers by the state's polling sites and he informed the president that Maryland's laws forbade militia soldiers from "menacing voters." Bradford emphasized to Lincoln that he could not see a distinction in these prohibitory laws for the federal army to do the same. The *Gazette* reprinted Bradford's complaint to Lincoln in a move which must have assured some voters that the governor tried to protect their political rights.²

A few politicians outside of Maryland backed Harris against Schenck. Senator Willard Saulsbury, a Delaware Democrat, cautioned a crowd of listeners in Baltimore that Schenck would, like General Butler before him, attempt to interfere in Maryland's elections. Although the record is not clear as to when Saulsbury first met or corresponded with Harris, the two men shared a similar ideology and became allies in Congress. In March 1864 Saulsbury introduced a bill to the Senate to "prevent Army and Navy officers from interfering in elections in the States," and Harris promised that he would attempt to introduce a similar bill in the House. While urging his fellow senators to support the bill, Saulsbury once more referenced federal interference in Maryland's elections.³

One matter during the campaign that angered Harris was the *Gazette*'s treatment of him. In 1863 he wrote to President Lincoln and asked that no Union forces be permitted to interfere in the election. The *Gazette* obtained a copy of the letter and criticized Harris' tone toward Lincoln. It was not the case, according to the *Gazette*, that Harris had been disrespectful to the president, but rather that Harris had not been forceful enough. The writer of the article went so far as to accuse Harris of supplicating himself to the president. Despite the *Gazette*'s tepid support of Harris, he triumphed over the two other candidates, Charles Calvert and Jonathan Holland. Neither of these two men championed secession or publicly called Lincoln a despot of tyrant, though they vowed to preserve slavery in the state.⁴

Election of 1863 and Early Legislative Activities

Harris' congressional campaign was unusual in that he not only advocated for an end to the war and promised to contest Lincoln's assertion of Executive Branch authority, but he also, once more, campaigned on a pro-secessionist platform. Unlike the Copperheads or Peace Democrats who merely campaigned on the basis to end the war or oppose emancipation, Harris went further. As a self-proclaimed protector of slavery and the supremacy of whites over African Americans, Harris articulated the "justness" of the Confederacy. Still, he realized that Maryland was unlikely to secede because of the large numbers of soldiers stationed in the state. Nonetheless, he believed that the results of the election would worry Lincoln into modifying the Union's war aims to protect slavery and renounce emancipation, or cause the War Department to cease arresting and prosecuting civilians in military trials. During the campaign, Harris represented slave owners in federal court against federal government officials who had used slave labor for the improvement of roads or the construction of fortifications. Apparently the federal officials had paid the slaves an income for their labor, but had not paid the slave-owners as was the custom at the time. Harris had enthusiastic support among southern Maryland's voters for his attacks against Lincoln and Congress over their abolitionist and military policies. These policies are contextually important for understanding southern Maryland's slave-owners' political reactions.[5]

Shortly after the war began, Congress passed the Confiscation Act (which became known as the "First Confiscation Act") which authorized the seizure of Confederate properties to include slaves. The law did not apply to Maryland, but Harris rightly believed it was a significant step toward abolition. The law vested federal courts with the jurisdiction to review challenges to a seizure, but it was unlikely that southern slave-owners could contest actions in the courts. Because of Confederate military victories during the war's first year, only a small number of seizures occurred. The next year Congress passed what came to be known as the Second Confiscation Act. This law enabled the prosecution of citizens who aided the Confederacy as well as the seizure of properties belonging to such persons, regardless of whether the person was a northerner or southerner. Perhaps the most important feature of the law was that slaves who fled from the southern states were protected from being

4. "A damning speech," the Roots of a Trial

returned to their "owners." While this part of the law did not affect Maryland, the presence of hundreds of escaped slaves also resulted in an increased number of Maryland's slaves who left their "owners," and sought freedom. The law was also thought to have enabled an expanded military jurisdiction, even though there was no specific language in the law to this effect. Union commanders in Maryland beginning with General Butler, a man that Harris utterly detested and accused of being responsible for the "Pratt Street Riots," refused to have slaves returned to whites who claimed ownership.[6]

By this time Harris realized that Congress was unlikely to reverse its stance on slavery unless more Democrats were elected. In November 1862, the Democrat Party gained twenty-seven seats in the House of Representatives and increased their number from forty-five congressmen to seventy-two. The Republicans suffered a loss of twenty-one seats, but maintained a presence of eighty-seven congressmen. Twenty-five congressmen belonged to the Unionist Party which aligned more with Lincoln than his opponents. Many of these men were not abolitionists but they accepted that emancipation had become a tolerable necessity to bring the war to an end. At the same time, some members of this party also sought to have slave-owners compensated for the loss of their slaves, particularly in the border-states which remained in the Union. Initially, this party was led by Thomas Swann, the former mayor of Baltimore and a future Maryland governor. At the outset of his campaign, Harris argued that he would be able to lead a coalition of Democrats and Unionists to protect slavery in the border-states.[7]

Six months after the 1862 mid-term elections, the War Department permitted Union officers to recruit African American men into the ranks of the Army in the border-states. More galling to Maryland's slave owners, was the fact Army officers were allowed to also recruit slaves who had left the southern states. Earlier that year, the War Department constructed "freedmen's schools" in Saint Mary's and the other southern counties. Undoubtedly, these two features of the war resulted in an increased resentment against Lincoln and the Army. It also enabled Harris to capitalize on the hatreds of the voting white male population. Harris could claim that he personally felt the effects of the Confiscation Acts and emancipation. Slaves fled from Saint Mary's County to the north and freedom. Often, Union soldiers aided their escape and transit. Equally galling to Harris was the perceived shift in the attitudes of freedmen toward their former masters, where the deference shown to white plantation owners speedily melted away. "Some pretended not to know their masters, ungrateful wretches, to wish to disown one who had been like a father," Harris' wife protested against their loss of status.[8]

In October 1863, a Union officer went to "Colonel" John Henry Sothoron's plantation. Sothoron shot and killed the officer, apparently under the belief that the officer intended to recruit slaves to the Army. In response, the Army confiscated Sothoron's plantation and forced his wife and children to look for sustenance and shelter elsewhere. Sothoron and his eldest son fled into Virginia and took up arms with the Confederacy. Prior to Sothoron's flight, Harris corresponded with him about the impending special election. Harris expressed his concern that "military interference," would cause him to lose the election once more, but added, "the people want nothing more than the tyranny of this administration to cause them to lose office at the ballot box." Harris made a promise to Sothoron that if elected to Congress, he would "remain quiet "until the defense of Maryland requires him to speak." After the murder of the officer, Harris prepared to defend Sothoron if the Union were to capture him and he intended to argue that the killing was justified to protect property. While campaigning, he reminded voters that he had stood by Sothoron.[9]

Harris also made it a point to repeatedly attack Schenck. In the two decades before the war, Schenck had been active in Ohio's Republican politics and cast his vote in the 1860 Chicago Republican convention for Lincoln. Like Harris, he was lawyer and began his political career as a Whig. In 1843 he was elected to Congress, worked to repeal the "gag rule," and joined with congressional opponents against sending the Army into Mexico in 1846. He had also served as the United States minister to Brazil. In 1860 he stumped across Ohio for Lincoln's candidacy against William Henry Seward and Salmon Chase. After South Carolina seceded from the Union, he volunteered for the Army and although he had no military experience, he was commissioned as a brigadier general. Schenck led a Union brigade at the First Battle of Manassas as well as in the Shenandoah Valley, but he was not an effective commander and Stanton reassigned him to command the VIII Corps. Although a Corps is a sizeable force usually composed of two or more divisions, the VIII Corps was exclusively assigned to "police" Maryland, and Schenck oversaw it until December 1863. Ironically, he was elected to Congress in November to Clement Vallandigham's former seat at the same time Harris won his election.[10]

In early 1863, a military commission prosecuted and convicted Vallandigham after he had publicly spoken against the war and opposed conscription. There is a historic consensus that this trial ranks among the most important in America's history. The twentieth century's leading

4. "A damning speech," the Roots of a Trial 89

scholars of the nation's legal history such as, Lawrence Freidman, Kermit Hall, and Melvin Urofsky, articulated that the Vallandigham trial and eventual Supreme Court determination in the case, is a rare landmark because the Court determined, for the first time in American history, that it did not have jurisdiction over the actions of the military in regard to its treatment of a citizen.[11]

First elected to Congress in 1858, Vallandigham embraced Stephen Douglas' "popular sovereignty" ideology. With the election of Lincoln in 1860, Vallandigham transited from being a "Douglas Democrat," to championing secession. Indeed, he argued that it was better to accept disunion than to fight to keep the Union as a whole, and no war to end slavery could be justified under any circumstances because slavery was inherently constitutional. Unlike Harris, Vallandigham was never a slave owner, but he became increasingly vitriolic after the Emancipation Proclamation. On May 1, 1863, Army officers overhead Vallandigham encourage a crowd to refuse to assist conscription. Four days later, General Ambrose Burnside ordered Vallandigham's arrest.[12]

Two weeks before Vallandigham's speech, Burnside, in his capacity as the commanding general of the Department of the Ohio, issued a general order prohibiting a number of activities such as "protecting, clothing, arming, or assisting enemy soldiers or Confederate agents." Additionally, Burnside forbade the transporting of confederate mail. As a military department commander Burnside possessed the authority under martial law to promulgate this order, or so Lincoln argued at the time. Captioned as General Order 38, Burnside's order generally comported with the prevailing law on treason. However, there were controversial prohibitions aimed at stifling dissent to the war. Most problematic was a section which stated: "The habit of declaring sympathies for the enemy will not be allowed in this department. Persons committing such offenses will be at once arrested, with the view toward being tried as above stated, or sent beyond our lines into the lines of their friends." This part of the order conflicted with the Bill of Rights' recognition of freedom of speech as an inalienable right. Of course, an arrest for criticizing Lincoln was not at all unique, but as of Vallandigham's trial, only non-descript citizens had been arrested.[13]

A military commission trial was quickly convened. Indeed, it began one day after the arrest, and unsurprisingly Vallandigham was determined to be guilty of violating Burnside's order. The commission sentenced Vallandigham to "be confined for the duration of the war." This trial caught Lincoln and Stanton by surprise, and a delegation of angry congressmen, including Republicans, confronted Lincoln over Burnside's conduct and Vallandigham's imprisonment. Vallandigham appealed to a federal judge who determined that the federal courts, in following *Dynes v. Hoover*, possessed no jurisdiction over military trials. Lincoln then ordered Vallandigham to be transported into the Confederacy, but within six months Vallandigham had traveled to Canada and re-entered the United States.[14]

Vallandigham's arrest and trial were covered extensively in newspapers across the Union. On May, 20, 1863, the *New York Herald*, a relatively neutral paper for its time, warned, "the military precedent of Vallandigham's case must be abandoned or the deeply excited popular elements of New York may be inflamed to the most fearful extremities of resistance." The *Saint Mary's Beacon* had reported on Vallandigham's activities as well. Other prominent northerners such as Melville Weston Fuller, a future chief justice of the Supreme Court, denounced Lincoln over the military trial and exile of Vallandigham. Harris seized on Lincoln's treatment of Vallandigham for political fodder. Although Vallandigham was not "front and center" of Harris' campaign, Harris was able to couple the former congressman's treatment with the arrests of southern Maryland's citizens who opposed the war.[15]

Like Vallandigham's trial, the contest for Maryland's Fifth Congressional district was well reported by the northern and Midwestern newspapers. On November 28, 1863, the *New York Daily Tribune* reported that Bradford certified the state election returns, and although Harris had been successful in his congressional race, so too had Henry Winter Davis, a fervent Unionist. "So vanishes the last hope of a Copperhead tangle in the organization of the House," the *Tribune* concluded. (Although Davis had been an outspoken abolitionist, he took a dim view of military tribunals over civilians.) Harris was to be a lone voice of his state's slave-owners in Congress. For instance, John Creswell, a provost marshal, was also elected to Congress with the promise of promoting emancipation not only in the southern states, but also in Maryland. Creswell served in the state's pro–Union state militia and assisted in the military arrest of civilians.[16]

When Harris arrived in Congress he quickly made friends with George Pendleton, an Ohio congressman who was first elected to the House of Representatives in 1856. By 1862 Pendleton was the leader of the anti-war Democrat faction. He was opposed to secession, but, like Taney, he believed that the use of armed force to compel the southern states to remain in the Union unconstitutional. Coupled with his staunch opposition to the abolition of slavery, Pendleton was as far in opposition to Lincoln as any congressman, until Harris was elected. Harris also befriended Congressman Fernando Wood of New York. Wood was a former mayor of New York City, and another leading pro-slavery Democrat. In 1861, while serving as mayor, Wood suggested that New York City secede from the Union.[17]

Harris' Early Legislative Activities and the Continuation of Military Authority

On February 5, 1864, Harris wrote to his friend Jonathan Dent that the "Republican enemy was glorying in its power," and that attempts to emancipate Maryland's slaves had to be opposed at all costs. Harris promised Dent, who by this time had been elected as the speaker of the House of Delegates, that he would undertake efforts to secure compensation for slave owners in the event emancipation occurred on a national level. But Harris also evidenced that he did not understand the ideological certitude of Congress' foremost abolitionist, Thaddeus Stevens. "I shall claim almost forty million for Maryland and shall endeavor by a polite course to obtain as near that sum as possible," Harris penned. "I have reason to believe that Thaddeaus Stevens is for a liberal amount." In reality, Stevens would not support compensation for the loss of slaves because to do so would be tantamount to financing the very evil he had fought against for two decades. Harris also derided the so-called "War Democrats," for secretly opposing the war's continuation, but then publicly supporting funding of the Army. "The War Democrats have almost all approved of it, but still continue the foolish game of blowing the blast of war, as a deception upon their people," Harris complained before concluding, "Not a very reputable course but as they say it is necessary for them in order to have any influence at home."[18]

Harris' first congressional votes occurred as a result of the House of Representatives internal administrative mechanisms. On December 8, 1863, the Republican majority elected Schuyler Colfax of as speaker of the House of Representatives. This was an election which the Democrat minority could not truly contest, since from the beginning of Congress' existence, the speaker has come from the majority party. Harris appears to have not taken part in the vote at all. Shortly after the selection of Colfax, a second vote was undertaken to determine who would serve as the clerk of lower house. This position is essentially the House of

Representatives' record keeper, and it has no political power, except that it possesses an inherent "marshalling authority." That is, the clerk is charged with maintaining the decorum of the representatives. Harris voted against the Republican favorite and ultimate appointee, Edward McPherson, a former congressman.[19]

Despite his congressional duties, Harris remained a participant in state politics, particularly in planning for a possible secession. On January 21, 1864, he met with several delegates to plan for a secession vote in the state legislature if abolition was forced on the state. He also became a victim of several rumors from both his allies and opponents. On February 4, 1864, the Ohio *Gallipolis Journal* placed on its front page the oddly erroneous news that Harris had succumbed to small-pox before showing its animosity to him by reminding its readers that Harris was a vocal detractor of Congressman Green Clay Smith, a staunch abolitionist. The Gallipolis newspaper concluded its report by hoping "a better man will fill Harris' place." One week earlier, the *Gazette* claimed that Harris had been arrested on his journey to Washington City, and that the Army was transporting him to Canada. Implicit in this story was that Harris endured similar treatment to Vallandigham. This too was untrue.[20]

Harris voted against Republican bills throughout January and February, but he maintained his silence in Congress. When, on January 28, Schenck asked the House to vote on Lincoln's bill to permit conscription, Harris voted with the minority in opposition. Despite his hatred of Schenck, Harris made no speeches against the bill, and the fact that several congressmen opposed conscription was hardly surprising. Historically the conception of draft has been unpopular. Indeed, during the War of 1812, Daniel Webster opposed conscription and a vote against a draft in the Civil War would not necessarily align a representative with the Confederacy. On February 16, Schenck introduced a bill to the House of Representatives to consider whether the citizens in Arkansas possessed an organized government and were entitled to be represented in Congress. Most of that state remained under a military government and Schenck wanted to ensure that the state could not impede the abolition of slavery when and if Lincoln introduced an amendment to Congress and the House of Representatives successfully voted by a two-thirds majority in favor of the amendment.[21]

In an act which must have appeared odd, Harris voted against a bill that would have the federal government pay loyal slave owners for the loss of their slaves through emancipation. He urged that under the Fifth Amendment, all slave owners had to be reimbursed for the loss of their

4. "A damning speech," the Roots of a Trial

slaves including losses not only caused by direct government action such as emancipation, but also losses resulting from runaways. He opposed the entry of Nevada as a state because this would give the northern states two more senate seats as well as a congressional district and he suspected that all three representatives would be Republican. Nevada became a state eight days before Lincoln's election to a second term and Congress appropriated monies to establish the Freedman's Bureau in spite of Democrat opposition on February 8, 1863. The same day he voted against the admission of Nevada as a state, he also voted against the establishment of the Freedmen's Bureau.[22]

His other votes prior to April included support for a reconsideration of the laws enabling the confiscation of property from persons in the service of the Confederacy. He also opposed permitting federal monies to be appropriated for the raising of "Colored Regiments." However, he was not always in the minority. He joined in an almost unanimous vote to empower the Committee on Commerce to study the means for protecting against ship collisions in the major harborways.[23]

On February 11, 1864, the *Gazette* lauded Harris' first month in Congress. "Our Readers have doubtless noticed the gallant and independent course of [Harris] in Congress," the newspaper began. "His vote often stands recorded 'solitary and alone' for he refuses to give any aid or assistance to the present disunion Abolition or war." The *Gazette* went on to claim that he was the only congressman from a border state who truly represented the interests of his constituents and then excoriated Lincoln for usurping the rights of citizens. The newspaper also apologized for its earlier criticism of Harris. Perhaps because of the widespread support he had amongst his constituents as well as from the *Gazette*, he became emboldened to break his promise to Sothoron of "quiet service." But there may have been another reason for him to become vocal. Once in Congress, Harris increasingly felt the effects of the war on his personal wealth. In March 1864 a sheriff seized four horses, one bull, four cows, three buggies, and one cider mill from him in order to satisfy a debt to the Saint Mary's Saving Institution, a local bank, and another to satisfy a debt adjudged in a Baltimore court at the behest of the Saint Mary's Seminary. This was not the worst of his loss. The sheriff also seized a seventy-acre tract of land containing a horse racing track.[24]

Ultimately Harris broke his pledge to Sothoron of quietly serving in Congress because, from his perspective, his constituents remained under the Army's authority. In early 1864, officers stationed in the District of Saint Mary's investigated dozens of citizens for aiding the Confederacy.

Most of the investigations did not result in arrests, and of those that did, twelve ended up in a military trial. What most troubled Harris was not simply the arrests of citizens actually caught physically aiding the Confederacy, such as the case of a Calvert County resident who smuggled a pistol to a prisoner of war, but rather the arrests of citizens who merely spoke out in support of the right of secession.[25]

On March 27, 1864, Army officers arrested a Mr. Conrad, "a grocer," and seized his store for the offense of "victualizing" refugees from Virginia that the officers suspected of engaging in anti–Union activities. "Mr. Conrad and the closing of his store will doubtless have the effect not only to prevent a repetition of the offenses by him, but will deter others from committing the crime," noted Lieutenant Jonathan Mix to Major Levi C. Turner, the Middle Department's judge advocate. Although Harris could have directed his anger at Turner, he was to soon focus his hatred on Turner's superiors, Edwin Stanton and Joseph Holt. Both of these men were to have a direct role in Harris' later arrest and trial, and to Harris, both of these men were the very "evil" which he promised his constituents he would defeat.[26]

Edwin McMasters Stanton was born in 1814 in Steubenville, Ohio. His father was a doctor and his mother a Virginian whose parents owned a slave plantation. However, Stanton's father was an abolitionist of Quaker descent, and even though his family no longer attended a Quaker church, they embraced that faith's anti-slavery tenets. When Stanton was young, his father unexpectedly died and left his family destitute. Stanton was able to attend Kenyon College but left before earning a degree, and instead studied law under the tutelage of a local lawyer. By the time of the Civil War, Stanton's personal life could be described as tragic. While he was never healthy, his first wife and one younger daughter had died. He had gained nationwide attention for his legal acumen in defending persons accused of political corruption and murder, including the first successful defense based on temporary insanity. In 1859 Congressman Daniel Sickles murdered Philip Barton Key, the son of Francis Scott Key. Sickles discovered that his wife and Key were having an affair and he shot and killed Key. Stanton defended Sickles in the ensuing trial and convinced the jury that Sickles was not guilty by reason of temporary insanity. Harris' writings and Martha Harris' diaries are silent on Sickles' acquittal, but there is an irony that Stanton defended the murderer of one of Harris' relations.[27]

Stanton argued before the Supreme Court not only in *Dred Scott v. Sandford* but also represented the state of Pennsylvania against a bridge corporation, as well as Cyrus McCormick, the inventor of a revolutionary mechanical reaper, in a patent dispute. A decade before the war, he befriended Salmon Chase, and worked for Buchanan's administration deciphering Mexican land grants in California. This was an important issue since, following the treaty with Mexico, the United States government promised to honor the Mexican government's grants of land to individuals, and hundreds of land tracts were disputed between new settlers and California's earlier residents. In December 1860, Attorney General Jeremiah Sullivan Black enlisted Stanton's aid in formulating legal arguments against the constitutionality of secession. Stanton served as attorney general for the last three months of Buchanan's presidency.[28]

From the time of his appointment as secretary of war through his resignation during Andrew Johnson's presidency, Stanton was a dynamic and forceful member of the presidential cabinet. He was also controversial and frequently made enemies including Secretary of the Navy Gideon Welles, Postmaster General Blair, and even his former ally, General George Brinton McClellan. Stanton not only prodded generals into action, he accused three generals of treasonous conduct. He also claimed that a vibrant "enemy from within," aided the Confederacy. The defeat of this internal enemy, he insisted, required an expanded military jurisdiction over civilians in both the southern states captured by the Union as well as in certain areas of the north. In the first three years as secretary of war, the Army jailed and prosecuted journalists, state judges, and people who publicly spoke against conscription. Stanton also convinced Congress to strip citizenship status from Army deserters and it was not until 1958 that the Supreme Court determined this law was unconstitutional.[29]

Joseph Holt was a loyal partner to Stanton, but the two men came from different backgrounds. Indeed, certain aspects of Holt's life aligned with Harris'. Born in 1807, Holt grew up in a slave owning family in Kentucky whose wealth exceeded that of his neighbors. At the age of fifteen he attended Saint Joseph's College, and later transferred to Centre College. Although Centre College was not thought of as being in the same category as Yale or Harvard and was also not a law school, its faculty stressed a classic education including "high oratory" and a mastery of both Latin and the common law. As a result, Holt could deliver long, forceful and eloquent speeches. In its history, Centre College graduated two Supreme Court justices, John Marshall Harlan and Frederick Vinson, and two vice presidents, Adlai Stevenson and John C. Breckenridge, who also began their political careers as well-respected attorneys. Considering that these four men graduated within a seventy-year span, it is a notable achievement for a comparatively small college without a formal law school, even in an era where most men became lawyers by apprenticing in a law office.[30]

Holt's early political affiliation made it appear unlikely that he would eventually ally with Lincoln and the Republican Party, let alone champion equal treatment under the law for African Americans. He represented slave-owners in addition to banks and other commercial entities which profited from slavery. In the early 1830s, Holt moved to Louisville where he opened a new law practice and became the assistant editor of the *Louisville Advertiser*. He first became involved in national politics in 1835 by campaigning for Martin Van Buren and gained national attention for eloquently defending Van Buren's running mate, Richard M. Johnson, a fellow Kentuckian. Johnson had been accused of corruption, but ultimately the accusation did not stop his ascension to the vice presidency. The following year, the Democrat Party rewarded Holt by selecting him as a delegate to their national convention in Baltimore. (He would not likely have encountered Harris at the convention since Harris still remained a Whig.) After the Democratic Party's Baltimore convention, Holt moved to Vicksburg, Mississippi, opening a third law practice. By this time, he was known throughout the south for his legal acumen, and Van Buren named him as a member of the Board of Visitors at the United States Military Academy. In essence, Holt became a *de facto* legal advisor to the academy.[31]

In the first of several personal misfortunes, Holt's wife died during a yellow fever outbreak in Vicksburg and he returned to Louisville. While in Louisville, he married again, this time to Margaret Wickliffe. This marriage connected Holt with David Yulee, a loyal Jacksonian serving as one of Florida's senators, as brothers-in-law. Yulee staunchly supported slavery and remained in the Confederacy, and even though he did not hold any political office in the Confederate government, he was imprisoned after the war. Holt's time in Louisville was short. Having amassed a small fortune, for a two-year period beginning in 1848, he left his legal practice and traveled extensively throughout Europe, Egypt, and the Ottoman Empire. During this time he appears to have first questioned the morality of slavery. Despite Holt's growing dislike of slavery, at no point before the war did he politically embrace abolition, and like Harris, he found the abolitionist movement a danger to the "natural order." James Buchanan, once observed, "[Holt] went further in his hatred of the abolitionists than Christian charity would have warranted."[32]

In 1852 Holt vigorously campaigned for pro-slavery northerner Franklin Pierce, a man he later claimed was a traitor to the Union. Four years later Holt abandoned his support for Pierce and campaigned for

Buchanan. In turn, Buchanan rewarded him with a position as commissioner of patents, and later as postmaster general, a position at the time deemed as one of the more powerful offices in the Executive Branch. Holt's performance as the director of the nation's mail evidenced a strong dislike of abolitionists. "It is amazing to see the insolent boldness of usurpation and the blind servile submission of party zeal," wrote future attorney general Edwin Bates. "The postmaster general has already authorized his deputies scattered through the country to judge whether the mail matter coming to their offices is fit to be circulated; and to that commit a felony by breaking packages and examining contents."[33]

Buchanan often turned to Holt on matters of international and Constitutional law throughout his four-year term. It has been aptly observed that Holt's presence in Buchanan's cabinet provided the president a measure of "backbone" to his otherwise indecisive vacillating during the crisis which occurred after Lincoln's election on November 7, 1860. Indeed, as war appeared increasingly likely following Lincoln's election victory, Holt expressed his unqualified support for the union to his fellow Kentuckians. After Lincoln took office, Holt drafted a letter to Lincoln's confidant James Speed which he intended for widespread publication. In it, he denounced secession, but he also faulted Kentuckians for seeking neutrality. He declared that there could be "no neutrality between that glorious flag that now floats over us, and the ingrates and traitors who would trample it in the dust." James G. Blaine, a Republican wrote of Holt in 1884, "[he] was the only southern man left in the Cabinet. A native of Kentucky, long a resident of Mississippi, always identified with the Democrat party and affiliated with its extreme southern wing." But Blaine also recognized the unique turn Holt took after the November election with South Carolina's threatened secession. "Without a moment's hesitation, he now broke all associations of a lifetime and stood by the Union without qualification or condition. His learning, his firmness, and his ability were invaluable to Mr. Buchanan in the closing days of his administration," Blaine concluded.[34]

Although Holt had ultimately sided with the Union, initially he was not a part of Lincoln's cabinet, or appointed to any position in government. However, with the appointment of Edwin Stanton as secretary of war, this would change. In early July 1862, General Henry Halleck, commanding the Union armies, pushed for a statutorily enacted Judge Advocate General's Department. Stanton agreed with Halleck and requested that Lincoln appoint Holt. Congress found Halleck's and Stanton's arguments compelling and on July 17, 1862, created the position of judge advocate with the accompanying rank of colonel. By the end of the year, the position was elevated to the rank of brigadier general.[35]

On September 3, 1862, Lincoln nominated Holt, and with Congress' rapid concurrence he became the judge advocate of the Army. Almost immediately, Holt proved his loyalty by siding with congressional Radical Republicans on the matter of emancipating slaves on the basis of confiscation and informed Lincoln that confiscation comported with the laws of war. States-rights southerners such as Harris would repeatedly argue that the laws of war were unconstitutional in their application to American citizens. But Holt urged the opposite and his position would contribute to Lincoln's decision to issue the Emancipation Proclamation.[36]

Harris was hardly the only critic of Holt and Stanton. As noted, Postmaster General Blair and Secretary of the Navy Welles criticized both men for asserting military authority over the nation. The Democrats tended to be more hostile toward Hold and Stanton than members of Lincoln's cabinet. As an example, Ransom Hooker Gillet, who had served in Congress from 1833 to 1837 and had also been an assistant attorney general under Franklin Pierce claimed that Holt was the author of "a modern Bloody Assize," a term that referenced a period in seventeenth century Britain when hundreds of suspected rebels were quickly tried and executed.[37]

Congressional Censure

On April 8, Congressman Alexander Long, an Ohio Democrat, denounced Lincoln in the House of Representatives. Long was an antiwar Democrat, but before the war, he had been a member of the Free Soil Party, a predecessor to the Republican Party, and, as a state legislator, he also had endorsed Salmon Chase's Senate candidacy in Ohio in 1860. Although many democrats had openly opposed Lincoln, Long's speech was particularly vitriolic. He accused the president intentionally foisting war on the nation and seeking dictatorial powers over its citizens. And he urged the nation to believe that Lincoln had goaded the southern states into secession and the war. "An unconstitutional war can only be carried on in an unconstitutional manner," he argued. In contrast to Lincoln's "illegal war," Long proclaimed the constitutionality of secession, and called Jefferson's and Madison's views "immortal." Like Harris, Long insisted that the Kentucky and Virginia Resolutions were the proof of secession's constitutionality because these documents embodied the beliefs of the authors

4. "A damning speech," the Roots of a Trial 99

of the Declaration of Independence and Constitution. Echoing Copperhead claims that the war was fought for ulterior motives, Long claimed the Republicans intended "to place the negro over the southern white," and derided the Confiscation Acts.[38]

He fired his angriest attacks on the administration's expansion of military law over civilians, and compared the Executive Branch unfavorably with European governments. "Military governors and their provost marshals override the laws, the echo of the armed heal rings forth as clearly now as in France or Austria," Long claimed. In France, long viewed by Americans as a fellow nation with democratic leanings, Napoleon III had, in fact, reduced individual freedoms granted in 1848 under the Republic, and sent the French army to invade Mexico. By 1864, Napoleon III was unpopular in the United States and any comparison to him was an insult.[39]

As Long's speech drew towards its conclusion, he harangued fellow Congressman Green Clay Smith over his openly stated desire to crush the Confederacy, calling Smith's words at odds with American principles. Pointing out to his fellow representatives that the United States supported Greek, Hungarian, Polish, Irish, and Italian independence, he argued it was hypocritical not to recognize the southern states as independent. In contrast, Long claimed, Lincoln's prosecution of the war was based on territorial ambitions "the equal of Russia." His final comments, undoubtedly designed to provoke Republicans, included a demand for an immediate recognition of the Confederacy.[40]

When Long finished, Congressman James Abrams Garfield walked to the front of the House of Representatives and denounced him as a traitor, leading to an exchange between the two men where Long disclaimed he was a member of the "Knights of the Golden Circle," a secret organization dedicated to the overthrow of Lincoln. Garfield next took the rare step of forwarding a resolution for the House of Representatives to expel Long. Allan Peskin, one of Garfield's biographers, in briefly noting the incident referred to Long as "an unknown Congressman." Peskin also concluded that while Garfield had gone too far in accusing Democrats of treason, his speech was "a fine campaign document."[41]

After Garfield attacked Long, Schuyler Colfax accepted Garfield's reasons for an expulsion vote and opened the House for a debate on this topic. The Constitution, under Article I, section 5, enables one of the houses Congress to expel its own members in a process somewhat akin to impeachment proceedings. If two-thirds of the representatives present at an expulsion vote, vote for a member to be expelled, then the member is removed from the House of Representatives. The House of

Representatives had already expelled three congressmen in the first year of the war, but Long's case was different. The three congressmen, John Bullock Clark and John William Reid, both of Missouri, and Henry Burnett of Kentucky had not only voiced support for the Confederacy, they served in the Confederate government at the time of their expulsion. Colfax tried to expand the basis for expelling Long beyond Long's speech and claimed that expulsion was necessary to prevent the British and French governments from recognizing the Confederacy as a sovereign nation. These additional reasons were not as specious as might be assumed. Up until Long's speech, and for much of the war, Lincoln's administration, congressional Republicans, and at least five of the Supreme Court's justices feared foreign governments recognizing the Confederacy.[42]

Although Colfax had a strong argument for highlighting the damage that Long's speech could have caused to the Union, it was unlikely to succeed because there were enough Democrats in the House to prevent an expulsion. Moreover, the Constitution grants remarkable free speech rights to congresspersons through its "Speech and Debate Clause." For instance, in 1971 Senator Mike Gravel of Alaska read aloud portions of what became known as "the Pentagon Papers" on the floor of the Senate. Nixon administration officials claimed that the documents in question contained highly classified information and the release of the information would be detrimental to national security. If true, had a citizen read the documents to the public, a prosecution might have succeeded. But because the Constitution's "Speech and Debate Clause" protects the right of legislators to espouse matters that they believe necessary to the public interest, it is very difficult to prosecute a legislator. An expulsion and a crime are different "creatures" and in theory the standard for expulsion is lower than the standard of "proof beyond a reasonable doubt" that is required in American criminal trials. Nonetheless, Long had allies that defended him. Samuel S. "Sunset" Cox forcefully argued that the expulsion vote was an unconstitutional abridgment of the "Speech and Debate Clause," let alone an act of trampling Long's freedom of speech. Following Cox, John Little Dawson, a Pennsylvania Democrat, defended Long's right to speak for his constituents, but made it clear that Long did not speak for the party as a whole. Dawson's arguments did not stop some of the congressional Republicans from badgering Long, but Long appears to have capably defended himself. When Schenck demanded expulsion, Long retorted, to the applause of his fellow Democrats, that while he had the utmost respect for the majority of his Republican opponents, he did not have any for Schenck.[43]

4. "A damning speech," the Roots of a Trial

By the following day, it became apparent that the most congressional Republicans could achieve against Long was a censure for his speech. A censure is nothing more than a rebuke which carries with it no loss of power. However, Harris unintentionally provided new life to the expulsion debate through his defense of Long. It is unlikely that Harris had interacted with Long prior to Long's speech. Indeed, neither Harris' nor Long's correspondences indicate the two men had met. In the morning, Harris strode to the front of the House of Representative for the first time in his legislative career. Harris' purpose was to defend not only Long's right to speak but also to attack Lincoln and the Republican Party. He began his speech by noting that while until that morning, he was unaware Long shared his sentiments towards the administration and the conduct of the war, he intended to "stand by [Long's] side, come weal or woe." He went on to challenge Garfield's assertion that Long's words constituted treason by asking, "can not a man get up and say, we do not admire your tactics; we would rather have peace than war?"[44]

When Garfield rose to interrupt Harris, he refused to yield the floor to the Ohioan, and continued defending his belief in the wrongness of the war. Unlike other Democrats, Harris admitted he favored secession over war and argued that a war for abolition was an evil. "I am a peace man, a radical peace man; and I am for peace by the recognition of the south, for the recognition of Southern Confederacy; and I am for acquiescence in the doctrine of secession," he proclaimed amidst the jeering of Republican and Unionist representatives. After his frank admission of rooting for the Confederacy, Harris returned to defending Long, equating him with the Roman Republic's great orator Cato the younger. Cato, Harris recalled, unsuccessfully fought against Julius Caesar's ambition to rule the known world in disregard of Roman law. Now, Harris argued, he and Long were in a fight against a modern Caesar.[45]

To Harris, that fight meant preserving slavery as a property right. He argued that slavery was central to the nation's fore-fathers determination in creating "a Union of states." He derided abolitionists, and then turned to his "Christian principles" by claiming his hatred of war was manifestly increased by its subversion of individual rights. The proof of this subversion, he claimed, was in the very chamber of government in which he now defended Congressman Long. Carrying on in his lofty rhetoric, Harris endorsed slavery, in the process proudly admitting he was a slaveholder "until Ben Butler stole my slaves away." Harris' hatred of Butler was evident in a number of speeches he made after 1863, and his speech in defense of Long was no different.[46]

Had Harris stopped speaking at this point, he might have only faced derision from the Republicans. After all, when Harris claimed that Long's speech proved that another "soul [had been] saved," this statement was met with laughter, but no demand for expulsion. However, Harris intended to protect slavery at all costs. Like many prominent southerners, he believed slavery was ordained in Christianity and sanctified by God. Harris' proof for his charge rested partly in the history of the nation itself. "The Puritans were first rate men," he claimed. "They approved of slavery; they looked at every corner of the Old Testament and in every line of the New Testament, and they could find nothing against slavery, and they approved of slavery." Moreover, he challenged northern congressmen whose descendants amassed fortunes based off the slave trade to admit the source of their wealth.[47]

After defending slavery, Harris transitioned his speech to a lengthy historic tirade, blaming the north for the war, in the process labeling John Quincy Adams an "old scold, the worst man whoever lived in this country," and then accused Adams for being responsible for the Civil War. Adams, according to Harris, had "cultivated the ground for war." He next attacked Secretary of State Seward as the apostle of "a supposed higher law." Northerners, he argued, arrogantly looked on their southern brethren as "poor white trash," but in the process were surprised by their prowess in battle. This prowess stemmed from one reason alone, Harris argued: the Republicans' erroneous desire to elevate blacks to equality with whites.[48]

As his speech moved on, he rapturously spoke of a southern victory ending with independence, and voiced a further attack on Lincoln. "He has proved himself unfit to be trusted for an hour," Harris yelled. Before he could continue, Congressman Henry W. Tracy, a Republican from Pennsylvania, interrupted Harris under the pretense of seeking a point of order. Initially Harris refused to yield the floor, but over both Harris' objection to yielding and Colfax upholding Harris' objection, Tracy was able to loudly inquire, "I desire to know whether such language is not treason."

Harris ignored Tracy, but before he was able to continue, Elihu Washburne, an Illinois Republican and Ulysses Grant's champion early in the war, asked for Harris' speech to be recorded so that the House could determine whether Harris had committed treason. Harris countered he had no objection to his speech being reduced to writing, claiming he endorsed every word of it. In response, Washburne objected to Harris' continuing his speech, and Harris retorted that Washburne was "a coward for being fearful of truthful words." If any of Harris' words came close to constituting treason—albeit only if spoken outside of Congress—it was the following statement articulated in the middle of his speech: "God Almighty grant that it never may be I hope that you will never subjugate the South. If she is to be ever again in the Union I hope it will be with her own consent; and I hope that that consent will be obtained by some other mode than by the sword. If this be treason, make the most of it."

At the conclusion of Harris' speech, Washburne motioned the House to expel both Long and Harris. The next day, the *New York Times* headlined that there was "great excitement in Congress," over the pending votes to expel Long and Harris. The newspaper also reported that Harris had excoriated some of his fellow Democrats for failing to protect Long. Two days later, the *Times* urged that any punishment of Long would violate the right of freedom of speech, even though the newspaper disavowed Long's position. Perhaps, because Long had once been a Free Soil Party member and campaigned for Salmon Chase's Senate candidacy, some Republicans were willing to forgive his remarks. However, the newspaper did not come to Harris' aid. Harris speech, the newspaper noted, "was couched in language of most outrageous insult to every loyal sentiment of the House," and concluded that there "was no sound principle of free debate that would protect or palliate an offence like his." The *Times* went so far as to question Harris' "manhood." Yet, Harris did have an unusual voice recommend against expulsion. While Thaddeus Stevens despised slavery, he cautioned Congress against expelling a representative for stating his beliefs, particularly when—as Stevens accused the Democratic Party—a number of other Democrats quietly shared the same belief.[49]

Although the *Saint Mary's Gazette* supported Harris and undoubtedly so too did the majority of the Fifth District's voters, his conduct was not lauded throughout the state or even in the capital. The *Annapolis Gazette* recognized that his speech was popular in Saint Mary's but countered that his "traitorous conduct" did not "do for the latitude or temperature of Maryland." More to the point, the newspaper's editors lamented that the House did not expel him. Even the *Easton Gazette,* a newspaper located on the state's Eastern Shore, criticized Harris for desiring the south's victory.[50]

Executive Branch and Congressional Response

After Washburne moved the house to expel Harris, Congressman Sydenham Ancona came to his defense and tried to convince the House to "table" any debate on expulsion, but Washburne convinced the House of Representatives to vote against the delay. Ultimately, eighty-four congressmen voted to open a debate to expel Harris but fifty-eight stood firm in opposition. The inability to achieve a two-thirds vote to open debate meant that Harris would either have to engage in other conduct that the majority found offensive before expulsion could occur. Ninety-eight congressmen voted for the House to censure Harris and only twenty stood by him. This meant that a number of Democrats crossed party lines against Harris. For instance, Joseph Baldwin, a Pennsylvania Democrat who had served in Congress for one term, sided with the Republicans in the censure. So too did James Cravens from Indiana. Cravens had served in the Mexican–American War and switched to the Unionist Party in the last days of the war. Moses Odell and John Benedict Neele, both New York Democrats, likewise broke with the party and voted for censuring Harris.[51]

Harris' speech, in point of fact, was not popular even with the most stalwart anti–Lincoln elements in his own party. For instance, Benjamin Wood, Fernando Wood's brother who also served in Congress, wrote to Manton Marble, the editor of the pro–Democrat *New York World*, "I had all the leading Republicans on trial, till that Harris stepped in to mar it all … he ought to have been censured if for anything else, then for spoiling our triumph over the niggers." Marble was, perhaps, the most prominent of the pro–Democrat journalists during the Civil War. Daniel Voorhees, an Indiana Democrat, likewise informed Marble that Harris was, in his opinion, "a fool of circumstance." Harris' strongest ally was not in the House, but rather it was Senator Saulsbury who came to his aid. Saulsbury informed his brother that he was prepared to represent Harris should any expulsion hearing occur in the future, and that he had tried to get the House Democrats to promise to vote against expulsion.[52]

On April 13 A.J. Mattson, a Washington, D.C., court clerk, wrote to Elihu Washburn his disgust with the House of Representatives' inability to expel Harris. "While I rejoice at the bold effort made to expel the traitor Harris from his seat, I have to regret that our Congress contained a single weak-kneed Republican," Mattson penned. "Our country wants men—sharper knives and more backbone." Washburn agreed with Mattson, but explained that without more Republicans, little could be done to Harris other than condemning him.[53]

One day later, Francis Lieber informed the clerk of House of Representatives Edward McPherson that he had heard Harris' and Long's speeches and asked McPherson for a transcript of both. By 1864 Lieber was not only known as a champion of abolition, he was a leading international law scholar who had headed a committee to devise a law of war code for the Union. Known as General Order 100, Lieber's draft code was adopted to the disciplinary systems of modern western armies. Lieber enjoyed close relations with Lincoln, Stanton, Holt, and General Halleck, and his son Guido Norman Lieber served as General Nathaniel Banks' judge advocate in Louisiana. At the time of his letter, Francis Lieber was working on defining the extension of military jurisdiction over treason and he would later defend the Union military trials of Milligan and other civilians who acted to disrupt the Union's war efforts. Leiber wanted the Army to prosecute Harris for treason.[54]

Conclusion

On April 10, Lincoln's bodyguard Ward Lamon offered to arrest Harris. "Is this not giving aid, counsel, and encouragement to the rebellion?" Lamon asked. "Can your administration afford to discriminate between traitors who are members of Congress and those who are not?" Judge Advocate General Holt suggested arresting Harris as well on the basis that a military trial could possess jurisdiction over Harris where the Speech and Debate Clause would not be considered as a jurisdictional impediment or defense. However, neither Lincoln nor Stanton had yet concluded that an arrest and trial of a sitting congressman could withstand constitutional scrutiny. Lincoln's decision to do nothing may have reflected a desire not to repeat the embarrassment the administration suffered over Vallandigham. But it also may have been a well-planned strategic decision. After all, if the administration left Harris alone, then he would remain a *de facto* appointed spokesman for the Democratic Party, and this could only serve to keep that party's leaders on the defensive in trying to distance the party from Harris. In light of Harris' conduct in the late summer at the Democratic Party's national convention in Chicago, Lincoln's decision to leave Harris alone would appear to have been a masterful stroke.[55]

5

The Democratic Party Convention of 1864

> "What you ask me to do is, in reality, to support the man who stabbed my own mother; and I for one—and I believe I speak for the whole delegation from Maryland—will never do it."
> —Benjamin Gwinn Harris, while objecting the nomination of George Brinton McClellan at the 1864 Democratic National Convention

At the beginning of the summer of 1864, it was by no means clear that Lincoln would be re-elected, or that the Republican Party would remain in the majority in the House of Representatives. Within the Republican Party, John C. Fremont threatened to run an insurgency campaign against Lincoln. Fremont had been the Republican Party's standard bearer and presidential candidate in 1856, and he was a veteran of both the war with Mexico and the Civil War. He was also a staunch abolitionist. Despite the fact the Union armies had won important victories at Gettysburg and Vicksburg the previous year, the war appeared to drag on with little end in sight. Moreover, shortly after the two victories, citizens engaged in widespread acts of defiance against the government, including riots which resulted in the loss of life in New York and other cities and towns. Disaffection with the war provided one basis for the Democratic Party's candidates to campaign. Democratic candidates also could campaign on constitutional issues such as the suppression of free speech. After all, Union generals like Ambrose Burnside and Robert Schneck had shut down Democrat oriented newspapers such as the *Philadelphia Evening Journal* and *Chicago Times*. Of course, opposition to emancipation was a powerful issue, particularly when it was coupled with allegations that the Republicans not only promoted racial equality, but also miscegenation.[1]

5. The Democratic Party Convention of 1864

Two factors internal to the Democratic Party would work to undermine their chances to become a majority party, notwithstanding that the Lincoln administration's enabling of the soldier vote as well as other measures made their quest to achieve the presidency and a congressional majority difficult. The first was the rise of radical militaristic groups such as the Knights of the Golden Circle whose pro-southern leaders espoused violence to the Union as a means to secure an end to the war. Men in this organization plotted armed uprisings to assist the Confederacy. Initially led by an adventurer and conman named George Bickley, the Knights of the Golden Circle tried to engage in piracy against the Union, and some of its members went so far as to plan raids on Union prisoner of war camps to free captured Confederate soldiers. In the late 1850s Bickley defrauded investors in schemes to topple the Mexican and Nicaraguan governments and on the eve of the Civil War his creditors had filed fraud charges with the Justice Department. He had posed in the Confederate Army as a surgeon, but was arrested within Union lines. After Bickley was arrested and interrogated by Judge Advocate General Joseph Holt's subordinates, the Knights of the Golden Circle broke apart, but quickly reformed as the Order of the Sons of Liberty. From inside of prison, Bickley corresponded with Manton Marble, and Holt had these letters examined. A few of Order of the Sons of Liberty's tangential members were prominent Democrats such as Clement Valladingham. It was problematic to the Democratic Party that Lambdin Milligan and his associates, all members of the Order of the Sons of Liberty, were arrested and prosecuted following the discovery of a large cache of arms and plans for an intended uprising in Indiana. Events such as this arrest made the Union's suppression of newspapers appear to be a reasonable necessity of war.[2]

Various studies on Copperheads and organizations such as the Sons of Liberty have resulted in differing opinions as to how powerful these movements were, as well as whether Lincoln's response to them was reasonable. For instance, Wood Gray, who authored the first such study in 1942, argued that there was a relationship between the Copperheads and Sons of Liberty so that both organizations posed a threat to the Union. Twenty years later, Frank Klement claimed that Lincoln's cabinet members, and in particular Secretary of War Stanton, had conflated the danger posed by these organizations to suppress civil liberties and maintain a Republican majority. Jessica Weber, in her more recent study on the Copperheads, concluded that these organizations possessed sufficient political power to shape the Democratic Party's approach to the 1864 presidential election. Harris had no association with the Sons of Liberty and he barely associated with the Copperheads but he independently championed their respective causes.³

The second internal factor which undermined Democrat hopes for the presidency had to do with the choice of presidential candidates. For instance, New York's governor, Horatio Seymour, was a possibility to become a candidate. Seymour had served two non-consecutive terms as governor of the nation's most populous state and he had made statements both supporting the war and criticizing Lincoln. He also had approved of the state's raising "colored regiments." When approached by prominent Democrats however, Seymour refused to be a candidate. Instead, the party leaders turned to General George Brinton McClellan. As an officer commissioned out of the United States Military Academy, and as a veteran of the Mexican-American War, McClellan could hardly be called a "political general," at least facially. In the first two years of the war, he held a dual command as the general in chief of the Army and the commanding general of the Army of the Potomac. In this later capacity, he commanded the Union's largest Army during the Peninsula Campaign, as well as at the battle of Antietam. But he also aggravated Lincoln and Stanton through his slow and deliberate maneuvering of the Army and he frequently overestimated the strength of his Confederate opponents. He also oversaw the Army's arrest of dozens of civilians, which was, to be sure, a platform issue for the Democrats. And, while McClellan was not a "political general," he fused his political views with his command to include opposing a war for emancipation. He was a flawed candidate, and it was Harris who would point out McClellan's flaws as vociferously as his Republican opponents would do.⁴

The Ideology of Maryland Democrats in the Election of 1864

In early August 1864 Harris traveled to Chicago as an "at-large" delegate to the Democratic Convention. In addition to Harris, Maryland sent eleven other delegates to Chicago. Three of the delegates were considered "delegates at large," while the others represented specific districts. Of all Maryland's representatives to the convention, the most prominent was Thomas G. Pratt. A decade older than Harris, Pratt was a long-term state legislator who served as Maryland's governor between 1845 and 1848. During his gubernatorial tenure, he battled with Pennsylvania's governor's refusal to return fugitive slaves, despite Maryland's victory in *Prigg v.*

Pennsylvania. Like Harris, Pratt began his political career as a Whig, but switched to the Democratic Party. When in 1850 Reverdy Johnson left the Senate to become attorney general, Pratt was appointed senator in his stead. In 1861, Union officials imprisoned Pratt on suspicion of pro–Confederate activities, but released him within two weeks of his arrest. The basis for Pratt's arrest is that his son-in-law had corresponded with Robert E. Lee in 1861.[5]

Union officers led by Major Donn Piatt, a judge advocate, arrested Pratt again in 1863, ostensibly for refusing to take a loyalty oath. This time, Pratt came into General Benjamin Butler's custody at Fort Monroe, Virginia, and by November, Butler had determined that Pratt should be treated in the same manner as Burnside had treated Vallandigham. Indeed, Butler planned to escort Pratt into the Confederacy, but before he did so, he sought Stanton's approval. Neither Lincoln nor Stanton wanted to repeat what had occurred in Vallandigham's case, where even Republican legislators criticized the former congressman's treatment. As in many of the Maryland cases, Stanton and Holt took sides opposite of Blair and the state Democrats. Blair went so far as to criticize Piatt and Holt to Lincoln over Pratt's treatment, but Holt countered that Pratt had supported secessionists in Maryland. Nonetheless, Lincoln ordered Pratt released. Ultimately Pratt had the distinction of serving as Jefferson Davis' counsel in 1866 for a trial which never occurred, in part, because Blair had lobbied Johnson to forgo prosecuting Davis.[6]

Harris' closest ideologue, Richard B. Carmichael, had served in Congress for a single term from 1833 to 1835 and attended the Democratic Party's conventions in 1856 and again in 1860. He also served as a state legislator in 1831 for one term, and then continuously from 1841 to 1866. He was initially a Constitutional Unionist in 1860, but like many men in this short-lived party, he became an anti–Lincoln peace advocate. In 1861 he pleaded with Senator James Pearce to denounce northern abolitionism. He also noted to Pearce that former president Franklin Pierce had written to him in the hopes that the country would let the southern states go without a war. Carmichael's hopes to convert Pearce to a pro-southern or pro-slavery position were misplaced. By 1862 Pearce was willing to sacrifice slavery to save the Union.[7]

Carmichael's most visible offense to the Union occurred while serving as a state judge in Kent County, Maryland. In 1861, he ordered a grand jury to indict federal officers who had imprisoned three men suspected of interfering in a local election. In early October 1861, Secretary of State Seward informed General John Adams Dix, "it seems to me that that functionary should be arrested, even in his court if need be and sent to Fort Lafayette. You may proceed accordingly." Dix later warned Governor Bradford, "Hon. R.B. Carmichael has for many months been one of the prime movers of disaffection and disloyalty on the Eastern Shore of Maryland." Bradford apparently agreed with Dix and did not object as to any actions Dix might undertake against the judge.[8]

In November 1861, the Army's provost marshal for Maryland notified Dix that he possessed proof Carmichael was "a traitor." In early spring 1862, Dix again considered imprisoning Carmichael, writing that if he had proof that "the judge uttered treasonable language to a grand jury, then he would order the arrest." Though this specific form of proof never came to Dix, on May 27, 1862, he finally ordered Carmichael's arrest. When Union soldiers and a marshal entered Carmichael's courtroom, he resisted being arrested and shouted out to the court sheriff to instead arrest the marshal and soldiers in the courtroom. In turn, the marshal assaulted Carmichael, and depending on who reported the arrest, the marshal either beat him unconscious, or he received a superficial wound.[9]

When Stanton became secretary of war, he took over the responsibilities of investigating persons suspected of disloyalty from Seward. On June 25, 1862, Dix reported to Stanton that he suspected Carmichael had supported secessionists in the state's legislature, but did not arrest the judge because he could not substantiate his suspicions. Instead, Dix assured Stanton, Carmichael's judicial efforts to undermine the military's governance in Kent County was the reason for his arrest. Carmichael's imprisonment continued after Stanton replaced Dix with General John E. Wool, and Carmichael was transferred from Fort Lafayette to Fort Delaware.[10]

During his confinement, Carmichael petitioned Lincoln for release claiming that he had not committed any treason and had remained true to the Constitution. Carmichael's supporters, including Harris, also appealed to Lincoln for the judge's release. "I was not favorably impressed by the judge," Lincoln told one of Carmichael's supporters before concluding with his classic logic: "the Judge was trying to help a little, by giving the protection of law to those who were endeavoring to overthrow the Supreme law—trying if he could find a safe place for certain men to stand on the constitution, whilst they should stab it in another place." But while Lincoln did not agree with Carmichael's supporters, he ordered the judge's release on December 2, 1862. Even the release was controversial. Former governor Thomas Hicks opposed freeing Carmichael, and warned Lincoln that Carmichael's freedom imperiled "the Union cause."

5. The Democratic Party Convention of 1864

Carmichael recovered from his assault and temporary imprisonment, and like Harris, he became an increasingly entrenched anti–Lincoln, anti-war Democrat.[11]

The fourth at-large delegate, Isaac D. Jones, was of a like mind to Harris on the twin issues of slavery and racial equality. During the 1864 state constitutional convention, Jones opposed any legislation to protect emancipated African Americans. He went so far as to advocate forcing emancipated slaves into the Confederate states so that they could be re-enslaved. Immediately after the war, while serving as the state attorney general, he proposed discriminatory laws to prevent African Americans from achieving equality under the law or economic emancipation.[12]

Of the other eight delegates, John Rankin Franklin had served in the House of Delegates alongside of Harris, as well as one term in Congress from 1853 to 1855. Originally a Whig, Franklin switched to the Democratic Party on the same basis as Harris. A nominal Unionist at the war's beginning, Franklin did not support emancipation. Nor did William R. Kimmel, who was born in 1812 and entered state politics after the war's outbreak, endorse continuing the war or emancipation. Kimmel claimed that emancipation without compensation from the federal government was a basis for secession. Marylanders later elected Kimmel to the state senate in 1866 and Congress in 1874 and again in 1876. The remaining delegates, Hiram McCullough, George H. Carman, A. Leo Knott, James A.L. McClure, Oden Bowie, and Spring Harwood, did not publicly speak on any matter during the convention. McCullough served alongside of Harris in Congress between 1865 and 1867. His reputation, according to a contemporary biography, was that of a quiet legislator who unfailingly voted with the Democratic Party minority.[13]

From the convention's beginning, it was clear Harris was the *de facto* leader of Maryland's delegation. Only one other delegate publicly spoke, and the delegation voted lock-step in all matters that Harris advanced. Thus, it can be easily concluded that Maryland's Democratic delegates embraced Harris' criticisms of Lincoln, supported the right of secession, and proclaimed the Constitutional efficacy of slavery. This last point is worthy of independent mention. The delegates came from the entire state and not all of them were slave owners like Harris. Kimmel is a case in point. At the time of the convention he was not a slave owner, and as a representative of small land-owners, slavery economically hurt his constituents. Yet his hatred of Lincoln and fear of emancipation arguably overtook his duties to protect the economic interests of his constituents. The majority of delegates from all states, however, certainly believed slavery was a matter of property rights and not an unintended omission from the Constitution's guarantee of individual freedom.

Harris and the Nomination of George Brinton McClellan

The National Democrats opened their convention on August 29 when August Belmont, a wealthy New York politician, called the delegates to order. A prominent financier, Belmont had never held elected office, but he campaigned for Franklin Pierce in 1852 and James Buchanan in 1856. He was also the Democratic Party Chairman. "Never since the formation of our government has there been an assemblage, the proceedings of which were fraught with more momentous and vital results, than those which must flow from your action," he began before listing the vices which Democrats believed plagued the nation during the prior four years. These "vices" included "misrule by a sectional, fanatical, and corrupt party," which "threatened to ruin the country." Belmont promised "a calamity to civil liberty" if Lincoln was re-elected and he urged that all Democrats, whether "war democrats or peace democrats," unify behind a candidate and avoid a repeat of 1860. As Belmont ended his speech, he nominated former Pennsylvania governor and senator William Bigler to chair the convention.[14]

Holt and Bigler had worked together during the secession crisis when Bigler served as one of Buchanan's special emissaries to the southern states. But Bigler's government service came to an abrupt end when Lincoln assumed office. In his speech, Bigler continued the theme of the nation's civil liberties being imperiled and promised that the Democrat candidate, whoever that might be, would bring unity to all sections of the nation. Absent from his speech was any recognition of the sacrifices of soldiers, an acknowledgment that the south might not desire unity as the price of peace, or that the cause of the war had been the south's secession. In one historian's analysis, Bigler set a tone of negativity that characterized the entire convention. Although Bigler maintained that the only lawful means to overthrow Lincoln was "by the ballot," he did not distance the Democratic Party from the Sons of Liberty, the Knights of the Golden Circle, or other subversive movements. His speech was as short as Belmont's, and it was followed by an invocation and then a series of resolutions designed to govern the convention's conduct, such as the appointment of conventioneers to various committees, and also to ensure that the party retain its unanimity. Leading the discussion of resolutions were Clement Vallandigham, Samuel S. Cox, Samuel Tilden, and George Pendleton, men whom Stanton, Seward, and Holt already concluded treasonously undermined the Union's war efforts. Indeed, it can be fairly stated that Vallandigham dominated the attentions of the conventioneers on first day. He was also appointed chairman of the committee on resolutions.[15]

After the termination of the first round of resolutions, Charles A. Wickliffe read aloud two letters from a military prison in Kentucky to the full convention. A Jacksonian Democrat, Wickliffe had served in Congress from 1823 to 1833 and later as Kentucky governor. In 1840 Wickliffe also served as President John Tyler's postmaster general. He returned to Congress in 1861 to serve one term as a Unionist, but became disillusioned with the war. Ironically, Holt had vigorously campaigned for Wickliffe's election through the fall of 1860 because he believed it was essential for Kentucky to remain in the Union. In 1862, Wickliffe vehemently opposed General David Hunter's attempts to enroll colored soldiers in the Army, and for this action, Holt withdrew his support.[16]

In 1863, Wickliffe ran for governor as a Peace Democrat, but was defeated within his own party. The first of the letters he read aloud was written by one John W. Leathers which asked, "is this our country?" Leathers begged the convention to campaign for "restoration of *habeas corpus* and trial by jury." The second, and far lengthier letter authored by a "J.R. Buchanan," urged the convention to fight against "Lincoln's bold schemes for the perpetration of his despotism." Buchanan also warned of a Republican led *coup d'etat* replete secret societies and "their hordes of negroes." When the convention next published its roll call of committees, it was apparent that the direction of the convention would be dominated by Peace Democrats. For instance, Alexander Long sat on the Committee on Credentials, while Harris was assigned to the Committee on Permanent Organization. The credentials committee was charged with the duty of determining the status of attendees, including deciding who had the authority to speak to the convention's plenary sessions. The permanent organizations committee contributed to developing the party's platform, and its members also were also responsible for determining the status of the various factions should any challenge arise from one of the presence of a faction. Thus, Harris and Long were well placed to ensure that their positions on slavery and support for secession were protected. Moreover, perhaps as a signal to how fractious the nomination process would become, when the first day ended with Vallandigham, and not Bigler or Belmont, adjourning the convention.[17]

The following morning, the Convention opened with a prayer which included recognizing the war's victims, including the soldiers from both sides. At mid-morning, Horatio Seymour gave an impassioned speech, appealing for party unity and lambasting the Republicans as "intolerant fanatics and bigots," beholden to "sectional prejudices." Seymour equated the bravery of southern soldiers fighting for rebellion to the devotion of Union men, and he scoffed at the notion of subversive bands in the north imperiling the Union. Although Seymour's speech was hardly offensive in comparison to what was to come, he too did little to distance the party from subversive movements. Instead, he mainly concentrated on the government's trampling of civil rights. Had Seymour's speech been adopted as the Democrat platform, the platform still would have included freedom of speech as its center piece, but it would not necessarily have welcomed the end of war short of reunion. In the end, Seymour's speech had little effect on the platform, and this was due in no small measure to Harris.[18]

Several speakers followed Seymour, though all were brief, and the convention adjourned at mid-day with only the promise to reconvene in the afternoon at four o'clock. When the convention regrouped, it heard the agreed upon party platform from Vallandigham. By now, Vallandigham was universally despised by Republicans and anything he took part in was likely to be deemed as treasonous by Lincoln's administration. Known as the "Peace Plank," the platform excited the conventioneers, but it hardly served the party well in the coming election. The first of the resolutions promised a reunion of all of states, without a plan of how this restoration was to be achieved. The second resolution, which proved the most politically carcinogenic and ultimately delusional, declared "after four years of failure to restore the Union by the experiment of war, during which, under the pretense of a military necessity, or war power higher than the Constitution, the Constitution itself has been disregarded in every part." The resolution then demanded an end to war without a promise from the Confederacy for reunion and went on to condemn "federal interference" in Maryland, Kentucky, Missouri, and Delaware. If the Democratic Party were to have any chance at regaining the presidency and increasing their numbers in Congress, they would have to dominate these four states. Finally, of note, it accused Lincoln of "shameful disregard," of imprisoning citizens. The resolution's last part, a tribute to the soldiers and sailors, was muted by the condemnations of Lincoln, Seward, Stanton, and Holt which encumbered the entire plank. During the reading of the resolution the conventioneers "totally drowned" the voice of the speaker, so that, according to the convention's own report, the plank had to be read again.[19]

5. The Democratic Party Convention of 1864

Neither Alexander Long nor Harris embraced the resolution. Both men complained that the Peace Plank did not go far enough. To Harris and Long, the war was a failure to adhere to the Constitution and the conflict had to come to an immediate end regardless of the result. Long took the first step in urging the convention to adopt the Kentucky and Virginia Resolutions. He invoked Thomas Jefferson in offering this amendment, which, if adopted, would have recognized a right of secession. The convention did not deliberate on Long's amendment, but rather tabled it for later consideration. Then the convention opened for formal nominations.[20]

George B. McClellan was the first candidate to be nominated. John Stockton, a New Jersey delegate, did the initial honors for McClellan, and in the process Samuel "Sunset" Cox of Ohio seconded the nomination. With representatives from two of the more populous and powerful states forwarding McClellan' name, it should have appeared that the general was assured the nomination. But other delegates nominated lesser candidates. For instance, Senator Willard Saulsbury from Delaware nominated Lazarus Powell, a former Kentucky governor and current senator. Powell had spoken against military arrests and decried Ulysses Grant's order expelling Jews from his theatre of operations as an unconstitutional act of bigotry. Grant had, in 1863, issued an order expelling Jews from his theatre of command, but Lincoln countermanded the order. Powell also opposed emancipation, even in the form of a Constitutional amendment. However, he appeared to see that he could not beat Lincoln and asked that his name be withdrawn.[21]

What happened next resulted in the Ohio delegation fracturing. Michael Stuart, an Ohio delegate, broke ranks with Cox and nominated Thomas Seymour. Seymour was a former Connecticut governor who had served in the Army during the war with Mexico. He was also a prominent anti-emancipation politician. This nomination was greeted by "loud and enthusiastic cheering, equal to that of McClellan's nomination." Worried over support for other candidates, McClellan's supporters tried to close the nomination process. Their attempts were unsuccessful, and when Wickliffe nominated former president Franklin Pierce to further applause, it appeared that McClellan's supporters would have to fight for his nomination to succeed. Before Pierce's nomination could be seconded, Harris rose to second Seymour's nomination. Although he proclaimed Seymour "second to no man in the country," whose record on individual rights, as Harris saw it, was unimpeachable, Harris reserved the majority of his speech to attack McClellan.[22]

"Admit the fact that all our liberties and rights have been destroyed and I ask you in the name of common sense, in the name of justice, will you reward the man who struck the first blow?" Harris rhetorically asked the convention. Two delegates tried to interrupt Harris, only to have Bigler admonish them that attempts to interrupt Harris' speech violated the very tenets for which the Democrats were now fighting. "He who will is not a true friend of the Democrat Party ... the gentleman from Maryland is in order," Bigler ruled. Horatio Seymour also rose in defense of Harris' right to speak. However, Seymour's reasons for protecting Harris stemmed from a desire for party unity rather than a desire to have McClellan defeated. With Bigler and Seymour ensuring him the podium, Harris was free to speak to the audience, and he began a lengthy invective against McClellan, in which he likened endorsing the general to supporting "the man who stabbed my own mother; and I for one, will never do it—and I believe I speak for the whole delegation from Maryland—will never do it."[23]

Another delegate broke into Harris' speech, with the purpose of asking whether criticizing a nominee was within the convention's rules when seconding another nomination. Once more, Bigler sustained Harris, and Harris launched into a history of the general's conduct over the prior four years. Calling McClellan a tyrant, Harris warned the convention he could sustain the same charges against McClellan as easily as he could against Lincoln and Benjamin Butler. "Maryland has been cruelly trampled by this man and I cannot consent, as a delegate from that state, to allow his nomination to go forward unopposed," he raged. After all, Harris reasoned, McClellan was culpable for the suspension *of habeas corpus*, the military's arrest and imprisonment of Maryland's citizens, and the military's interference in state elections. Even McClellan's military record came under attack. "Why as a military man he has been defeated everywhere," Harris argued, "the siege of Richmond was not, I think a success; the battle of Antietam was not a success, and in him as a military leader you have nothing whatever to brag of."[24]

Harris finished by calling McClellan "Lincoln's assassin of State rights" before reiterating his refusal to support the general. When a delegate questioned Harris whether he refused to abide by the convention's determination if it nominated McClellan, Harris responded, "I am free to say that I will not do it." As he returned to his seat, a New York delegate confronted Harris and Harris pushed him to the ground. At the end of the day, Harris quietly clarified that he would vote for whichever candidate the convention chose, but clearly his criticisms of McClellan later benefitted the Republicans.[25]

Several delegates rose to defend McClellan against Harris' charges, but it would be impossible to undo all of the damage to McClellan that Harris caused. The Connecticut delegation had not intended to vote for Thomas Seymour, apparently because its members did not know beforehand that Seymour was going to be a candidate. While the state delegation did not outright endorse Seymour, after hearing Harris' speech, its leader lauded Seymour's candidacy. Toward the end of the nomination process, the only other Marylander to speak, Isaac D. Jones, rose in defense of Harris, and reminded the convention that McClellan had imprisoned the state legislature. Although Jones was willing to concede that McClellan had been misled by "false witnesses," this still remained a reason to oppose the general.[26]

Following Jones, Long once more sided with Harris. Long argued that McClellan had "gone further in suppressing free speech and hindering elections than has Abraham Lincoln himself." And, he reminded the Democrats that McClellan "has acquiesced in the emancipation proclamation." Although Long promised to vote for the nominee, he implored "give us a candidate for President, anyone except George B. McClellan, any one whose hands are clean." Again, several delegates rose to defend McClellan, but by now McClellan's supporters were on the defensive. When the convention adjourned on its second day, it was evident that while the majority of delegates nominally supported McClellan, the convention was hardly united.[27]

The following day when the delegates voted, McClellan received a majority of votes. In the first round of votes, he garnered one hundred and seventy-four votes to Thomas Seymour's eighty-nine. But this number fell short of the required majority. Of the three other candidates, only Horatio Seymour gained more than ten votes. Maryland cast its seven votes for Thomas Seymour, while Ohio split its votes ten and one half for Seymour and eight and one half for McClellan. Maine, Kentucky, Vermont, Delaware, Indiana, Wisconsin, California, and Oregon also split votes in varying degrees between Thomas Seymour and McClellan. Clearly Harris had an impact. However, the state delegations began to internally shift to McClellan after the lesser candidates withdrew from consideration. In the second and final round of voting, McClellan garnered enough votes to become the party's nominee for the presidency. Absent from McClellan's two hundred and two and one half votes were any from Maryland, and he had a less than a complete set from Ohio, Delaware, Indiana, and Missouri. Still, McClellan enjoyed support from Cox and Vallandigham as well as the majority of delegates. Equally damaging to Democrat hope was that the convention appeared to have bound McClellan to its Peace Plank. The vice presidential selection of George Pendleton, an anti-war Democrat, was more to Harris' liking. In this respect, the convention was not a complete loss for Harris.[28]

As the convention drew to a close, its speakers reminded each other that they were the heirs of Andrew Jackson, James Madison, and Henry Clay. (Clay was an odd choice since he had been a Whig and repeatedly sought compromise on the issue of slavery.) The conventioneers also proclaimed that the nation did not "spill a drop of blood" in dealing with public opposition to the War of 1812 or the South Carolina "Nullification Crisis of 1833." The Democrats exited the convention lockstep in their revisionist convictions that the Republicans had forced the war as a means to "unconstitutionally" end slavery and force racial equality. Convinced of their inherited wisdom and past record of success in avoiding conflict, they became equally certain that they would sweep into office and bring peace and unity back to the states. On August 31, 1864, this optimism was partly merited, if one ignored that the Union armies were progressing against the Confederacy outside of Virginia and the naval blockade had a significant effect on the south's ability to continue the war. It was true that the Army of the Potomac and its supporting forces were seemingly bogged down near Richmond, and Union soldiers stopped a Confederate force from threatening Washington, D.C., earlier in the summer, but elsewhere there were signs that the south was exhausted. The Union appeared to have the resources to continue to wage war almost indefinitely.[29]

Ultimately Democrat optimism was grossly misplaced. Having produced a platform which called the war a failure, Union soldiers would hardly support the candidate, and these soldiers would vote in large numbers. Additionally, the fact that General William Tecumseh Sherman's Army captured Atlanta proved a falsity to the convention's claim that the war was a failure in the minds of the majority of voters. Shortly afterward, news that a Sons of Liberty conspiracy to overthrow the Indiana governor and force the state into rebellion had been discovered also caused the Democrats to confront the possibility that some of their supporters had taken up arms against the Union. Worse, the Judge Advocate General's Department issued a well publicized report on subversive activity within the ranks of the Democrat Party. Finally, the 1864 Convention could hardly be said to have unified the Democrat Party's voters, which was precisely what the convention was supposed to accomplish.[30]

On October 18, 1864, Alexander Long led a group of disaffected Democrats in Cincinnati into another convention. He believed that McClellan could not win against Lincoln, because the election choice had to be between war and peace, instead of between two competing principles of how the war should be fought. With the exception of Long, the men who attended this convention were mostly local politicians with little national prominence, though one attendee, James Washington Jewett, entered the national stage as a congressman after the war. In spite of his agreement with all of the Cincinnati Convention's principles, Harris was absent from it. He had come to believe that although McClellan was an unworthy candidate, a third party guaranteed Lincoln's re-election. Instead, Harris directed his energies to try to defeat the adoption of a new state constitution and campaigned for local Democrat causes.

Long explained to the Cincinnati Convention that because McClellan's acceptance letter did not endorse the Peace Plank, a separate independent peace party was essential. The conventioneers had originally proposed to Long that he become the presidential candidate, but he declined their offer. Instead, he insisted that the convention's platform was all that was required. Other members were divided between Long's positions, and a desire to actually nominate a candidate to contest the election. Clearly none of the conventioneers were satisfied with the Chicago Convention, and foremost amongst their complaints was the Democrats refusal to incorporate the Resolves into the platform. "For sixty-five years, the Kentucky and Virginia Resolutions for State's rights have been the basis of the Democracy: They are the scriptures of the party," the Cincinnati conventioneers declared while lamenting that out of weakness, in Chicago, their party abandoned this core principle. In the end, Long prevailed over the convention not to nominate anyone, but rather to pressure McClellan and the Democrat congressional candidates to embrace the Peace Plank, and decry emancipation.[31]

The Cincinnati Convention became an exercise in futility. After proclaiming that the Democratic Convention had failed to nominate a true peace candidate, the conventioneers hearkened to Jefferson's opposition to Adams, once more stating that the Virginia and Kentucky Resolutions were the correct constitutional view of secession. "That as Jefferson made the rugged issue of doctrine with Adams as we must make it with the Federal Administration, if we would resist effectually the infinitely greater dangers which surround us," they determined. This was missing from the Chicago Convention, whose members only went so far as to agree to negotiate for reunion. The Cincinnatians pledged to exit the war at any cost, including recognition of the Confederacy. Like the Chicago Convention, the Cincinnati delegates criticized paper money, protective tariffs, conscription, military arrests and trials, the "fettered press," and "bayonet elections." These men went further through. They openly disavowed abolition, favored agriculture over industry, and called "the people of the Confederate States, brothers in blood."[32]

Aftermath: Election of 1864

As in the case of Harris' speech and censure, not all of the state's newspapers supported his conduct at the convention. The *Saint Mary's Gazette* favorably reported on Harris. But the *Easton Gazette* reported that he "so forgot his character and mission as an ambassador for peace that he knocked down some impertinent fellow who assumed he was a traitor in a style of pugilism that would have done credit to Tom Hyer." Hyer was, in the mid-nineteenth century, a "bare-knuckle" boxer of some renown.[33]

Although McClellan had no contact with Harris, he was not pleased with the conduct of the Maryland delegation and he let Manton Marble know of his anger. On September 16, 1864, McClellan wrote to Marble that he received "an indignant protest from some Maryland secessionists," against his promise to restore the Union. McClellan did not mention Harris by name, and there is little indication in the letter of any understanding of the damage that Harris or the Peace Democrats might have caused to his campaign. But McClellan at least knew that not all of the Democrats supported him.[34]

Noah Brooks, a correspondent and one of Lincoln's confidants kept the president informed of the Chicago Convention proceedings. Through a number of other sources, Lincoln knew that the Peace Plank was not universally lauded within the Democratic Party and McClellan was not popular in his own party. As to Harris' role in the Convention, Brooks informed Lincoln, "as you are aware, a few malcontents, like Long and Harris, refused to the last to vote for the nomination. Maryland, Kentucky and a great part of Ohio and Indiana refused to support McClellan in convention in any way, and they kept their promise, not voting for him." Lincoln's earlier decision not to arrest Harris and turn him into a Democrat cause célèbre paid handsome dividends. Harris was instrumental in fracturing the Democratic Party during its most critical stages in the presidential campaign. His conduct at the Chicago Convention was well publicized, and it left a lasting imprint. In 1884 Republican James G. Blaine reminisced that his party faithful kept abreast of Harris' conduct during the convention and that Harris had unintentionally contributed to Lincoln's success.[35]

5. The Democratic Party Convention of 1864

In early 1864, the Maryland legislature switched its congressional races to the same date as the presidential election, meaning that Harris, in reality, had only served a half of a normal term in Congress. He did not have a difficult campaign in his district. His district would not vote for a Republican for several elections after the war. Indeed, after Harris decided not to run for re-election in 1866, he was succeeded by Frederick Stone, a Democrat who defended Dr. Samuel Mudd in the military commission which sentenced Mary Surratt and three others to death. Harris did not campaign for McClellan throughout the state because, as he informed his constituents, he believed the general would continue the war and disregard the Peace Plank. During the late summer and into the fall, Harris campaigned for other Democrats who ran in neighboring districts. In this he was largely unsuccessful. In the 1864 elections, Maryland's voters elected Hiram McCullough as the only other Democrat. The state's voters also elected Charles Edward Phelps who had fought in the Union Army during the previous three years, Edwin Hanson Webster, an unconditional Unionist, who served as a colonel in the Union Army, and Thomas Francis who campaigned as a Unionist. Maryland not only remained decidedly aligned with Lincoln, Harris had other difficulties.

On October 13, Marylanders voters approved, by a vote of 30,174 to 29,799, a new state constitution which emancipated slaves without compensation to their owners. This infuriated Harris. He had spent much of his energies trying to defeat the new constitution and was embittered when he was unable to do so. There were reasons for the close ratification. Marylanders who had left the state to fight for the Confederacy could not vote, and the Union soldier vote overwhelmingly supported the new constitution by a margin of 2,633 to 262. To Maryland's slave owners, this was bad enough, but Harris found other aspects of the constitution galling. Traditionally the slave populations had been counted in the apportionment of legislative districts. The new constitution only considered white voters. Thus, the new state constitution diminished the political power of the slave districts and Saint Mary's County was threatened with the prospect of becoming a county with little influence.[36]

There was, to Harris and his fellow slave owners, one last legal argument to enforce a type of quasi-slavery in spite of the new constitution. One of the state's old slave codes enabled slave owners to compel African American children into apprentice work. Many of the state's slave owners, according to Professor William Starr Myers, a historian of the Republican Party and Woodrow Wilson acolyte, tenaciously took advantage of the code. In response, General Lew Wallace, a general in command of the

Middle Department encompassing Maryland, Delaware, and Pennsylvania, established that department's Freedmen's Bureau headquarters in Baltimore and issued General Order 112. This order authorized officers to arrest whites who tried to enforce the slave code. After several arrests, in January 1865, the state legislature removed the code and Wallace rescinded his order.[37]

On October 26, 1864, Union forces arrested a Democrat state agent and three state elections inspectors in Baltimore. The four men were in the process of registering voters, including amongst the soldiers stationed in the area. They also claimed to be uncovering fraudulent votes from being counted. However, Stanton accused the men of creating false registrations and destroying Republican registration cards. Harris argued, as he had done throughout the war, that the arrest was further proof that Republicans used the Army to subvert free elections. Although Democrats in Maryland were inclined to agree with Harris, the threat of the Army undermining the democratic election process was not enough to have the state re-embrace the Democratic Party.[38]

When the nation went to the polls in November, the Democrats were swept from legislative office. Maryland's voters also carried the state for Lincoln in what must have appeared to be a remarkable turnabout from 1860. After the 1862 election, the Democrats held seventy-two congressional seats to the Republicans eighty-two. The Republicans maintained a majority based on an imperfect alliance with twenty-five Unionist congressmen. The 1864 elections radically changed the congressional dynamic because it produced a Republican super-majority. The Democrats were reduced to thirty-eight seats. Holding 136 seats, the Republicans no longer needed an alliance with a third party, though they maintained it with the Unionists who held onto seventeen seats. Harris well understood that the Thirteenth Amendment was going to become a reality and there would be little the Democrats could do to stop it, unless, of course, Lincoln pushed for the amendment vote before the new Congress came into being.[39]

This is precisely what occurred. The Emancipation Proclamation was a war measure and following its issuance, it was never clear as to whether the Supreme Court would uphold it at war's end. Arguably, Lincoln possessed the authority to free slaves in the southern states which had not yet been occupied by the Union, but this act was not legislated, and there was no provision for the compensation of slave owners. Harris had argued that the "Takings Clause," of the Constitution, which prohibited the government from seizing private property without fully compensating the property owner, required the government to pay slave owners who lost their slaves as a result of Union actions. Indeed, Congress possessed the constitutional authority to dismantle the Emancipation Proclamation through the passage of legislation and certainly Democrats such as Pendleton and Harris considered this possibility if, and when, the Democratic Party achieved a congressional majority in the future.[40]

The process of a enacting a constitutional amendment to end slavery was well underway before the election. On April 8, 1864, the United States Senate passed a measure to abolish slavery as part of the Constitution's amendment process. The Senate's vote was unsurprising as the Republicans possessed over two thirds of the votes in that body. In June, the House of Representative failed to pass the measure, although ninety-three representatives voted in favor it and sixty-five representatives voted against. Harris was not present for this vote, and for reasons that are now lost to the historical record, it can only be speculated on as to why he did not travel the short distance to Washington, D.C., to vote. However, on January 31, 1865, the House of Representatives voted again and this time the measure passed by two votes. On February 3, 1865, despite Harris' efforts, Maryland became the fourth state to ratify the amendment. By March 1, eighteen states ratified the Thirteenth Amendment thereby destroying the institution of slavery.[41]

The passage of the Thirteenth Amendment was a tremendous defeat for Harris' constituents. The end of slavery destroyed the very economic foundations that had enabled the ancient "planter class" in southern Maryland to maintain their statewide power. Then there came news of Lee's surrender at Appomattox. Harris did not shy from expressing his dismay at the Confederacy's collapse and he lamented that Lincoln "would be sitting in Jeff Davis' reception chairs." His wife penned in her diary, "terrible news from the Army. Lee surrendered to Grant, I fear there is no longer hope for the south." To be sure, southern Maryland's white elites maintained their power through the enactment of racial codes. But, within the state government, the strength of the planter class would diminish and in its place the influence of the cities and industry would grow. Although Harris likely predicted that his constituents would lose their aristocratic status, the last weeks of the war created a different problem for them.[42]

Conclusion: The Assassination of Abraham Lincoln and Southern Maryland

In March 1865 Henry Winter Davis, a Maryland Republican, introduced a bill to the House of Representatives prohibiting the military from prosecuting northern citizens. Davis was a fervent abolitionist and deplored northerners who sympathized with the Confederacy, but he also believed that military trials of citizens were unconstitutional. This placed him at odds with Thaddeus Stevens, and although the two men wanted to enforce the Radical Republican plan for Reconstruction, Davis believed that the government had to adhere to the Constitution placing the Army subservient to the civil government. Davis noted that he had opposed the arrest of Maryland's legislators in 1861 and in an odd, albeit brief alliance, Harris sided with Davis. One congressman who rose to oppose Davis would later attempt to have Harris removed from Congress altogether. John Franklin Farnsworth, an Illinois Republican challenged Davis that Maryland had been encumbered by secessionists from the time that "a mob" attacked the Massachusetts Regiment in the so-called "Pratt Street Riots," through the war. Franklin, along with Steven, prevailed in convincing the House of Representatives to "table," Davis' draft bill. The determination of the House not to take up the bill enabled the continuation of military trials of citizens through the summer of 1865.[43]

On the night of April 14, 1865, a disaffected pro–Confederate actor named John Wilkes Booth not only assassinated President Lincoln, he led a conspiracy to upend the Executive Branch's ability to both continue the war and reunify the country. A Booth accomplice named Lewis Powell (aka Payne) attempted to murder Secretary of State Seward, and a related plan to kill Vice President Andrew Johnson was aborted. The conspirators hoped that the Union government would fall into chaos and the Confederacy be preserved. Harris did not know any of these men, but when Booth tried to flee arrest, he headed toward southern Maryland to the home of Samuel Mudd, a medical doctor and slave-owner. One of Booth's key coconspirators, John Surratt, the son of Mary Surratt, was acquainted with Mudd. Just as it is likely that Booth and Mudd knew each other, it is also likely that Harris and Mudd knew of each other. Mudd lived in neighboring Charles County which was part of Harris' congressional district. The distance between their two homes was much less than a half day's horse ride, and Harris had campaigned in Charles County. This fact would soon bring Harris back to Stanton's and Holt's attentions.[44]

6

The Military Prosecution of a Congressman

On April 16, 1865, Radical Republicans led by Ohio Senator Benjamin Wade visited with President Andrew Johnson and gained the president's assurance that the Army would be used to police the southern states and ensure that Reconstruction would commence without hindrance. Wade, a longtime abolitionist who chaired the Joint Committee on the Conduct of the War, had sided with Thaddeus Stevens in trying to pressure Lincoln to commit to full abolition and equality. Had Johnson embraced Wade's and Stevens' vision of Reconstruction, the Army would have taken over law enforcement duties in the southern states for several years, and military arrests and trials would have continued for several years. But for the intervention of the Supreme Court in 1866, military trials might have also continued in the northern states. For the first few month of his presidency Johnson gave little indication to the Radicals that he would not be their ally. Commensurately, he also caused fear throughout the southern states that he would oversee a vindictive victory. The War Department's treatment of Benjamin Gwinn Harris would provide credence to this fear.[1]

Indeed, on Johnson's ascension to the presidency, Martha Harris expressed in her diary that any hope of a peaceful restoration of the Union was dashed because of who and what she believed Johnson represented. Johnson was born into poverty in North Carolina in 1808, but moved to Tennessee while plying his trade as a tailor. He served in the state legislature and then in House of Representatives from 1843 to 1853, in the Senate between 1857 and 1862, and he was also appointed as the military governor of Tennessee after leaving the Senate. Johnson replaced Hannibal Hamlin as vice president in March 1865, and in less than two months, he rose to the presidency. He remained a pro–Union Democrat during the war but was never an abolitionist. Indeed, he intensely disliked African Americans with a bigotry that mirrored Harris' hatreds as well as those of the Copperheads. But he also hated the institution of slavery and large plantation slave-owners because he believed they consigned the majority of white men and women into a form of serfdom. Johnson was, in essence, a poor man who hated the institution that kept his family in poverty and Martha Harris realized that as slave owners, they represented the very thing that the new president despised the most.[2]

The Arrest of Harris

On the afternoon of April 26, 1865, Benjamin Gwinn Harris provided a dollar apiece to two paroled Confederate prisoners of war. The two former soldiers did not know Harris, and it appears from the historic record that the meeting was a happenstance. What also appears to have occurred was that the paroled soldiers had two discussions with Harris, and in between the two discussions, they sought out a Union officer named Major Waite to obtain a pass to enter Baltimore. On May 21, 1862, Governor Augustus Bradford appointed Waite as a first lieutenant and recruiting officer to the Third Maryland Volunteers, and assigned him to Saint Mary's County. Waite fought at Harper's Ferry in 1862 during Lee's invasion of Maryland which culminated in the Battle of Antietam. After being injured at Antietam, Waite returned to Saint Mary's County as an adjutant to the commanding officer of the VIII Corps. Harris would later allege that Waite had ordered the paroled soldiers to entrap him in an act of treason. However, on April 22, General James Barnes, the commander of the District of Saint Mary's County ordered Waite to grant passes to paroled prisoners of war who undertook a loyalty oath in the presence of two officers. Thus, whatever Waite's motivations were at the time, he was performing his military duties.[3]

Because southern Maryland contained prisoner of war encampments, the region swarmed with recently paroled prisoners, and so a meeting between a civilian and a parolee was not unusual. Indeed, the *Easton Gazette* reported that throughout April and May, "numbers of guerrillas and rebel soldiers have at various times crossed the Potomac and been welcomed into these counties." The newspaper added that blockade running had been common in Saint Mary's County. The rules governing paroled prisoners were such that they were prohibited from returning to their homes until they undertook a loyalty oath and promised to take no

6. The Military Prosecution of a Congressman 127

further action against the United States. A parolee could face a military trial and a death sentence for violating a loyalty oath. Additionally, there were no provisions in the United States Treasury to pay for the transit of prisoners to their homes, and until the end of May 1865, a paroled prisoner was responsible for paying for their own transport home. Other rules further constrained paroled prisoners of war. Citizens were not permitted to aid parolees to enter the southern states or return to their homes before a paroled prisoner took a loyalty oath. Undoubtedly it was a crime to aid a released prisoner of war to return to the south with the intent that the prisoner would rejoin in the fight against the Union. Likewise it was a well-known offense under the law of war to encourage a released prisoner to take up arms once more. In spite of these rules, a Union civilian who assisted paroled prisoners of war returning home likely would not be the Army's primary concern after the night of April 14, 1865.[4]

In the immediate aftermath of Lincoln's assassination, War Department agents scoured Maryland and Virginia and searched not only for Booth and his known accomplices, but also for evidence of a far deeper conspiracy. Judge Advocate General Holt was unequivocally convinced that the assassination conspiracy originated with Jefferson Davis and the conspiracy reached as far as Canada because there were several confederate agents there. But Holt was also provided information that Harris, along with other southern Marylanders had assisted the conspiracy. As a result, Harris became ensnared in Holt's quest to bring the full conspiracy to justice. Booth had traversed in a direction toward Harris' home and Doctor Samuel Mudd was acquainted with Harris. During the military trial of Mary Surratt and her fellow conspirators, Holt would reference various witnesses' associations to Harris.[5]

After the assassination, Holt assigned Major Levi Turner, his long-serving judge advocate, to investigate subversive citizens in Maryland and northern Virginia. By May 1, Turner's investigations led to the arrests of seventeen citizens. With the exception of Doctor Mudd, none of the arrested citizens were indicted for taking part in the assassination or for assisting the conspirators in their escape attempts, but several civilians were imprisoned for months at the Old Capitol Prison nonetheless. Included in their number were Austin Adams, a Maryland farmer reported to have helped Booth and his accomplice David Harold escape from the capitol, and Walter M. Barnes, a saloon keeper, "cognizant or implicated in the murder of the president." Barnes was neither cognizant nor implicated in the assassination, though he publicly exulted in Lincoln's murder. Likewise Adams was innocent of wrongdoing. Also innocent of complicity in the assassination was Edward Barry of Leonardtown, Maryland, who shared a cell with Barnes. Once at the Old Capitol Prison, they were not far from the solitary cell of Benjamin Gwinn Harris, their congressman. Turner believed that each of the three men were a potential link between Harris and the assignation conspiracy.[6]

Turner also caused James M. Farr, a Dranesville, Virginia, farmer to be arrested on April 22, 1865, for "having been in the plot to assassinate the president," simply because Farr had entered Saint Mary's County in the hours after Booth's act. Based on Turner's investigation, federal forces arrested Washington Traumill "in the plot to assassinate the President." Traumill, like Harris, was from Leonardtown. The evidence was, in each case, unsubstantiated because there simply was no link between these individuals and the president's murder. Nor was there any true link between Booth and Harris or between Harris and Surratt other than perhaps a shared political ideology. Ultimately, the existence of any tie between Harris and the assassination was patently absurd. But Harris had engaged in other acts "against the Union" which were far easier to prove.[7]

Harris' arrest was different than that of the others for the simple fact that the president knew that the arrest was to occur beforehand. On April 29, Charles A. Dana, the assistant secretary of war, ordered General Christopher C. Auger, a successful general who was recently appointed as commanding general in Maryland, to arrest Harris and convey him to the Old Capitol Prison in Washington, D.C. Dana informed Johnson that he had issued this order and the president had time to either countermand it or release Harris from arrest at a later time. But in the time between the arrest and trial, Johnson did not order any relief for Harris. Importantly, Johnson's presidential papers are noticeably silent on Harris over any matter, including his later order to have Harris released from prison. Martha Harris penned in her diary that she suspected the arrest had been justified by "falsehoods told by men hired for that special purpose." Moreover, she penned the blame for these falsehoods on Waite and concluded that he was "a miserable puppy."[8]

Personalities and Anatomy of a Trial

On May 1, 1865, the adjutant general's office in Washington, D.C., while acting under Stanton's authority, ordered a court-martial to determine whether Harris violated the Articles of War in assisting parolees return to their homes, or committed treason. Although technically the

6. The Military Prosecution of a Congressman   129

War Department prosecuted Harris in a military commission, the record of the trial was reported within the War Department, to the newspapers, and to Congress as a court-martial, and therefore these terms are interchangeably used. As in the case of other significant military trials, Stanton appointed the officers who sat in judgment of Harris. These officers included major generals John G. Parke, A.A. Humphreys, Orlando Willcox, and John A. Rawlins; brigadier generals William H. Morris and G.H. Sharp; and colonels T.S. Bowers, William Gamble, and Charles Albright. All of these officers had seen considerable combat during the war. So too had Major William Winthrop, the judge advocate assigned to prosecute Harris.

Winthrop's appointment troubled Harris. A descendant of John Winthrop, the first colonial governor of Massachusetts and a relative of both Robert Charles Winthrop, the last Whig speaker of the House of Representatives, and Theodore Dwight Woolsey, the president of Yale University, Winthrop was a fervent abolitionist. Like Harris, he had attended both Yale and Harvard. Unlike Harris, his early law practice included working with fellow abolitionist Richard Henry Dana aid fugitive slaves against southern slave-owners. In 1859, he assisted in writing the Minnesota state constitution which enabled male suffrage regardless of race, and he enlisted in the Seventh New York Militia after South Carolina soldiers fired on Fort Sumter. From 1861 to 1863 Winthrop was an officer in the First United States Sharpshooters. He fought on the Peninsula, at the Second Battle of Manassas, Antietam, and Fredericksburg, and was twice promoted for gallantry. After being shot in the stomach by Confederate soldiers during the "mud march," of early 1863, he was commissioned a judge advocate and assigned to the Bureau of Military Justice.

The Bureau of Military Justice acted as a quasi "court of appeal" though it had no appellate court authority. That is, judge advocates such as Winthrop reviewed records of trial and recommended to Holt, Stanton, and occasionally Lincoln, that because a court-martial had been unfairly conducted, conducted contrary to legal principles, or overly extreme, a finding of guilt or sentence should be overturned. This advice, however, was in no way binding on the War Department or president. The Supreme Court, in 1881 in *Ex Parte Mason*, upheld the legal construct of courts-martial including the non-binding nature of the Bureau of Military Justice's advice and the lack of judicial oversight. There were only thirty-three congressionally mandated officer commissions for the Judge Advocate General's Department, and Winthrop and competed with over one hundred other applicants to gain a permanent judge advocate commission. But he had the support of Senator Charles Sumner as well as Minnesota governor Alexander Ramsey. Both of these men were staunch abolitionists.[9]

As a result of his abolitionist fervor and legal acumen, Winthrop impressed Holt. Winthrop drafted the government's legal brief in *Vallandigham*, and at the end of 1864, he published the first ever compilation of judge advocate determinations on military law which the Supreme Court cited decades after the war. By 1863, Holt reported to Stanton that Winthrop was one of the two best judge advocates in the Army. During periods when Holt was absent from the capitol, he entrusted Winthrop to oversee the Bureau of Military Justice. Holt was fully occupied with prosecuting Mary Surratt and the other suspect conspirators and he assigned Winthrop to prosecute Harris. That Holt himself did not prosecute Harris was not a reflection on the importance of the prosecution to the War Department. Both Stanton and Holt had expected the Harris trial to become a matter of national importance.[10]

Despite Winthrop's vehement abolitionism and his role in *Vallandigham*, he was not uniformly zealous in arguing for an expansive military jurisdiction over civilians. On June 20, 1865, Winthrop advised Stanton against prosecuting citizens who publicly applauded Lincoln's death. Prior to prosecuting Harris, he also informed Stanton that a citizen who robbed a soldier in Baltimore was not prosecutable in a military commission and had to be tried in a civil court. Six months after Harris' trial, he advised General O.O. Howard, the commander of the Freedman's Bureau, not to expand the military's jurisdiction to matters pitting former slaves against white citizens until Congress expressly authorized the bureau to do so. While Winthrop understood that the civil courts would be prejudiced against former slaves, he cautioned against a move which would establish a military government in the south without Congressional approval. He insisted that Harris had violated the laws of war by aiding the enemy.[11]

A judge advocate in a nineteenth century military trial was not synonymous to a prosecutor. A judge advocate, while representing the Executive Branch, had a tripartite role. To be sure, the primary duty of the judge advocate was to present evidence of guilt to a panel of officers. But because courts-martial did not, until 1969, have a military judge, the judge advocate also was required to serve as a legal advisor to the panel of officers. The panel of officers, in turn, had the duty to make not only factual determinations of innocence or guilt, but also to make legal decisions as to whether to exclude evidence. In the absence of a formal trial judge, the ranking officer, referred to as the "president of the court," determined whether, under the law, the rest of the empanelled officers could consider evidence that either the judge advocate or the accused person had objected to. In the majority of courts-martial and military commissions, persons accused of violating the Articles of War, were unrepresented by counsel. In such instances, the judge advocate was also required to serve as an advisor to the accused person. In essence, a judge advocate was responsible for safeguarding the rights of persons accused of crimes. This system had its opponents. For instance, in 1872 Ransom H. Gillet, a former assistant attorney general, criticized the practice of courts-martial, writing, "although in theory the judge advocate protects the accused and causes justice to be done to him, whether he has counsel or not, still in practice in most cases, he is a severe public prosecutor and resorts to all possible means to secure a conviction." Gillet concluded his criticism by decrying the lack of judicial oversight in courts-martial. Since Harris was an accomplished lawyer, he represented himself and was eventually represented by a defense counsel, Winthrop relieved of the duty to advise him. He was not, however, relieved of the duty to ensure Harris was prepared to defend himself.[12]

A Civil War military trial was different from a civilian trial in several other respects. The person accused of committing a crime was referred to as "the Accused," instead of as "the defendant." Under the Articles of War, Stanton could order a court-martial or military commission to reopen for the purpose of introducing new evidence if the officers serving in these trials voted for an acquittal. For reasons that remain somewhat murky, this practice which originated in the early seventeenth century Swedish Army and was adopted by the British, continued in the United States until 1920. As a result of controversies in World War I, Congress and the judge advocate general responded to public pressure to end this practice. The officers sitting in judgment were not randomly selected white male property owners such as what would occur in a federal or Maryland trial. The adjutant general of the Army selected the officers, subject to Stanton's approval. Some trials ended in acquittals in spite of these features of courts-martial, but there were no barriers to prevent the secretary of war from "stacking the panel," against Harris. Whether this occurred is difficult to know. Earlier in the war, Fitz John Porter, a disgraced general, claimed that a panel consisting of General James Garfield and General David A. Hunter, a staunch abolitionist, as well as other generals assigned by Stanton was designed to secure a conviction against him. Montgomery Blair and Senator Reverdy Johnson would later argue that this was the case, just as Blair would argue to Andrew Johnson that Harris' trial was designed to secure a conviction. Another unique feature of military trials was that if the military trial were to find Harris guilty, it would assign a sentence without taking more evidence. An accused person on trial would have to, at the same time as he or she argued for innocence, argue as well for leniency. Finally, an accused person would not immediately find out a verdict and sentence. Indeed, after deliberations, the verdict and record of trial was sent to the Bureau of Military Justice for a quasi-appellate review and then approved or disapproved by the judge advocate general and then the secretary of war. Thus, Harris, along with hundreds of others, could be forced to wait for a verdict.[13]

Along with these differences from a civilian criminal trial, there were similarities between nineteenth century courts-martial and criminal trials. An accused person was not permitted to testify in their own defense, because it was believed that a prosecutor would unfairly manipulate him into making statements which could lead to guilt. It did not matter that Harris was an attorney since the prohibition governed all accused persons. Because for much of the trial Harris represented himself he was able to produce his version of the events through the questioning of witnesses. A second similarity had to do with the evidentiary rules. Nineteenth century courts-martial were required to utilize federal and state rules of evidence as well as common law practices. Thus, while Harris was prosecuted in a military tribunal, he had knowledge of its basic procedures.

The officers sitting in judgment of Harris were significant participants in the Civil War. General Orlando Willcox graduated from the United States Military Academy and was a Mexican War veteran. He was also not a stranger to either courts-martial or the law. Like many officers, he left the Army in the early 1850s to pursue other employment. Prior to the Civil War, he was admitted to the bar, worked as an attorney in Detroit, and on occasion represented the city in federal court. He had also been court-martialed as a cadet at the Academy for "imbibing in intoxicating liquors." Likewise, General John G. Parke, a trained engineer, was admitted to the New York bar and became a patent law expert. After the Civil War, he published two treatises on land use law. When in 1864 General Ulysses Grant removed Ambrose Burnside from command of the independent Ninth Corps, he appointed Parke in his place. At the time of Harris' trial, Parke was Willcox's commander. This was problematic to notions of fairness because, in theory, Parke could try to order Willcox to vote for a finding of guilt. In modern courts-martial, such a relationship would be grounds for dismissing one of the officers from the trial, but it was not so at the time.[14]

6. The Military Prosecution of a Congressman 133

Andrew A. Humphreys was a career officer who graduated from the Academy in 1831. Like Parke, Humphreys was commissioned into the engineers. He first saw combat during the Seminole Wars, fought against Mexico, and then commanded divisions during the battles of Fredericksburg, Chancellorsville, and Gettysburg. After Gettysburg, Humphreys served as chief of staff to General George Meade, the commanding officer of the Army of the Potomac. In this position, he oversaw thousands of courts-martial records processed through the Army of the Potomac and on to the Bureau of Military Justice.[15]

John Rawlins practiced law in Illinois after passing an oral bar examination in 1854. When the war began, he served as Ulysses Grant's aide de camp. He was loyal to Grant, and his promotions occurred commensurate with Grant's. When Grant was appointed commanding general of the Armies, he brought along Rawlins as his chief of staff. Rawlins was also an ardent Unionist who, like Grant, was raised in an impoverished family in Galena, Illinois. He believed that southern slavery depressed northern families who could not compete with slave labor.[16]

To Harris, the most troubling officer appointed to the court-martial was Theodore S. Bowers. Born in Philadelphia in 1832, Bowers migrated to Mount Carmel, Illinois and educated himself as a printer and newspaper reporter. Shortly after the Union defeat at Bull Run, Bowers recruited a volunteer infantry company, but refused a commission in it. He was appointed a clerical assistant to Grant in early 1862. Early in the war, Grant became impressed with Bowers' work ethic and personal bravery. In late 1862, Confederate raiders captured Bowers, but he destroyed Grant's correspondences and managed to escape shortly after. On February 19, 1863, Grant appointed Bowers as judge advocate to the Tennessee Department. However, after Rawlins was promoted from Grant's adjutant general to a higher military office, Grant, in turn, promoted Bowers to Rawlins' old position. On August 30, 1863, Bowers left his duties as the Tennessee Department's judge advocate, but he remained on Grant's staff through the end of the war. In March 1866 he was killed when, while accompanying Grant to the United States Military Academy, he slipped under a train and was crushed under the train's wheels.[17]

Based on Harris' objection, Bowers was removed from the trial, as was William Morris. In their place, Stanton added John G. Foster and Joseph A. Haskin. An important feature of the trial was that Winthrop objected to the removal of Bowers and Morris, but both officers, with the concurrence of the other officers serving on the court-martial, determined that in the interests of fairness, their removal was required. Foster, a descendant of New England Puritans, was born in New Hampshire. He graduated from the United States Military Academy, fought in the war against Mexico, and assisted in Fort Sumter's construction. In 1862 he assumed command of the Department of North Carolina and created settlements for runaway slaves. Joseph Abel Haskin was the oldest of the officers sitting in judgment of Harris. Born in New York in 1818, he graduated from the Academy in 1830, fought in the Mexican War, and after being shot in that conflict, a surgeon amputated his arm. For most of the Civil War he was placed in garrison commands, but he was promoted to general for his efforts in countering a Confederate raid on Washington, D.C., in 1864.[18]

Court-Martial: The Military's Prosecution of Harris

Harris' trial began on May 2, 1865, without an opening statement from either side as was the custom in military trials. He had determined to represent himself in the trial, but in doing so, he ultimately confirmed the adage that "a lawyer who represents himself has a fool for a client." The major eastern newspapers, including the *New York Times*, *Baltimore Sun*, *Philadelphia Inquirer*, and *Washington Post*, as well as Harris' local paper, the *Saint Mary's Gazette*, reported on the trial. Even the far-away *New Hampshire Farmer's Cabinet*, a small-town newspaper, reported on the trial, and the *Freemont Journal* of Sandusky, Ohio, argued that if Harris were found guilty, he should "meet with the punishment so heinous an offense merits." Northern and Maryland newspapers were not the only source of coverage on Harris' arrest and trial. The *Houston Tri-Weekly* listed the charges against Harris on May 29, 1865. The importance of these newspapers was not simply that they reported on the trial and often evidenced their political partisanship, but also that their reporting provides context to aspects of the trial that the record of trial cannot do such as presenting the varied political and regional opinions toward Harris and the trial, as well as toward Reconstruction.[19]

Winthrop began the trial by calling Sergeant Richard Chapman as the first witness against Harris. Chapman had been born in Baltimore but like many of his peers, he crossed into the Confederacy to fight for secession. He testified he served in Confederate Army and had been taken prisoner in late 1864. He then explained that on April 25, while in Leonardtown, Major Waite provided passes to himself and a Private William Read to

6. The Military Prosecution of a Congressman 135

transit to the Union lines, but warned them not to cross into Virginia south of Fredericksburg or north of Baltimore without being given further permission to do so. These limitations were unnecessary because Chapman's mother lived in Baltimore, and he intended to go there. In order to travel home to Baltimore, Chapman was required to take a loyalty oath to the Union, and he had not yet done so because Waite could not find another officer to witness the oath. Chapman explained that, after meeting with Waite, he and Read went to Harris' house and asked for a place to sleep, but Harris instead gave them money. He also told the court-martial that Harris informed him that he was a congressman and under Army surveillance, and because of this, the two released prisoners could not stay in his house.[20]

The most damaging aspect of Chapman's testimony was not that Harris provided a small sum of money to Chapman and Read, but rather in the conversation the three men had. Chapman claimed that Harris advised him against taking the loyalty oath, and then called Ulysses Grant, "a damned rascal." He testified that Harris lauded Jefferson Davis as "a great man and a gentleman in every respect," and approved of Lincoln's assassination. Amongst the population of southern Maryland, Harris was not alone in these sentiments, and perhaps not even the most hardened twenty-first century prosecutor could convince herself or himself that Harris' words constituted treason. What Harris did next, if true, was unlawful. According to Chapman, Harris encouraged the two former soldiers to violate their paroles, return to Virginia without taking an oath of allegiance to the Union, and take arms against the Union once again. Implicit in Chapman's testimony is that Harris intended to support the south's armed forces against the Union.[21]

Harris cross-examined Chapman, but he did not at all undermine the salient points brought forward in Chapman's direct examination. He was able to show that Chapman had visited Waite twice: once before Chapman met Harris, and then after. However, there was some dispute as to whether Chapman's and Read's second visit to Waite occurred at Harris' suggestion. In response to Harris' question as to whether Chapman and Read wanted to stay at his house, Chapman replied, "you hesitated a moment and said you did not know what to do; that the Yankees had their eye upon you; that you would prefer giving me some money; and that we could go back to the hotel." As to whether Harris encouraged Chapman to break his parole by returning to Virginia, Chapman steadfastly repeated his direct examination by testifying, "you said I could go home on my parole without taking the oath of allegiance, and moreover you advised me not to take the oath of allegiance." Without Harris' prompting, he added that Harris called Grant a "damned rascal."[22]

Part of Harris' defense tactic was to test Chapman's memory and to this end Harris fleshed out the conversation between the two men further than Winthrop had accomplished in direct examination. But, in this case, the expanded conversation did not add to Harris' defense. Harris established that Chapman had five brothers killed during the war, that two of the deaths occurred during the siege of Richmond, and that Chapman had informed Harris of this point. This evidence bolstered Chapman's testimony that Harris encouraged him to continue fighting, because, after all, Chapman had a reason to blame the Union for the deaths of his brothers.[23]

What likely made Chapman appear to have been sincere in his testimony was that he did not, of his own volition, report Harris to Waite. Rather, before his return to Waite's office in Leonardtown, a sergeant had overhead the conversation between Harris, Chapman and Read, and reported this conversation to Waite. In concluding his cross examination, Harris futilely attempted to undermine Chapman's credibility in pointing out Chapman wore a Union Army coat and that Waite provided him the coat. Chapman admitted Waite gave him a coat, but only after Waite informed him it was against "the rules to wear a rebel uniform in federal lines."[24]

On redirect examination, Winthrop asked Chapman whether Harris volunteered to provide each man a dollar, or whether Chapman or Read asked for money. Chapman testified the provision of money was entirely Harris' idea. Winthrop also asked whether Harris inquired how long Chapman served in the Confederate Army and how it came into the conversation that Chapman's brothers were killed during the last year of the war. Chapman responded that he volunteered that particular information, but then Harris continued the conversation by blaming Lincoln and the Union for the death of Chapman's brothers.

As in the case of twenty-first century courts-martial, the conclusion of the judge advocate's questions did not end the witness' testimony, because the officers empanelled on the court were also able to question witnesses. The record of trial, however, does not indicate which officer asked Chapman a question and instead leaves the reader of the record the impression the questions were "collective" in their origin. The officers inquired whether Chapman volunteered or was conscripted into the Confederate Army. Chapman had volunteered in July 1861 and had served almost continuously with the Thirty-Second Virginia. This regiment had fought in the Peninsula Campaign, and then at Fredericksburg, Drewry's

6. The Military Prosecution of a Congressman 137

Bluff, and Cold Harbor. It also defended the Confederate lines during the siege of Petersburg. Most of the soldiers in the regiment came from the area around Williamsburg, Virginia.[25]

After Chapman testified, Harris notified the court-martial that he would later motion the officers to exclude Chapman's testimony in its entirety as well as that of the next witness, Private William Read, because both men "were public enemies of the United States" and therefore were not competent to testify against a citizen of the state of Maryland. Under Maryland law, it was true that certain classes of persons were not considered competent to testify in a criminal trial. For instance, African Americans were not permitted to testify against white citizens, and a foreign spy was not permitted to testify against a loyal Marylander. The question as to whether service in the Confederate Army precluded testimonial competency had not been addressed by the War Department, but as of 1865 no Maryland court had accepted the arguments Harris raised. And it was unlikely that, regardless of the fact that military trials adopted state rules of evidence, the court-martial would apply the rule Harris advanced. Winthrop opted not to formally respond to Harris' notification and called Private Read to the stand.[26]

Like Chapman, Read testified he served in the Thirty-Second Virginia and was captured during the siege of Petersburg. Read's testimony was consistent with Chapman's regarding their parole from prison and their journey towards Leonardtown, as well as their interaction with Harris. Unlike Chapman, however, Read was illiterate and his testimony was often strained. Read related that he and Chapman had initially traveled to see Waite so that they could take an oath of allegiance, but Waite informed both soldiers that they would have to wait until the morning to take their oath. Instead, Waite gave both men a pass to travel to a Mr. Clarke's house, roughly three miles outside of Leonardtown. On the way to Clarke's house, the two soldiers encountered Harris and had hoped to spend the night there. However, according to Read, Harris told both men he "did not want to get into any trouble" and instead gave a dollar to each man. Harris also made clear to both men he was a serving congressman. Read buttressed Chapman's testimony as to Harris' demeanor, particularly on the issue of taking a loyalty oath. Like Chapman, Read testified Harris encouraged both men not to take an oath and instead "go home ... and fight them again." Although Read was unsure of whether Harris had rejoiced in Lincoln's death, or the proclaimed rightness of Booth's act, he made it clear that Harris was "in favor of a southern confederacy and believed its cause was just."[27]

Harris' cross examination of Read was as ineffective as his earlier cross examination of Chapman. The trial record indicates Read was not an articulate soldier, and Harris was able to establish Read was illiterate. Yet Harris did more harm than good to his defense when he produced a copy of Read's pass. Since Read could not read the pass, Harris spoke it aloud and then confirmed Read had shown him the pass. It is a common-sense litigation rule for attorneys never to ask a question if the answer is unknown and the record of trial shows Harris breaking this very rule in the next series of questions. He clearly wanted to establish that Chapman and Read were bribed or compelled to testify based on the government's long standing animus against him, but no evidence came out to this effect.[28]

Read quickly debunked the idea that Waite or other officers ordered him to go to Harris' house. Indeed he testified that he had no idea who Harris was in the first place. In response to Harris' query on how Read and Chapman initially told Union Army officers of their meeting, Read informed the court-martial that he and Chapman discussed their conversation outside of a store in Leonardtown. He surmised their conversation had been overhead by a Union Army sergeant outside of the store, because the sergeant approached Chapman and took him aside. This differed somewhat from Chapman's testimony who claimed that the sergeant had overhead the conversation from a place near Harris' house. Read could not recall seeing a sergeant near Harris' house. Read recollected that Harris was "a hot-headed man" who spoke loudly.[29]

After the officers on the court-martial questioned Read, he conceded that when the conversation between Harris, Chapman, and himself took place it was already evening and dark outside. Read also opined that there were several large trees on Harris' lawn, and therefore it was possible for a person to have overheard the conversation without him knowing. This was particularly so, given Harris' raised voice.[30]

Based on Read's testimony, Winthrop recalled Chapman to testify. His purpose in doing so was to build further facts on how the sergeant noticed the conversation between Read, Chapman, and Harris. Chapman claimed that after their conversation, and with Read several yards downhill and presumably out of earshot, the sergeant noted to Chapman he overheard Harris call Grant "a damned rascal." Chapman testified that he believed that he had no choice but to confirm his conversation with Harris to the sergeant. Harris' cross-examination of Chapman again yielded little in his defense, and while he pointed to a few inconsistencies between the two men, a number of statements further corroborating Read's testimony were also adduced.[31]

6. The Military Prosecution of a Congressman 139

In order to further corroborate Chapman's testimony, Winthrop recalled Read who reaffirmed that when the two soldiers left Harris' house, Read was at least a minute in front of Chapman. He also corroborated Chapman's memory of the conversation with the Union sergeant. As during Chapman's testimony, Harris' cross-examination only resulted in Read agreeing with Chapman.[32]

After Chapman and Read had finished testifying, the *New York Times* reported that the court-martial sat "with open doors," and it retracted its earlier reporting that Harris had been accused of being complicit in aiding Booth's getaway. The *Philadelphia Inquirer* erroneously noted that Harris' court-martial was "held in abeyance for the trial of Booth's fellow assassins." On May 4, the *Inquirer* reported that little progress had been made in the trial. Contemporaneously, the *Chicago Tribune* listed the charges against Harris and noted that while Harris objected to Chapman's and Read's competency to testify based on their treason against the United States, it was likely that Winthrop could produce witnesses to testify to Harris' disloyalty. On the same day, the *Baltimore Sun* reported on its front page the details of Harris' trial beginning with the charges and specifications leveled against him. The paper also noted Harris "thoroughly cross examined Chapman and Read," and predicted an acquittal. But its version of the trial was overly optimistic. Not so the *Cleveland Leader* which reported that Winthrop had offered to prove Harris' disloyalty and that the court-martial closed to deliberate Winthrop's offer of proof.[33]

On May 3, neither Winthrop nor Harris produced any witnesses because Harris had objected to Read's and Chapman's testimony based on their status as "public enemies," testifying against "a citizen of Maryland and of the United States." Winthrop responded to Harris' objection with a proposal to introduce two or more witnesses to prove Harris' reputation for disloyalty to the Union. He argued that such testimony would be admissible to show that Harris acted out of sympathy for the two prisoners of war, and the cause they once served. While the existing evidentiary rules permitted type of character evidence, such evidence was highly prejudicial. As such, Harris opposed the admission of any testimony as to his disloyalty to the Union. The court-martial decided to adjourn for the remainder of the day while ruling whether it would allow Winthrop to present this additional testimony.

The following day, Winthrop's next witness, the sergeant Chapman had spoken with, failed to arrive at court, causing the court-martial to adjourn for another day. Additionally, the court-reporter, Mr. R.R. Hitt, was replaced by one Mr. D.F. Murphy. On May 5, the court-martial again heard no witnesses. Instead, the transcript of Chapman's and Read's testimony was reread to the court-martial and, following the trial procedures of the time, the officers serving on the court-martial, as well as Winthrop and Harris, approved of the record's accuracy. Winthrop's sergeant witness was still in transit to the court-martial, and more importantly, Harris smartly concluded he was in need of counsel. His first choice of counsel, a J.W. Carlisle, was unavailable for the remainder of the day.[34]

On Saturday, May 6, the court-martial resumed and Winthrop called Sergeant Reuben R. Stewart to the stand. Stewart testified that he commanded six other soldiers under orders to arrest Harris, adding that after the arrest, Harris admitted he provided money to both Chapman and Read, and refused to let the two men stay at his house. Stewart also claimed Harris openly stated that he informed both Chapman and Read they were not required to take a loyalty oath to the Union, with the implication that Harris did not believe his actions were illegal. Stewart next assured the court-martial that Harris had volunteered these statements without any coercion. This is an important point, and one which Harris did not contest. Although there was no rule of law mandating the exclusion of statements taken by authorities when a suspect was physically coerced or threatened, a court-martial could determine that such statements were unreliable and therefore had to be excluded from evidence. Perhaps the most damaging part of Stewart's testimony was that he claimed Harris had admitted he offered Chapman and Read money without the two paroled prisoners asking for the money first.[35]

For reasons not contained in the record of trial, Harris remained without counsel and cross-examined Stewart on his own. Harris' cross-examination of Stewart was as unsuccessful as his questioning of Chapman and Read. At one point, when Harris strayed from the direct examination, Winthrop objected. Relying on a military law treatise, Harris argued he had a right to elicit the full details of his conversation with Stewart. In the end, the court-martial determined only that the form of Harris' questions were objectionable, but not the substance and permitted Harris to ask Stewart to complete the facts of the entire conversation between himself and Harris. Thus, the court-martial overruled Winthrop in part, and during the time it took to consider Harris' objection, his defense counsel arrived.

The counsel was not J.W. Carlisle, but rather a retired state judge named Peter W. Craine (sometimes spelled Crane). There is little information on Craine today, but he represented slave owners in the Maryland courts in the 1850s, and he had been a frequent guest at Ellenborough. Indeed, during an earlier period when Martha Harris recorded that they had been abandoned by friends, she noted that Craine had remained loyal. Despite the addition of Craine, Stewart's answers were not helpful for Harris. He noted Harris used the term "damn abolitionism," and "damned black republican," in reference to a black cat who appeared in a fight with another cat during their conversation. When Craine tried to raise the possibility his comments to Stewart were made in jest, Stewart responded, "I took it in connection with the remarks made about Republicanism." Craine tried to commit Stewart to admit that a "Mr. Maddox" was present during their conversation, but Stewart only acknowledged Maddox's presence at one of several conversations he had with Harris. While the two men quibbled over Maddox's presence, the court-martial was left to inquire who Maddox was. Ultimately, both Winthrop and Harris agreed that the "Mr. Maddox in question" was Harris' son-in-law. At the conclusion of the day, the *New York Times* noted Stewart's testimony was consistent with Chapman's and Read's, particularly in regard to Harris providing both men money and encouraging them to travel to Baltimore.[36]

After Stewart's testimony, Winthrop introduced the terms of Lee's capitulation to Grant into evidence. Prior to closing, Winthrop sought to modify one of the specifications against Harris by purging it of the words "it's too late to kill him now." Craine objected to this change, but was overruled. The objection's basis was that the record showed Read made the statement "it's too late to kill him now," rather than Harris having done so. The officers on the court-martial panel recalled Chapman to clarify whether or not Harris had used the words "it's too late to kill him now," and Chapman affirmed that this was the case. This consisted of the Army's evidence against Harris.[37]

On May 7, the *New York Times*, under the headline "Treason at Home," reported that Chapman and Read had essentially proven Harris' guilt, and two days later the paper reported that the arrival of Judge Craine had not altered the proof. The next day the *Philadelphia Inquirer* reported that Harris agreed that he had spoken with Read and Chapman, and that Craine made a belated appearance for the congressman. That same day, the *Chicago Tribune* called for an amnesty for all Copperheads, but did not mention Harris as a candidate for such amnesty. On May 11, the *Saint Mary's Beacon* optimistically reported that the people of Saint Mary's County looked "forward to an honorable acquittal of Mr. Harris with a high degree of confidence and hope." This hope was grossly misplaced.[38]

Harris' Defense

Thus far, the quantum of evidence against Harris was enough to sustain a conviction, under the Articles of War, notwithstanding the question of jurisdiction. While the motives of Chapman and Read, as well as the other participants to the trial had to be considered, it is a rule of law that a person may be convicted on the testimony of a single witness, and that certainly two witnesses can form the basis for a conviction. That is, given Harris' conduct, a panel of officers sitting in judgment could conclude he possessed the intent to aid enemy soldiers to continue fighting against the United States.[39]

On Tuesday, May 9, Harris called Aloysius Fenwick as his first and only witness to testify. Harris and Fenwick were neighbors, and from the beginning of his testimony it was clear to the court that Fenwick politically supported Harris. Fenwick's testimony on direct examination only established that Chapman and Read approached him the same evening the two men met with Harris, and after a brief conversation Fenwick determined not to accommodate the two paroled soldiers for the night. Fenwick also added to his testimony that "a negro," named Mr. Lawrence George lived in the vicinity of Harris' home. Winthrop's cross examination established that Fenwick voted for Harris. (Harris unsuccessfully objected to the question of Fenwick's voting record.) While in modern courts-martial a witness' voting record is almost always inadmissible as evidence, in the nineteenth century, under the common law applicable to all criminal trials, questions regarding political affiliation could be asked of witnesses to establish a witness' bias. Winthrop also was able to commit Fenwick into testifying that Harris knew that Read and Chapman were paroled prisoners of war at time Harris provided money to them. Both Winthrop and Harris were determined to prove which direction Chapman and Read took after leaving Fenwick's house. Fenwick was reluctant to answer Winthrop's questions claiming only, "I can tell you where I think they went." From that point Fenwick admitted it was possible the two soldiers slept in his barn without his knowledge, but he could not be sure of it.[40]

On Thursday May 11, after a one day recess in the trial, Harris introduced evidence that the prisoner of war rolls—that is the formal military documents assigning soldiers to specific regiments and brigades—related to the 32d Virginia Regiment of infantry did not list either Chapman or Read. In direct examination, Union brigadier general G.H. Sharpe, who had been called by Winthrop, attested to the authenticity of the prisoner rolls. However, Sharpe also noted he could not testify as to the accuracy

6. The Military Prosecution of a Congressman 143

of the rolls. The reason for Sharpe's hesitation was simple: The 32d Regiment was part of "Corse's brigade," in "Pickett's division," and that Marylanders were often not formally placed into the rolls of other states' regiments. The available muster rolls indicated some of the 260 Marylanders who were prisoners of war and assigned to Corse's brigade also might have been in the Thirty-Second Virginia, but the rolls for the Thirty-Second Virginia contained only forty-two men. This occurred as a result of the individual captains placed in command of smaller units known as companies, not placing their soldiers in the proper muster rolls upon their capture. As Chapman and Read were not listed on the Thirty-Second Virginia's rolls, Harris hoped to undermine their testimony.[41]

Sharpe explained how the disintegration of Lee's Army eroded the record keeping abilities of Union adjutants and provosts. On the eve of Lee's surrender, Sharpe claimed so many Confederate units were merged, it became difficult to affix a prisoner of war to a specific regiment. To Sharpe, the rolls provided no proof that Chapman and Read were either paroled prisoners, escaped prisoners, or imposters who had never served in the Confederate Army. But the fact that Chapman and Read were held in a prisoner of war camp evidenced a strong likelihood that they had, in fact, been captured while wearing Confederate uniforms. (Contained in the National Archives are two rolls which detail that Chapman and Read were both assigned to the Thirty-Second Virginia, and that Chapman's recitation of his military tenure was largely correct.)[42]

On the afternoon of May 11, Harris, rather than Craine, read to the court-martial his closing summation. He began his argument by urging that because he was "in no way connected to the land or naval of the United States or the militia in its service," the Constitution prohibited the Army's assertion of jurisdiction over him. This was basically the same argument which Lambdin Milligan and his peers would later employ to prevail over the government before the Supreme Court in 1866, and had President Johnson not intervened resulting in an imprisoned Harris appealing to the Court, the justices would likely have overturned his conviction as well.[43]

Because the government had asserted that his offenses were capital in the sense that the offenses could be punishable by death, he also argued that he was entitled to have the evidence investigated by a grand jury before a trial occurred. Although the Fifth Amendment to the Constitution provides this right in federal trials, the amendment itself exempts military trials from the grand jury requirement. Because the Supreme Court had more or less placed courts-martial as a trial akin to state criminal trials and the Court had not determined whether state trials had to have a grand jury predecessor, it was unlikely that the denial of the right to a grand jury investigation would create any sympathy for Harris.

Harris next attacked the government's evidence as weak and unreliable, but his arguments were exacting. For instance, he urged that as paroled prisoners of war, neither Chapman nor Read could be considered to be "an enemy force," such as the charges against him required. And, even if the two paroled prisoners were "an enemy force," the giving of a dollar was an act of "Christian charity" rather than treason. In 1945, the Supreme Court in *Cramer v. United States* would note that treason is partly a crime of intent, but also the crime had to be proven by the production of two witnesses who observed not simply the act, but also direct evidence of the treasonous intent. This requirement is supposed to prohibit a person from being convicted for merely being an unknowing accomplice in another person's treasonous act. Harris was not actually charged with treason. Rather, he was charged under the Articles of War with aiding enemy soldiers and inciting or encouraging them to continue fighting. Likewise, Harris also called the Union sergeant who overheard the discussion between Harris and Read and Chapman "a myth, akin to Hamlet's ghost."[44]

Harris' strongest argument was rooted in the First Amendment's right to freedom of speech. However, he was a century too early to succeed. "A citizen may condemn the course of his government as unjust and really sympathize with the enemy, the victim of its injustice, and yet be guilty of no act to thwart its purpose or object," he claimed. "It was the case in England during our revolutionary struggle, when the great historic names of that country boldly proclaimed, in the hearing of their monarch, their sympathies with whom they thought the monarch suppressed." Thus, to Harris, if, as a matter of freedom of speech, there was a right to sympathize with secession, there could be no crime in encouraging a prisoner of war not to take a loyalty oath.

In the military trials of the time, the accused provided the first closing argument and the judge advocate responded with the final word. Winthrop, in his closing argument, countered that the two articles under which Harris was charged were "closely allied to treason" before reciting the legality of the extension of military jurisdiction over citizens in Maryland. Winthrop's proof of the legality, though, was the prevailing military law texts as well as the fact that military commissions trials had occurred in Maryland throughout the war. He also reminded the court-martial that the Supreme Court had settled the issue of jurisdiction in *Vallandigham*.

But here Winthrop was in error. The Court had not determined where military jurisdiction ended. Rather, the Court had deferred the issue of jurisdiction by asserting that the justices had no authority to determine the issue of military jurisdiction. This, of course, was soon to change in *Milligan*, but neither Winthrop nor Harris could have known of this.

Moving past the issue of jurisdiction, Winthrop had an easy time convincing the officers sitting in judgment of Harris' guilt. After all, Harris did not deny giving Read and Chapman a dollar apiece and he did not deny specifically making the comment that the taking of a loyalty oath was unnecessary. And, if the military had jurisdiction, then its ranking officers possessed the lawful authority to issue orders to the local population. This is what Burnside had done in Ohio that led to Vallandigham's arrest and trial, and therefore the War Department's order prohibiting aiding paroled prisoners of war was equally enforceable. Winthrop then argued that if, as Harris asserted, Chapman and Read possessed slightly different versions of the conversation, none of this negated evidence of Harris' criminal intent. Winthrop characterized Chapman and Read as simple minded soldiers, while Harris presented himself "not as a patriotic citizen, faithfully observing the Constitution and the laws of his country, by which he had a sworn duty to abide, but as an ardent sympathizer with the public enemy."

Winthrop concluded with the argument that because Harris was a congressman, his liability to the laws was far greater than had he been a normal citizen. "He had a duty to sedulously comport himself as a loyal citizen and as a supporter of that government in its struggle for life with rebels in arms," Winthrop argued before reciting to the officers the oath that Harris took prior to being seated in Congress. He conceded that the trial presented a "case of first impression," that is, a trial unique in American history, but it was only so because of Harris' actions and not the war or the Army. Winthrop then closed his argument by reiterating that because Harris was a congressman his offenses were "far graver than if he were a private citizen."[45]

Verdict and Sentence

The military trial unanimously found Harris guilty and sentenced him to three years in prison as well as a lifetime prohibition against serving in a government office. The part of the sentence which prohibited Harris from further government service, in reality, had no basis in law. Neither statutory law including the Articles of War and the Constitution enabled the Army to prohibit a person from being elected to Congress as part of a criminal sentence. Only Congress could have passed such a law and given the historic distrust of standing armies, it is highly unlikely that Congress would have done so. On May 13, 1865, Holt recommended to Stanton to approve the findings of guilt and the sentence imposed by the court-martial. Holt noted that Harris had been represented by "four able counsel," though only one of the counsel had been present and only for part of the proceedings. The other three attorneys only came to Harris' aid after the summation and were in the process of petitioning President Johnson for redress. Holt concluded that while Chapman and Read had served the Confederacy, their deportment evidenced disinterest in the outcome of the trial and therefore proof of their honesty, while Harris had been in sympathy with the Confederacy since the start of the war. Stanton almost immediately approved the findings and sentence, and Harris returned to his cell at the Old Capitol Prison.[46]

Harris' prison conditions were not onerous, and he was able to conduct business from his confinement, particularly in tobacco sales from his farm. On May 22, 1865, he wrote to his daughter that he "was very well and in excellent spirits," and that he found prison food "wholesome." He shared a room with North Carolina's governor Zebulon Vance and Georgia's governor Joseph E. Brown, and the three men were able to have full access to the prison yard. He also acknowledged that while he was under the stress of waiting for a verdict in his trial, Capitol Prison superintendent, a Mr. Wood, ensured that the south's former political officers, along with Harris, were not treated as convicts.[47] On May 29, Stanton offered Harris a reprieve from prison provided Harris swear to a loyalty oath to the Union. Steadfast in his belief of being right, Harris refused to do so and he determined to remain in prison until legally vindicated.[48]

7

Aftermath of the Trial, 1865–1892

> "I am an old line Democrat and I believe in the Doctrine of Secession."
> —Benjamin G. Harris, 1866

On October 12, 1865, the *Annapolis Gazette* reported that President Andrew Johnson not only pardoned "Colonel" John Sothoron, he also ordered the Army to return Sothoron's estate to him. The newspaper noted that the Union officer who Sothoron killed had attempted to enlist slaves in the Army and threatened Sothoron at gunpoint. Apparently, the *Gazette* considered the killing a justified defense of property. As a result of Johnson's order, Sothoron escaped prosecution for an act far more egregious than the behavior which resulted in Harris' arrest and trial. One month later, the newspaper informed its readers that although Johnson had been inaugurated vice president as a "drunken sot" and an ally of the Radical Republicans, he had since become a "dignified" president. Of course, Johnson's quick transition from a feared Radical ally to a president who sought conciliation with the south might have been, in hindsight, predictable. After one month as president, Johnson began to grant pardons to Confederate officials held in federal custody. The pardons did not automatically restore civil or political rights, but several governors and other officials were released to return home.[1]

Harris did not appeal to Johnson for amnesty. Indeed, one of Secretary of War Edwin Stanton's officers inquired to Harris whether he would be willing to take a loyalty oath—the same loyalty oath given to former Confederates—but Harris refused to do so, arguing that he had not committed any crime, the military trial lacked jurisdiction, and he had been assiduously loyal to the Constitution. Democrat congressmen largely abandoned Harris and only Alexander Long appears to have thought of coming to his defense. Yet Long made no public speeches against Harris' imprisonment and Clement Vallandigham advised Long that it was unwise to do so because any defense of Harris would "agitate" the Republican majority who "were now in their boldest form." Vallandigham further cautioned Long that if the Republicans were "aroused" they would "destroy the cause of state's rights and sovereignty." Harris also had no help from any of Maryland's prominent politicians in the federal government or the state governor. On March 9, 1865, Governor Augustus Bradford accepted the General Assembly's nomination of John Creswell to replace Senator Thomas Hicks. Creswell championed abolition, and during the war he served as a state adjutant general and oversaw the arrests of citizens. Harris protested this appointment, but to no avail, and Creswell had applauded Harris' arrest and trial. Likewise, Senator Reverdy Johnson evidenced no interest in publicly supporting Harris. Ironically, the only person of any political influence who would come to Harris' defense would be one of Lincoln's former cabinet officers.[2]

President Johnson's Release of Harris and Montgomery Blair's Attempted Alliance

On May 31, 1865, President Johnson granted former postmaster general Montgomery Blair an audience in the White House. Blair brought with him a Saint Mary's County attorney named John Camalier who had collected dozens of affidavits in support of Harris. The affiants swore to Harris' loyalty to the Constitution. Some of the affidavit writers challenged Chapman's and Read's integrity and mistakenly urged that the two men had never served the Confederacy's forces. One affidavit, written by a former Confederate soldier, claimed that Major Waite had promised Chapman and Read their transit home in exchange for testimony against Harris. Another former Confederate soldier named J. Passano claimed that Chapman had forged his own parole papers, and then later stated to Passano that "Mr. Harris had done nothing, but that he had a bad scrape and had to get out of it by any means." A third person alluded to Chapman and Read being ordered by Waite to entrap Harris. There is nothing recorded on Blair's conversation with Johnson but, that afternoon, Johnson exercised his presidential prerogative to release Harris and remitted the sentence. The specific language contained in Johnson's order read: "Additional evidence and affidavits, however, bearing on this case and favorable to the accused having been presented to me and considered by me since the sentence aforesaid, I deem it proper to direct that the sentence in the case of said Harris be remitted and that he be released from imprisonment." Johnson did not expressly overturn the conviction—indeed the order began with a statement that the findings of Harris' guilt were "affirmed"—and when he invited Harris to dine with him, Harris refused to do so.

There is a feature of military law which enables a commanding general, the secretary of defense, the service secretaries, and the president, to disapprove of a court-martial finding or sentence. Although in 1865 the position now known as secretary of defense did not exist, during the Civil War, the secretary of war overturned hundreds of courts-martial. In 2013 a ranking Air Force general overturned a court-martial verdict of a fighter pilot who had been found guilty of sexually assaulting a woman. This action drew a degree of public and congressional ire, perhaps not seen since Nixon's act of freeing an officer found guilty of egregious war crimes during the Vietnam conflict. Indeed, the freeing of Harris seems to have drawn less congressional ire than the overturning of the pilot's court-martial conviction some three years before the publishing of this book.[3]

Johnson's act of freeing Harris has almost universally gone unnoticed by historians of the Civil War and Reconstruction, including scholars who have studied Congress' attempts to impeach Johnson. Both Judge Advocate General Holt's and Secretary of War Stanton's correspondences are silent as to their opinion of Johnson's actions. As of June 1865, Holt, Stanton, and Johnson had yet to feud, and it may have been the case that Holt did not know of Harris' release until after it had occurred. Holt was consumed with his duties as lead prosecutor in the trial against Mary Surratt and the others implicated in the conspiracy to assassinate Lincoln. Stanton's attentions were not only focused on that trial, but also the occupation of the southern states, the expansion of the Freedman's Bureau, and he had entered into a public feud with General William Sherman. Winthrop would later note that Johnson possessed the lawful authority to free Harris, but his existing correspondences are likewise silent on his opinions of Johnson's actions. He would also, in his scholarly writings on military law, claim that the president's sustainment of the conviction was proof that the military could prosecute civilians for aiding an enemy force as a law of war measure. Although Winthrop was a brilliant constitutional scholar, it would be difficult to reconcile his opinions on the Harris trial with *Ex Parte Milligan*.[4]

Blair's actions on behalf of Harris appear perplexing if his own political ambitions were to be ignored. Blair flirted with running for governor in Maryland. On January 24, 1866, he spoke to the Maryland legislature and critically characterized the Freedman's Bureau as an instrument designed to maintain Republican control over the federal government. By this time his prior abolitionism gave way to rampant racism. He opined that the character of freedman were "tropical, and given to despotism," and declared equality among the races was an impossibility arguing "as we cannot amalgamate with the blacks, we cannot make them participants and equals in government."[5]

Blair's relation by marriage, John Fitzgerald Lee became his surrogate for finding allies in Maryland and Lee courted Harris. Lee had been the judge advocate general of the Army from the end of the war with Mexico through the first six months of the Civil War. However, he was also a slave owner and Lincoln's administration forced his resignation after several disagreements regarding the Army's arrest of citizens. In August 1866, Lee approached Harris to ascertain whether Harris would support a Blair candidacy for governor. Lee informed Blair that while Harris was not opposed to his quest for the governor's office, he could not expect for Harris to campaign for him. In March 1867, Lee reported to Blair that Harris still enjoyed widespread support in St. Mary's County, and had been considered as a possibility to replace Reverdy Johnson in the Senate. This time Lee secured Harris' backing for Blair's gubernatorial ambitions, but Blair decided not to run for office. Harris willingness to back Blair did not last for long. In 1870, Lee approached Harris once more. This time, he reported to Blair that Harris "refused to endorse any democrat who did not support southern rights." Although Blair opposed the Fourteenth and Fifteenth amendments, he could not go so far as to argue for compensation for former slave owners.[6]

The newspaper reporting of Harris' release varied from angry opposition to complete support. On June 2, the *Philadelphia Inquirer* not only called Harris "a traitor, guilty of treasonable acts," it hoped that Congress would declare him "an unworthy member, and promptly expel him." The next day the *Chicago Tribune* reported that Johnson had released Harris based on the affidavits Blair provided to him, but implicit in their reporting was that while Harris was actually guilty, Johnson's magnanimity was laudable. Not surprisingly, the *Baltimore Sun* took the opposite position than the *Philadelphia Inquirer*. On May 31, its editors hoped that Johnson would grant Harris amnesty, and on June 3 the *Sun* reported that Harris had been released from the Old Capitol Prison based on evidence that exonerated him. At the same time, the *Sun* urged Congress to support

Johnson and recognize that "Negro suffrage" was purely a state matter that should be free from federal control. On June 7, the *Sun*'s editors proclaimed military trials to be inherently unconstitutional and unfair. "The forms and practices of our civil courts in taking and receiving testimony are the experience of ages and cannot be set aside with any safety to personal liberty," its editors concluded.[7]

Other newspapers that carried news of Harris' release simply reported on the president's action. The *Indianapolis Daily Sentinel* noted on June 6, that Johnson had ordered Harris' release. But the article was overshadowed by reporting on the assassination conspiracy trial. Likewise the *Dayton Daily Empire* printed that Johnson had been favorably impressed with the affidavits on Harris' character and found these compelling enough to order his release, though not so in overturning the verdict. The Wheeling, West Virginia, *Daily Intelligencer* also reported Johnson's order, though its editors made sure to stress that the president had upheld the verdict. On June 22, the New Hampshire *Farmer's Cabinet* approvingly reported on the conviction, but equally approved of Johnson's act in remitting the sentence.[8]

Despite being freed by Johnson, Harris remained in Holt's "cross hairs," if not for a later prosecution, then at least as a means for discrediting witnesses called by the defense counsel in the conspirators' trial. For instance, on May 30, when Mary Surratt's defense counsel called a Mr. J.Z. Jenkins to testify that as an intimate friend of Mary Surratt, he had never heard her to utter any statements disloyal to the government, Major John Bingham, a judge advocate and Ohio congressman assisting Holt, called a Mr. A.V. Roby to rebut Jenkins by casting an aspersion as to Jenkins' motives. Harris served as Bingham's vehicle for the aspersion. Roby testified, "I asked how [Jenkins] could vote for Mr. Harris, he said he wanted the south to succeed."[9]

Harris' Return to Congress: December 1865–April 1867

After his release from prison, Harris faced a challenge from several Maryland politicians who sought to unseat him prior to the 1866 election. Led by John C. Holland, a Baltimore Republican, their challenge fell short. In 1860 Holland campaigned for Constitutional Unionist, John C. Bell. Three years later Holland ran against Harris for the Fifth District's congressional seat. In 1864, Holland had tried to run for Congress once more but because he had been serving in the Union Army as a provost marshal and his campaign managers were unprepared for the election, he was unable to have his name secured on hundreds of ballots. Moreover, as a provost marshal he might have been ineligible to run for federal office under the laws of Maryland since he had the duty of ordering soldiers to guard the Fifth District's voting polls. Holland's argument to replace Harris in Congress was two-fold. First, Harris' sentence to be barred from government service remained intact because Johnson had not pardoned him. Second, because Holland had run for Congress and been deprived of a full ballot count, he was entitled to take Harris' seat. But no court in Maryland was willing to grant Holland a hearing and Congress traditionally did not interfere in state elections. Holland might have hoped that Congress would quickly make an exception since Harris had already been censured, but this was not be.[10]

Instead, on December 18, 1865, the first day of the new legislative term, Congressman John Franklin Farnsworth, an Illinois Republican who had first taken his seat in the House of Representatives in 1857, introduced a resolution recommending that the House Committee on Elections investigate Harris' conduct. Farnsworth left Congress in 1861 after obtaining a colonelcy and being placed in command of the Eighth Illinois Regiment. In 1862 he was promoted brigadier general, but in 1863 he resigned his commission to sit in Congress once more. One month before the assassination of Lincoln, Farnsworth led the House of Representatives to "table" a fellow Republican congressman's bill to prevent further military trials of civilians in the northern states. It was clear that the intended investigation of Harris was not designed to assess the propriety or fairness of the court-martial, as Farnsworth's resolution began: "Whereas it is alleged that Benjamin G. Harris, a representative in this house from the 5th district of the State of Maryland, was, in the month of May last, before a very respectable and intelligent court-martial, tried, and by said court convicted." On January 8, 1866, Speaker of the House of Representatives Schuyler Colfax informed Congress that he supported Farnsworth and then ordered a vote to have the House of Representatives open an investigation. One hundred and thirty-eight congressmen voted in favor of an investigation, while twenty-one opposed, and another twenty-one, including Harris, simply did not vote.[11]

Oddly, on December 19, 1865, the *Alexandria Gazette*, a Virginia newspaper, stated that Harris resumed his seat with no opposition. Two days later, the *Annapolis Gazette* informed its readers that Harris "pronounced by the last Congress as unworthy," arrived in Congress and took a loyalty oath to the Constitution. The *New York Times* reported that

7. Aftermath of the Trial, 1865–1892   153

Harris "stealthily slid into his congressional seat," and "escaped a formal protest to such behavior." From the *Times*' reporting, one might adduce that Harris had no friends in the legislature. The newspaper claimed that none of the Democrats would vouch for him in taking the oath of office on that opening day, and the Republicans glared at him. The *Times* did not, however, immediately report on Farnsworth's resolution.[12]

In early January 1866 Harris fell through a sheet of ice and was ill for much of the winter. It was not until the end of March that Harris was able to return to Congress. This delay might have provided him a needed absence so that the Republican majority could turn their attentions to matters other than him. Farnsworth tried to push the House to quickly investigate Harris, but senior congressmen were already focused on the Civil Rights Act and a growing feud between Stanton and Johnson. Moreover, the Supreme Court in *Milligan* determined that military trials of citizens in states in which the civilian courts functioned were unconstitutional. This decision extended to allegations of treason committed by citizens in the northern states and the majority of justices went so far as to conclude that even Congress did not possess the constitutional authority to statutorily create military trials over civilians when the civilian courts functioned. A brief further analysis of *Milligan* is important because, for other reasons, the decision mooted arguments that Harris had been convicted in a lawfully recognizable trial and was therefore ineligible to sit in Congress.

On March 5, 1866, David Dudley Field and Jeremiah Sullivan Black, two of the nation's foremost constitutional scholars, argued to the Supreme Court against the encroachment of military jurisdiction over United States citizens. Field, the older brother of Supreme Court justice Stephen Johnson Field, had been an outspoken abolitionist since he joined with anti-slavery Democrats to form the Free Soil Party in the late 1840s. Moreover, as a Republican Party member since its formation in 1856, he had supported Lincoln's candidacy in 1860 as well as the president's military and anti-slavery policies throughout the war. Although Black had not been a staunch abolitionist and had served as attorney general and secretary of state under President James Buchanan, he was a highly regarded constitutional lawyer and remained a loyal Unionist during the war. The two men were joined by one of Harris' political enemies, James Abrams Garfield. Garfield had remained a loyal Republican—indeed he voted to impeach Johnson—but because Garfield vigorously argued that military trials of civilians were unconstitutional, he could not join Colfax or Farnsworth in arguing that the evidence taken in Harris' trial served as a viable means to remove Harris from Congress. Thus, the same congressman who had forcefully argued to have Long and Harris removed from Congress in 1864, now resisted Farnsworth and Colfax. Ultimately, the Supreme Court sided with Field, Black, and Garfield. In more than one sense, the arguments and outcome were pivotal for Harris. After all, he had argued the very opposition to military jurisdiction that Milligan raised in his trial and Field, Black, and Garfield challenged before the Court. Harris could reasonably argue that if Milligan's trial was illegal, then so too was his. Harris' fate in Congress would then also have to be based on a much different question than whether he had been convicted of treasonable activities. Instead, Congress itself would have to determine whether Harris had acted in such an unworthy manner as to justify his expulsion. Even with a strong Republican majority, under these circumstances, it would be unlikely that the House of Representatives could expel him by the necessary two-thirds vote.

The Supreme Court was to further weaken the Radicals' reconstruction plans by finding that test oaths to enter the profession of law were unconstitutional. In a decision captioned *Ex Parte Garland*, the Court determined that the exclusion of former Confederates from the legal profession could not withstand constitutional scrutiny. Put another way, a person's prior political affiliation could not be used as a basis from barring an attorney from the courts. Harris would have probably viewed Chief Justice Salmon Chase as an untrustworthy enemy because of Chase's past abolitionism, service as secretary of the treasury during Lincoln's first term, and his concurrence in *Milligan* in which he agreed that military trials of citizens were unconstitutional but only when conducted in the absence of an express congressional mandate. Harris did not know that Chase wanted the southern states to economically recover. "I am exceedingly anxious for the complete recovery of the Southern States from the evils of war. They are a most important part of the country," Chase wrote to a United States District Court judge in explaining *Garland*. "I do not regard it as denying the right of Congress to require the oath as a prerequisite to entertaining the duties of an office where the appointment has been made since the act: but only as denying the right to impose the oath as a condition of continuing to exercise an office or profession." Importantly, the person who challenged the test oath, Augustus Garland, was a former United States senator from Arkansas who joined the Confederate government, and Congress had attempted to bar him and hundreds of his peers, from practicing law in the federal courts. Garland would return to the Senate and in 1885 President Grover Cleveland appointed him Attor-

7. Aftermath of the Trial, 1865–1892 155

ney General of the United States with little Senate opposition. Harris could have argued that based on *Garland*, his removal was unconstitutional.[13]

Despite *Milligan* and *Garland*, Farnsworth's efforts to unseat Harris were brought to the House of Representatives once more. In response, Harris determined to defend himself in a manner similar to his defense of Long two years earlier. On June 14, when Harris spoke to the House of Representatives, he might have been inspired by the Sixteenth Century German religious reformer, Martin Luther. Luther allegedly used the words in his defense against the Papacy's challenge to his teachings before a jury of cardinals at the Diet of Worms: "Here I stand, I cannot do otherwise." Harris began his speech, "I now stand as I stood before the war was declared; as I stood in the last Congress when I received its crown of censure; as I stood in prison and before that infernal instrument of tyranny, the court martial." Nor did Harris offer any excuses for his opposition to Reconstruction in stating, "I am an old-line democrat, and believe in the doctrine of secession." Although Harris had a constitutional basis for his right to remain in Congress and although he could have attacked the constitutionality of military trials over civilians, he muted the legitimacy of his speech with a wide ranging tirade. He wrongly attacked President Johnson for wanting to enforce equality between the races. He also railed against "Mormonism, Millerism, free-loveism, and strong-minded Massachusetts women." But this was not all, he lauded Justice Taney, and insisted that *Dred Scott* remained the true law of the land, and therefore "negro citizenship" was a farcical idea. To Harris' political opponents, the most offensive part of his tirade, and one which could have resulted in another censure if not removal, occurred when he favorably compared John Wilkes Booth and Mary Surratt to John Brown. He claimed that Booth's body had been grossly mistreated and Mary Surratt executed without due process. To Harris, John Brown had been given a fair trial, the chance to appeal, and time to place his will and last testament in order. Implicit in Harris' message was that Booth and Surratt were martyrs and Brown, a villain for an "evil idea." And yet, Harris concluded his speech as being hopeful for a full reconciliation between north and south. He did not argue for a resumption of slavery, but rather a rapid restoration of the southern states to the Union which placed citizens immediately on their prewar footing. In other words, he sought the admission of an unreconstructed south where African Americans remained second-class persons, not citizens though no longer slaves. Harris also informed Congress that he would not run for office again.[14]

One week after his speech, the *Saint Mary's Gazette* called it a "vigorous and manly speech." A week later, the newspaper clarified its support to Harris noting that "while we dissent, as we believe the majority of his own constituents do, from some of Mr. Harris' political views, we cannot too warmly applaud the spirit in which they were enforced." The newspaper also encouraged him to run for office once more. Although Harris would survive all efforts to remove him from Congress, he adhered to his decision to not seek federal office. Instead, he determined to become the south's spokesman in the absence of southern legislators in Congress. On September 14, 1866, he spoke to the National Democratic Party Convention and claimed that the southern states and Northern Democrats wanted a speedy reunion. However, he challenged the conventioneers that the foremost impediment to reunion was the test oath and he decried the Radical Republicans' unwillingness to compromise on this issue. He also opposed the Fourteenth Amendment and he succeeded in having Maryland vote against endorsing it. (Maryland would not accede to the amendment until 1959.) But he failed to keep the amendment from becoming a part of the Constitution.[15]

In June 1866, the *Saint Mary's Gazette* informed its readers that it would endorse Harris if he decided to run again for office. "The present incumbent bravely and ably defended throughout the dark and perilous hours of our civil distractions," it reported. Harris refused, however, to change his mind and insisted he would not run for Congress. He reasoned that he needed to focus his efforts on Maryland from enfranchising African American males and to try to stem the rapid loss of his personal wealth. At war's end his wealth was estimated to be slightly over $3,000 including his debts even though his property remained valued at $40,000. This was less than a quarter of his pre-war worth. Without slave labor to till and harvest his fields and orchards, he found that he had to sell several properties including a large tract of land to Reverdy Johnson.[16]

In addition to outlasting the Congressional investigation, which appears to have been tabled as Congress geared to impeach Johnson, Harris was to enjoy another success. In early 1867 Radical Republicans pushed Congress to keep the United States Naval Academy in Rhode Island where it had been moved during the war. The Radicals intended to punish Maryland for opposing the Fourteenth Amendment by keeping the Academy away from Annapolis. In the last months of his congressional tenure, Harris led the state's congressional delegation to oppose the measure, and President Johnson along with Gideon Welles did not lend their support to the Radicals. The defeat of the Radicals over the location of the naval academy was Harris' last success in Congress.

7. Aftermath of the Trial, 1865–1892

Return to Saint Mary's County and Political Aspirations

Shortly after leaving Congress, Harris published an editorial in the *Baltimore Sun*, which the *New York Times* reprinted. Under the headline "Views of a Maryland Democrat on the Situation," the *Times* reported that Harris championed the nation's return to the Democratic Party's principles "which it recognized before it was paralyzed by the ambition of [Stephen A.] Douglas and the imbecility of [President James] Buchanan." Harris claimed that a new embrace of that party's belief in the limits on the federal government was essential to protect "the rights and liberties of the people." Of course he meant only the rights of white men and women, and he blasted the Republican Party for enabling the enfranchisement of African American men. Perhaps surprisingly to his fellow northern Democrats, he concluded that the restoration of the Democrat Party to political power should occur "peaceably if we can, forcibly if we must." For a nation that had endured well over a half million deaths, and with over a million injured survivors of the war, the idea of restoring a defeated political ideology by force would have little appeal. Harris did not stop with this idea. He also criticized his fellow Democrats who served with him in the Thirty-Eighth and Thirty Ninth Congresses by claiming that "out of timidity they spoke in favor of continuing the war," but behind the scenes they too had hoped for emancipation to fail and the war to peaceably end regardless of whether the southern states either rejoined the union or gained their independence. Harris could have found himself under arrest once more by both the federal government and Maryland's government based on the article, because of his advocacy for violence. He also urged that without full compensation to former slave-owners, the Thirteenth Amendment was unconstitutional. Without compensation, he claimed, Maryland's former slave owners had a right to use any means to regain their "property." And he exhorted his listeners that *Dred Scott* remained the nation's law regarding relations between African Americans and whites, regardless of any amendments to the Constitution.[17]

Harris was not one to let the issue of compensation rest. Indeed, as late as 1892 he tried to petition Congress on behalf of Maryland's former slave owners. He also attempted to re-enter politics on at least two occasions. In 1868, Maryland's southern democrats tried to convince the state legislature to appoint Harris as a senator in place of Reverdy Johnson. An anonymous letter in the *Gazette* went so far as to claim that Harris was a modern-day "Cato," and Reverdy Johnson a "traitor as bad as [General Benjamin] Butler." The two issues which concerned Harris, compensation to Maryland's former slave-owners and depriving African Americans the right to vote, were intertwined, and both issues predated his departure from Congress. On January 5, 1866, with Harris' congressional fate far from certain, he began to advocate Congress as well as his state legislature for compensation to Maryland's former slave owners, reasoning that since Maryland had been a loyal state, the emancipation of all slaves was a taking of private property without constitutional compensation by the federal government. He would fail to convince Congress to debate the issue since the Radical Republicans had taken the majority of seats and compensation for a loss of the central matter over which the war was fought would have been repugnant to the majority party. Curtis Jacobs, one of the pre-war re-enslavement movement's leaders, aligned with Harris on this issue and urged Senator Creswell that Harris was correct in demanding remuneration for Maryland's former slave owners. But Creswell unsurprisingly refused to advance Harris' argument.[18]

Harris next tried to lead a movement to oppose a new state constitution unless it provided compensation and disenfranchised African Americans. His position on compensation proved unpopular because it would have required the state's taxpayers, including property owners who had never owned slaves, to contribute to the wealth of former slave owners. There was a large number of white Marylanders who opposed extending the right to vote to African Americans. Harris likely alienated some of his potential allies after comparing supporters for a new constitution which failed to address compensation to "Judas Iscariot." He opposed other aspects of the draft constitution. One the proposed amendments to the constitution was to have African Americans deemed fully competent to testify in any proceeding including against the interests of white citizens. In response, Harris argued that expansion of voting rights as well as the ability of "colored persons" to testify in trials against white citizens was antithetical to "biblical law."[19]

Although Saint Mary's voters nominated Harris as a delegate to the constitutional convention in Annapolis in May 1867, he refused to attend even after John F. Dent, the former speaker of the House of Delegates, implored him to do so. Dent even went so far as to try to organize a campaign for Harris to run for governor. Harris' intentional absence may have weakened his future political chances. President Andrew Johnson was present for the convention's opening, as a symbol that while he supported emancipation, he would never support equality. In introducing the

7. Aftermath of the Trial, 1865–1892   159

president, Governor Thomas Swann—Bradford's successor—warned that the Republicans intended to transfer "a whole section of the country from the Anglo-Saxon to the African race" and to "establish the negro in the Governmental control of a large section of our country." The convention's second speaker before Johnson took the podium was Richard Carmichael, Harris' fellow delegate from 1864. Carmichael proclaimed Johnson as a hero and in turn the president enthusiastically endorsed the conventioneers. In the following days, Carmichael and Swan successfully opposed permitting African Americans standing to testify as competent witnesses in the civil courts. The new constitution contained features in it which Harris supported. The 1864 constitution prohibited over twenty-five thousand former voters from voting in the future as a result of having served in the Confederate Army. The new constitution returned the voting rights and rights to hold political office to these individuals. Still, to Harris and those that aligned with him, the new constitution had troubling aspects to it.[20]

    In several respects, the 1867 constitution adopted a broader rights enumeration than its predecessor, including trial by jury, religious freedoms, and freedom of the press. Even after its adoption, Harris vociferously opposed the new constitution because it failed to remunerate former slave-owners for the loss of their property, and permitted former slaves to testify as competent witnesses in criminal trials. One of his long-timer supporters, a Baltimore attorney named Jonathan Norris penned to his son "we had a very large ratification meeting in monument square. As large as I ever saw in that place and which has had a good effect on the state. Ben Harris is opposing the instrument but he is only hurting himself by his course which I am deeply sorry." In spite of Harris not siding with the majority of Democrats in adopting the state constitution, he still remained politically viable, given the views of his former constituents.[21]

    At the same time Harris campaigned to defeat the state constitution, he became an executive officer for the Mutual Life Insurance Company of Baltimore. This corporation was founded through a legislative charter in 1838, and by 1880 it was the city's largest insurer. Harris also began to represent debt collectors over loans to farmers and merchants made during the war. Following the Confederacy's defeat and with emancipation, southern Maryland's slave-owners, including Harris, had difficulty repaying loans to banks and holding companies. Harris was able to finance his personal debts through the sale of property as well as by his legal practice. However, small property owners were not as fortunate as Harris and were confronted with the loss of their farms and businesses. Harris went further than court litigation in obtaining fees. He purchased debts and then was able to recover the value of debts, interest, and legal fees though court actions. He also partnered with William Merrick, the former federal judge who Seward had ordered placed under house arrest during the first year of the war.[22]

In March 1868 Marcus M. "Brick" Pomeroy, the editor of the *La Crosse Democrat*, a Wisconsin newspaper, tried to convince Midwestern democrats to support a Harris presidential campaign. Pomeroy had been a copperhead and ally of Vallandigham during the war, but Vallandigham had lost a congressional election to Robert Schenck. Pomeroy had another reason for not supporting Vallandigham. Despite campaigning against African American suffrage and the Fourteenth Amendment, Vallandigham tried to distance himself from his earlier Copperhead activities. Pomeroy became convinced that only Harris could remain true to the 1864 election platform. Likewise, Johnathan Norris led a movement to have the state legislature appoint Harris as a senator in place of Reverdy Johnson in 1868. Southern Maryland's Democrats wanted Harris to support Andrew Johnson during the impeachment crisis, or, in the absence of Johnson remaining in the White House, declare secession. "We had the hon Benjamin G. Harris speak for us a few days ago (I mean our dear Dem Association). He looks well and is straight out a repudiationist as we all are," Norris wrote to his son, before adding, "He is, however, for paying the soldiers and widows their pensions." Norris, like Harris' other supporters, were unrealistic about Harris' chances, as well as those of the Democrat Party in the forthcoming presidential election. They believed that New York's governor, Horatio Seymour, and his vice presidential candidate, Frank Blair, would sweep into office over Ulysses Grant. Harris, however, feared that Grant would prevail in a landslide election. On election day in November 1868, Harris and his wife attended church to pray for the nation to elect Horatio Seymour. In this instance, Harris at least had a realistic appraisal of Seymour's slim chances.[23]

During the 1868 election, Alexander Long attempted to convince Chief Justice Chase to resign from the Supreme Court and run as the Democratic Party nominee. Long tried to convince Harris to join him, but Harris would not support a former abolitionist. In a letter to Chase written on October 3, Long conveyed his impression of Vallandigham as untrustworthy and unelectable: "His ambition overcame his judgment and he runs to be defeated." Long informed Chase that he had tried to bring Harris into the campaign and he encouraged the justice to "seize upon the last and only hope left of this county from anarchy and despotism by adopting your platform and yourself and General Franklin, or some other such man with you as candidates." Twelve days after sending the first letter to Chase, Long again exhorted the chief justice to resign from the Court and run for the presidency, writing, "hesitate not in accepting as the candidate of the great conservative as the only hope for the preservation of civil liberty and Constitutional government." Chase, however, did not inspire the Democratic Party's convention and remained on the Court.[24]

By 1870 Harris' law practice spanned Maryland and stretched into the nation's capitol and Virginia. He represented the Baltimore and Ohio Railroad in the state courts in Baltimore, Annapolis, and throughout southern Maryland. Perhaps more important, in light of *Garland*, he was able to represent clients in federal court and the railroad paid him a large retainer for a matter in New York. Harris also campaigned across Maryland's southern counties to ensure that the state would not vote in favor of the Fifteenth Amendment. His efforts proved successful and it was not until 1973 that Maryland's legislature voted in favor of the amendment. Nonetheless, the Amendment became a part of the Constitution. Yet the reality of the Fifteenth Amendment which recognized that all African American males over the age of twenty-one had the same voting rights as white males, was that it became unenforceable once Reconstruction came to an end in 1877. Southern states rapidly disenfranchised their African American population though restrictive laws and violence. By the 1900, most of the states south of Maryland had wholly eliminated the rights of African Americans to vote, while service to the Confederacy had almost become a political necessity to succeed in elections.[25]

Harris believed himself to be a viable candidate throughout the 1870s, particularly as former slave owners and southerners sought to end Reconstruction. In 1871 his nephew Joseph Harris wrote to a friend in Port Tobacco that while in Kansas City, Missouri, Democrats asked him to encourage his uncle to run for Congress once more. Harris was reticent to do so because other Democrats who had associated with him during the war had to defend themselves against accusations of disloyalty and he warned that he would have to do the same. In 1869 George Pendleton, while running Ohio governor, was accused of embracing treason for voting against removing Long and Harris eight years earlier. It was not until 1878 that Pendleton was able to re-enter politics as one of Ohio's senators. In April 1870 Harris tried to lead an insurgency within the state Democratic Party against its leaders accepting the Fifteenth Amendment. Some of the state party leaders concluded that they could recruit African American voters and thereby strengthen the party. But Harris refused to accept that the state would allow African American males to vote and urged "the rank and file" to dissolve the party. He faced ridicule in the nation's newspapers for campaigning on issues tied to the war without addressing the national debates on organized labor or federal monetary policy. In 1870, the *New York Herald*, in an article titled "Antiquity," reported that Harris "takes for his platform some relics of antiquity recently discovered in Cheops" before listing the "relics" as his opposition to the Fifteenth Amendment as well as his adherence to states' rights.[26]

In the election of 1872, Harris openly campaigned against the Democratic Party's candidate, Horace Greeley even though Greeley challenged Grant. Harris claimed that Greeley could not embody the traditional principles of the Democratic Party because he had sided with Lincoln and the Republicans during the war. As a newspaper editor, Greeley had served half of a single term of Congress as a Whig in 1848, and he had excoriated pro-slavery interests in the decade after. In October 1872 Harris spoke to the state Democratic Party and argued that southern voters would not vote for either Greeley or Grant. At the same time he implored the party's leadership to name him as an elector the Electoral College so that he could wage a campaign against Greeley as he had against McClellan. But this was not to be. It was not the case that Harris had become *persona non-grata* within the Democratic Party. Rather, Saint Mary's voters decided to name Dent as an elector instead. Harris had intended to witness Grant's second inauguration, but, as Martha recorded in her diary, he decided to remain at Leonardtown as "Grant has a bitter day for his inauguration, the thermostat is lower than it has been this winter. It stood at 17 this morning, the wind blowing a gale and shaking the house." Harris' went to Washington, D.C., to meet with Cox and Wood to discuss the possibility of his returning to Congress in the next election. One of the reasons he felt compelled to run for Congress was that in the election of 1872, the Fifth District's voters narrowly elected a Republican named William Julian Albert to the district's congressional seat. Albert had opposed secession and supported the Freedman's Bureau.[27]

In 1874 Harris once more sought the Fifth District's congressional seat, but five candidates campaigned for it. During the campaign, Harris ignored political issues such as federal financial policy, labor unrest, and immigration. Instead he accused Grant's administration of failing to adhere to the Constitution's protections against property seizures and promised that if elected, he would push to have all former slave-owners compensated. He also opposed the use of the Army in the south to defeat the Ku Klux Klan's efforts to terrorize African Americans and destroy

7. Aftermath of the Trial, 1865–1892   163

Reconstruction programs such as freedmen's schools. His campaign promises were unique in the sense that southern candidates tended to shy away from the issue of slavery and secession and concentrated instead on reconstruction and disenfranchising African Americans. Harris' rhetoric gained attention as far away as Omaha, Nebraska, where a newspaper reported that it was to Maryland's credit that "Harris election chances are exceedingly slim."[28]

At the same time he tried to establish a candidacy for Congress, a small group of southern state legislators approached Harris to run for president. Harris initially flirted with the idea, but realized that any campaign for his seeking higher officer would simply strengthen the Republicans. He suggested to his erstwhile supporters that they try to influence the Democrat platform for the 1876 presidential election by specifically calling for a repeal of the Fourteenth and Fifteenth Amendments as well as pass a new amendment prohibiting non-white men from serving in Congress. Not only did the local newspapers report on Harris' ambition to repeal the two amendments, the Helena, Montana, *Weekly Herald* informed its readers on Harris' activities.[29]

The next year, with a Democrat majority in the House of Representatives for the first time since the war, Fernando Wood sought to have Harris employed as the clerk of House, replacing Edward McPherson, the man who tallied the legislative votes for the Thirteenth, Fourteenth, and Fifteenth amendments, as well as for the vote of censure against Harris. Wood failed to have Harris appointed as clerk because northern Democrats favored George Adams, a former Kentucky congressman. Adams was, in several respects, Harris' opposite. In 1861 he raised a regiment for the Seventh Regiment, Kentucky Volunteer Infantry, and fought for the Union. He served as a congressman from 1873 to 1875 and opposed that compensation for former slave-owners. Harris did not record in any surviving correspondence whether he was angered over Congress' vote for Adams.[30]

Like many Democrats, Harris looked to the 1876 election as their chance to recapture the White House. Grant's presidency was mired in several scandals and had become unpopular. The Republicans turned to Ohio's former governor, Rutherford Hayes, as their candidate. A Harvard Law School graduate and veteran of the Civil War who had fought at Antietam, Hayes had approved of extending the vote in Ohio to African American males and he campaigned in for the Fourteenth Amendment in 1866. He was elected governor the next year and tried to implement equal rights to African American males in Ohio. But a Democrat legislature influenced by George Pendleton thwarted his plans. In 1868 Hayes publicly spoke in favor of Congress removing Andrew Johnson though the impeachment hearings. The next year, Ohio's voters returned him to the governor's office for a second term in an election in which he not only triumphed over George Pendleton, his party gained a majority of seats in the state legislature. From 1871 to 1876 Hayes remained outside of politics and in 1876, the Republican Convention elected him on the seventh ballot over James G. Blaine. Although Hayes became president over Samuel Tilden, the Democratic Party candidate, the election result was controversial and only decided by a special commission involving Congress and the Supreme Court. Neither candidate had achieved the requisite number of electoral votes. Harris assumed that since the contested votes were in southern states, the presidency would go to Tilden and he publicly rejoiced that a Democrat would return to the presidency. During this time Harris traveled to Washington to once more confer with his Democrat allies, but because he championed secession and reimbursement to former slave-owners, Tilden's backers wanted nothing to do with him. Indeed, Tilden and his supporters wanted a unified nation, and talk of secession would have been embarrassing to them. Unable to find an audience, Harris returned home to his law practice.[31]

Again in 1878, Saint Mary's democrats nominated Harris to run for Congress for the Fifth District. Local politician John Chapman, in advancing Harris' candidacy, declared, "nothing I could say would add to his high character and brilliant reputation. His experience and high ability demand the confidence of this convention." Chapman then returned to the theme of Harris being in the right during the war and challenged that Harris' "manly course, unswerving fidelity to principle, and gallant defense of constitutional rights" demanded Maryland's gratitude. Chapman conceded that Harris had not adopted the recent principles of the Democratic Party, but these principles were not founded upon "Jeffersonian integrity" and rather reflected only policy needs. Harris once more campaigned on the basis of compensation for former slave-holders and a promise to disenfranchise African American voters, but he continued to ignore other political and economic issues. In the end, the Democrat, Eli Henkle, a doctor already serving in Congress, was returned by the voters to Congress.[32]

In 1880 Harris campaigned for Winfield Scott Hancock throughout Maryland against James Abrams Garfield. He justified his willingness to campaign for Hancock, who had a distinguished record as a Union general during the Civil War, as a necessity to defeat the congressman who tried to suppress freedom of speech. Once more, the nation's voters elected the Republican. However, Garfield was shot by an assassin named Charles

Guiteau on July 2, 1881, and died on September 18 of that year. His successor, Vice President Chester Arthur, proved unpopular within the Republican Party, and James Blaine became the party's nominee in 1884. After a campaign which was marred by an unusually high degree of personal slanders and false accusations, Grover Cleveland, a Democrat, was elected president. But although Cleveland had not served in the Union Army during the war, he also was never a champion of compensation or disenfranchisement. Nonetheless Harris gleefully attended the inauguration. Although Saint Mary's County remained staunchly Democrat, the Fifth District elected two Republicans, Hart Benton Holton and Sydney Mudd, to single congressional terms before Harris' death. In 1888 Republican Benjamin Harrison narrowly defeated Cleveland, but the voters returned Cleveland to office in 1892. In March of 1892, Harris forwarded a petition from Maryland's former slave-owners to Vice President Levi P. Morton seeking compensation for the loss of their "property." Morton forwarded the petition to the Senate, but that body declined to vote on the petition.[33]

Conclusion

Harris remained politically relevant in Saint Mary's County as well as to adherents of the "lost cause" until his death in 1895. In June 1881 an agent of Jefferson Davis reached out to Harris and asked him to review his biography. There is no longer any documentary evidence as to what Harris agreed to do, but he wrote at least one letter of praise to Davis. One year later, when the book came up for sale, Martha Harris recorded that he still held "admiration, thinking with him, as he does, in every point." On December 1889 when the *Saint Mary's Gazette* reported Jefferson Davis' passing, it also informed its readers that while Harris had never personally met Davis, he held the former president of the Confederacy in high esteem and then went on to note that Harris continued protest against the right of African Americans to vote. Harris also, almost bi-annually, tried to petition Congress and the courts to take up the issue of compensation. In 1892, he did so for the last time, but no representative appeared to have any interest in debating the issue in Congress. A South Carolina governor who was elected to the Senate by his state legislature in 1895 passingly referenced Harris as a champion of the south in also proclaiming the justness of compensation. That governor, Benjamin Ryan Tillman, could have been a protégé of Harris,' but there is no evidence the two men personally corresponded or met.[34]

Conclusion

> "A leading member of the bar; member of the Maryland Legislature, Constitutional Convention, and Served two terms in Congress. A Man of Undoubted Courage, Holding Sacred his Obligations to Duty"
> —epitaph on Harris' grave

After the controversy surrounding Rutherford Hayes' election, the nation retreated from Reconstruction, and throughout the southern states a movement to reduce African Americans to a level of serfdom gained ascendancy. Sectional politics evolved so that few northerners in Congress cared about the Confederate military service of southern congressmen or the rise of "Jim Crow" laws. Indeed, in 1896 in *Plessy v. Ferguson*, the Supreme Court informed the nation that governments and private enterprise alike could discriminate on the basis of race. By 1900, it was almost inconceivable that an African American male would be permitted to vote in any of the southern states, and a new generation of political leaders such as Benjamin Ryan Tillman in South Carolina, Henry G. Connor in North Carolina, James Vardaman in Mississippi, and Thomas Watson in Georgia, would symbolize the desire of the south's white voters to keep African Americans from taking full part in the nation's political and economic machinery.

Harris wholly approved of the reduced legal status of African Americans. After all, he had campaigned against the Thirteenth, Fourteenth, and Fifteenth Amendments, and even after the passage of these amendments, he still argued that the rights contained in them were both illusory and unconstitutional. To the end of his life he was convinced in the justness of slavery, and so, he could not reconcile himself to a United States with its African American citizens technically "free." In May 1893, Bradley J. Johnson, the commander of the Confederate Soldiers Home in Maryland, and a former Confederate general, invited Harris to give a speech to invalid veterans residing in the home. While he replied that an illness prevented him from accepting their offer, the contents of his letter—one of his last correspondences—detail his objectives during the Civil War. Harris began with praise for the southern cause, "It would have afforded me great pleasure to have had such an opportunity of expressing the admiration and affectionate regard which I entertain for the brave soldier and noble patriot of the Southern Confederacy who fought not only for their own rights and liberties, but those of their enemies in the field." He went on to lambast Lincoln, Stanton, Holt, and Grant, as "treacherous tyrants," and lamented that while such men were "villains," they were men of the "greatest minds and most highly talented."[1]

It was in his voting record where Harris took the most pride. "When in Congress I was always found, when present, voting in the negative on all propositions for furnishing men and money to carry on the iniquitous invasion," he claimed. He also took particular pride both in his objections to Congressman Green Clay Smith's December 17, 1863, resolution to raise colored regiments, as well as his defense of Alexander Long. Indeed, it was in his defense of Long, where he wanted to be memorialized. In closing his letter, he noted he wanted his headstone to read the very words which earned him censure, "God Almighty grant you may never subjugate the South." Unrepentant to the end, he also insisted on adding, "the hypocritical tyrants tried, but failed to expel me, but madmen like, they did succeed in censuring me which adds fame to the prayer."[2]

Harris died on April 4, 1895. He had outlived his wife by two years, and on his death he was surrounded by his daughter, Delia Harris as well as four granddaughters, a nephew, and local men of prominence. The *Saint Mary's Gazette* eulogized him as "a man of undaunted courage, of unswerving fidelity to what he believed right, and one who for a life longer than usually allotted bore without abuse the old name of gentleman." The newspaper recalled that Harris had been an advocate of religious tolerance, and characterized him as a "kind slave-owner." The *Baltimore Sun's* editors likewise lauded him as being made "of sterner stuff," than politicians in the "present generation." His death was reported by the *New York Times*, and the far away *San Francisco Chronicle*. When, in September 1895, the Saint Mary's County circuit court commenced its docket of cases, a number of attorneys and local men venerated Harris. He was called "an honored officer of the court," with "a mind well adopted to the science of law," and "a man of clear judgment." None of the newspaper reporting indicated that Harris had championed a cause that was at odds with the basic tenets of universal freedom, but rather, that he defended states' rights and property rights of Marylanders against federal encroachment.³

Like Harris, Fernando Wood, undertook an effort to undermine efforts to keep Taney's belief in a nation with exclusive white citizenship alive. Indeed Wood did his utmost to undermine the Army's role in Reconstruction. His means for accomplishing this goal was to target the general officer most closely associated with the ideal of racial equality, General Oliver Otis Howard. Wood's attack on the Freedman's Bureau failed. President Grant and his allies valued the continued existence of the agency. With venom similar to charges against Republicans he earlier made, Wood's attacked Howard as favoring "racial amalgamation," and in 1870 he accused Howard of "personally enriching himself," with government funds. The charge was malicious. For all his shortcomings as a field commander, Howard was an officer of impeccable character. He demanded a court of inquiry, a function unique to the military, to exonerate himself. Howard's demand, in effect, was akin to a civilian demanding a grand jury to prove innocence. The court of inquiry, headed by General William Tecumseh Sherman exonerated Howard.⁴

Harris outlived Clement Vallandigham. Beginning in 1870 Vallandigham initiated a new political movement within the Democratic Party called the "New Departure Policy." In 1871 he led Ohio's Democratic Party to embrace the Thirteenth, Fourteenth Amendments and Fifteenth Amendments as irrevocable law. He claimed that this was necessary to re-establish the party to assert its other principles, namely a limited federal government. Harris could not accept Vallandigham's shift, but Vallandigham insisted that acceptance of the amendments was necessary to end Reconstruction. Harris never had the chance to directly challenge Vallandigham. In June 1871 Vallandigham accidentally shot himself in the stomach. He had attempted to practice a closing argument to team of defense counsel before trying to prove to a jury that a client was innocent of murder.⁵

George Pendleton unsuccessfully ran for Ohio's governor against Rutherford Hayes in 1869. A decade later he was elected by the state legislature to the Senate, and he quickly worked on reforming the "spoils system" endemic to American elections. In 1883, after Garfield's assassination, Congress passed an act bearing Pendleton's name. The new law required merit as a consideration in federal appointments, and although the law did not eradicate patronage, it brought some respectability to the federal agencies. Although Harris believed he was close to Pendleton, there is no record that they corresponded after Harris left the House of

Conclusion

Representatives, and Pendleton never joined in any cause seeking compensation for former slave owners.

Although Harris became a lone voice for compensation, he left a legacy in both Maryland and the nation. To be sure, even without Harris, bigoted men would have tried to keep Taney's determined opinion that African Americans could never be citizens. But Harris had remained a symbol of a racist cause throughout the southern part of Maryland. southern Maryland's democrats repeatedly tried to disenfranchise the state's African American voters. Even though Maryland's voters refused to ratify the Fifteenth Amendment, from 1870 onward, African Americans had the right to vote. But Democrats tried to imitate the southern states an enact barriers to full male suffrage. Likewise, several schools were opened to educate African American children but arsonists destroyed eleven schools between 1865 and Harris' death, and teachers were assaulted by whites. In 1904, the state's attorney general, John Prentiss Poe, a Princeton University educated Baltimore native lead a movement to deny African Americans the right to vote, segregate schools, and prohibit access to the Chesapeake's oyster beds to African Americans. When, in 1909 President William Howard Taft nominated John Phillip Clayton Hill as United States Attorney for the state, Hill faced bitter opposition from the state's majority Democrat party. It was not the case that the opposition existed because Taft was a Republican, but rather, that because Hill had the temerity to lead the fight to defeat Poe. Hill did share a character trait with Harris. Both men were exceedingly stubborn. Hill opposed prohibition and manufactured wine in his house with the intent of being arrested. Unlike Harris, however, the court which adjudged Hill nullified the evidence against him and acquitted him. Hill became a judge advocate in World War I.[6]

Obviously Harris would be appalled at the United States' present social structure in which the Supreme Court beginning with *Brown v. Board of Education* in 1954 and the civil rights laws of the 1950s and 1960s reduced discrimination in housing and employment and enabled federal enforcement. Of course he would be livid that a southerner belonging to his party named Lyndon Johnson spearheaded the passage of a sweeping civil rights law. Harris would have likely left the Democratic Party in the same manner as Strom Thurmond and other southern politicians between the late 1940s and into the early 1960s and he would have signed the "Southern Manifesto," opposing integration. In 2008 forty-two percent of Saint Mary's County voters voted for President Barak Obama. This percent remained consistent in 2012. In 2008, Maryland's voters overwhelming cast their votes for Mr. Obama, and so too did the Fifth

District. The Fifth Congressional District has voted for the Democrat candidate since 1975. The last two congressional representatives, Gladys Spellman and then Steny Hoyer, the current House Minority Whip, had a commitment to civil rights and voting equality than Harris would have tolerated.[7]

Whether Harris was guilty of violating the Articles of War is a question that could be debated, whether or not one assumes as a predicate that Chapman and Read testified honestly. The debate would center on Harris' intent in providing money to the two former prisoners of war. On top of this, it would be difficult to assess if the officers sitting in judgment of Harris could have dispassionately reviewed the evidence against him before determining his guilt. None of their personal collections contained any reference to their service on Harris' military trial. In one sense, the Supreme Court in *Ex Parte Milligan* lifted the guilty finding against Harris. After all, the nation's highest court determined, by implication, that Harris' military trial was unconstitutional. Had the Court determined an appeal titled *Ex Parte Harris* or *Harris v. Stanton*, undoubtedly Harris would be well known in our modern times. And then, perhaps, arises the most interesting question of all. How would that decision have shaped assertions of Executive Branch authority from World War II to the present? And this question would have left an indelible legacy for Harris instead of leaving him in an obscurity which lasted for over a century.

Chapter Notes

Introduction

1. OR, Ser. II, Volume III (1899 edition), 632; Harris was specifically charged with violating the Fifty-Sixth Article of War.

2. Trial Transcript of the Harris court-martial (hereafter trial transcript), 1. It must be noted that the War Department, the predecessor to the Department of the Army, captioned Harris' trial as both a court-martial and a military commission. Thus, in this book, the two terms are interchangeably used.

3. See, e.g., Diary of Martha Elizabeth Harris [MDHS/MS 1585, hereafter MEH] entries for July 9, 1862, and September 9, 1862. For a contextual appraisal of Martha's Harris' views on Maryland politics, see Claudia Floyd, *Maryland Women in the Civil War: Unionists, Rebels, and Spies* (Charleston, SC: The History Press, 2013), 19–20, and 22–25.

4. On the Sacco and Vanzetti trial see Felix Frankfurter, *The Case of Sacco and Vanzetti: A Critical Analysis for Lawyers and Laymen* (Boston: Little, Brown, 1927); Bruce Watson, *Sacco and Vanzetti: The Men, the Murders, and the Judgement of Mankind* (New York: Viking, 2007), 292–295. On the Mooney trial and appeals see Henry Thomas Hunt, *The Case of Thomas J. Mooney and Warren K. Billings* (New York: Da Capo Press, 1927, reprint, 1971). On the Rosenberg trial see Melvin Urofsky, *Division and Discord: The Supreme Court under Stone and Vinson* (Columbia: University of South Carolina Press, 1997), 178–183; James Haynes and Harvey Klehr, *Early Cold War Spies* (New York: Cambridge University Press, 2006), 143; Joseph Sharlitt, *Fatal Error: The Miscarriage of Justice That Sealed the Rosenbergs' Fate* (New York: Scribner's, 1989), 15.

5. On Merryman's arrest see, OR Ser. II, Vol. 4, 574–578. See also William Marvel, *Mr. Lincoln Goes to War* (Boston: Houghton-Mifflin, 2006), 62; Brian McGinty, *Lincoln and the Court* (Boston: Harvard University Press, 2008), 68. On the court-martial of General Fitz John Porter see Joshua E. Kastenberg, *Law in War, Law as War: Brigadier General Joseph Holt and the Judge Advocate General's Department in the Civil War and Reconstruction* (Durham: Carolina Academic Press, 2011), 78–89. Montgomery Blair, *Hon. Montgomery Blair: Postmaster General During Lincoln's Administration to Fitz John Porter, written on January 26, 1874* (DC: 1874), 2.

6. 17 F. Cass 144 (1861). See also Marvel, *Mr. Lincoln Goes to War*, 62.

7. The offense Burnside charged Vallandigham with was General Orders No. 38, Department of the Ohio, dated April 13, 1863. On the arrest and trial of Vallandigham see *The Trial of Hon. Clement L. Vallandigham by a Military Commission and the Proceedings Under his Application For a Writ of Habeas Corpus In the Circuit Court of the United States For the Southern District of Ohio* (Cincinnati: Rickey & Carroll, 1863), 11–12. For further pertinent analysis see Phillip Shaw Paludan, *A People's Contest: The Union and the Civil War, 1861–1865* (Lawrence: University Press of Kansas, 1996), 240–241; Brian McGinty, *Lincoln and the Court*, 176–192; William Hubbs Rehnquist, *All the Laws But One* (New York: Alfred A. Knopf, 1998), 63–64. Dynes is found at 61 U.S. 65 (1858). On *Dynes v. Hoover* see Joshua E. Kastenberg, "A Sesquicentennial Historic Analysis of Dynes v. Hoover and the Supreme Court's Bow to Military Necessity," *University of Memphis Law Review* 595 (2009).

8. David M. Jordan, *Winfield Scott Hancock: A Soldier's Life* (Bloomington: Indiana

University Press, 1988), 176–182; *Army Navy Journal*, July 8, 1865, p. 728; Mary Bernard Allen, *Joseph Holt, Judge Advocate General (1862–1875): A Study in the Treatment of Political Prisoners by the United States Government During the Civil War*, Ph.D diss., University of Chicago 1927. See also James Wilford Garner, *International Law and the World War*, Vol. II (London: Longman, Greens, 1920), 103.

9. For the varied background information and opinions on Wirz and the prison, see Ovid Futch, *History of the Andersonville Prison* (Gainesville: University of Florida Press, 1968), 9–62; Norton P. Chipman, *The Tragedy of Andersonville: Trial of Captain Henry Wirz, The Prison Keeper* (San Francisco, 1911), 32; R. Fred Ruhlman, *Captain Henry Wirz and Andersonville: A Reappraisal* (Knoxville: University of Tennessee, 2006), 185; Lewis Laska and James M. Smith, "Hell and the Devil: Andersonville and the Trial of Henry Wirz," *Military Law Review* 68 (1975): 77–131, 88. The most recent use of Wirz's trial is *Hamdan v. Rumsfeld*, 584 U.S. 557 (2006). Chipman was a prosecuting judge advocate in Wirz's trial who later served in Congress and as a judge in California.

10. See, for example, William O. Douglas, *An Almanac of Liberty* (New York: Doubleday, 1954), 72; William Rehnquist, *All Laws But One: Civil Liberties in Wartime*, 98. For another judicial conservative view see Harold Hitz Burton, "Two Significant Decisions: *Ex Parte Milligan* and *Ex Parte McCardle*," *American Bar Association Journal* 41 (February 1955): 121–130. Burton served on the Supreme Court from 1945 to 1958. On the importance of Milligan, two decisions arising from later wars speak for themselves: Justice Hugo Black in *Duncan v. Kahanomoku* (1946), and Justice Sandra O'Connor in *Hamdi v. Rumsfeld* (2004).

11. Weber, *Copperheads*, 147–150; Charles Fairman, *Mr. Justice Miller*, 91.

12. Benn Pittman, ed., *The Trials for Treason at Indianapolis* [hereafter Dodd Record], 9. Thomas R. Marshall, *Recollections of Thomas R. Marshall* (Indianapolis: Bobbs-Merrill, 1925), 30; see also Frank Klement, *Dark Lanterns: Secret Political Societies, Conspiracies, and Treason Trials in the Civil War* (Baton Rouge: Louisiana State University Press, 1984), 175, quoting *Indianapolis Daily Journal*, August 19, September 5, 1864. On Hovey, see Ezra Warner, *Generals in Blue* (Baton Rouge: Louisiana State University Press, 1964), 235–236.

13. Rehnquist, *All Laws But One*, 86. See *Milligan v. Hovey*, 4 Am. L. T. Rep U.S. Cts 136 (1871).

14. William Marvel, *Mr Lincoln Goes to War*, xiv-xv; William Marvel, *Lincoln's Autocrat: The Life of Edwin Stanton* (Chapel Hill: University of North Carolina Press, 2015). There is no mention of Harris in Marvel's biography of Stanton, even though he ordered the congressman court-martialed. For a poignant review of Marvel's Stanton biography, see Harold Holzer, "Character Assassination: Edwin M Stanton, Lincoln's Secretary of War, was fierce conniving and unlikeable. But he built the army that won the war," *Wall Street Journal*, June 7, 2015.

15. See, e.g., *Bond v. Floyd*, 385 U.S. 116 (1966), in which the Georgia legislature was determined not to have the authority to evict one of its own duly elected members, simply because that member exercised the right to speak in opposition to the United States' involvement in Vietnam. See also *Powell v. McCormack*, 395 U.S. 486 (1969), in which the Court determined that the House of Representatives had unconstitutionally removed a duly elected member.

16. Mark Neeley, *The Fate of Liberty: Abraham Lincoln and Civil Liberties* (New York: Oxford University Press, 1992); Joanna D. Cowden, *"Heaven Will Frown on Such a Cause as This": Six Democrats Who Opposed Lincoln's War* (Lanham, MD: University Press of America, 2001). Harris is even absent from a recent successful movie on Lincoln's success in influencing the House of Representatives to approve the Thirteenth Amendment.

17. On Napoleon III, see John Bierman, *Napoleon III and His Carnival Empire* (New York: St. Martin's Press, 1988), 85–104; on the fear of standing armies, see Stanley Elkins and Eric McKittrick, *The Age of Federalism: The Early American Republic, 1788–1800* (New York: Oxford University Press, 1993), 716; Walter Millis, *Arms and Men: A Study in American Military History* (New York: G.P. Putnam and Sons, 1956), 48.

18. See, e.g., Lawrence Friedman, *Law in America: A Short History* (New York: Random House, 2002), 1–19.

19. Frankfurter to Minton, January 25, 1950 [Robert H Jackson Papers / 163].

20. A good discussion of this model can be found in William W. Freehling, *The Road to Disunion: Vol. II, Secessionists Triumphant, 1854–1861* (New York: Oxford University Press, 2007), 530–534. Also see Sean Wilentz, *The Rise of American Democracy: Jefferson to Lincoln* (New York: W.W. Norton, 2005), 465–481.

21. Jonathan Norris to his son, April 22, 1868 [MDHS / MS 1379]. On Norris, see H. Charles Ulman, *Trow's Legal Directory and Lawyers' Record of the United States* (New

York: James Trow, 1875), 455. Harris is listed on 474.

Chapter 1

1. See "Charles County Court," *Port Tobacco Times*, 28 August 1845; "Charles County Court," *Maryland Republican*, November 15, 1845. In 1936, the Supreme Court, in *Palko v. Connecticut*, determined that a state trial courts could prosecute a citizen who had been acquitted in a federal court for the same offense. However, most states, to include Maryland, had already determined that double jeopardy was prohibited within a state's criminal justice system. Nonetheless, this prohibition did not serve to protect Caesar. See *Palko v. Connecticut*, 302 U.S. 310 (1937).

2. See "Insurrectionists Found Guilty," *The Voice of Freedom*, October 9, 1845; Court Session, *Port Tobacco Times*, September 4, 1845. On Harris' involvement see "Public Meeting," *Saint Mary's Gazette*, April 4, 1859; Christopher Phillips, *Freedom's Port: The African American Community of Baltimore, 1790–1860* (Urbana: University of Illinois Press, 1997), 30–31.

3. William W. Freeling, *The Road to Disunion: Vol. II, Secessionists Triumphant*, 194–195; see also Christopher Phillips, *Freedom's Port: The African American Community of Baltimore, 1790–1860*, 206–209.

4. See, e.g., Curtis Jacobs, *The Free Negro Question in Maryland: Slavery and free negroism incompatible ... able letter of C.W. Jacobs on this all absorbing question* (Baltimore, 1859).

5. Henry Dorsey Richardson, *Sidelights on Maryland's History With Sketches of Early Maryland Families* (Baltimore: Williams and Wilkins, 1903),156.

6. Carroll T. Bond, ed., *Proceedings of the Maryland Court of Appeals* (Washington, D.C.: American Historical Society, 1933), 26. Bond was the chief judge of this Court at the time he authored this study.

7. "The Harris Family," *Saint Mary's Beacon*, May 23, 1901; Helen West Ridgely, *Historic Graves of Maryland and the District of Columbia: With the Inscriptions Appearing on the Tombstones in Most of the Counties of the States and in Washington* (New York: Grafton, 1908), 44–47. The Harris family lineage was researched by an attorney named George Forbes in the 1930s. See George Forbes, "Joseph Harris of Ellenborough," *Maryland Historical Magazine*, Vol. XXXI (December 1936).

8. MEH diary entry, January 1, 1869.

9. Anon, *The 1850 Census of Saint Mary's County, Maryland* (Saint Mary's County: Genealogical Committee of the St Mary's Historical Society, 1978), 43; Edwin N. Beitzell, "Hon Benjamin Gwinn Harris," *Chronicles of Saint Mary's*, 37.

10. Barbara Jeanne Fields, *Slavery and Freedom on the Middle Ground: Maryland During the Nineteenth Century* (New Haven: Yale University Press, 1972), 1; Bernard C. Steiner, *The Institutions and Civil Government of Maryland* (Boston: Ginn and Co., 1899), 5–16.

11. On Harris breeding race horses, see "Leonardtown Jockey Club News," *Saint Mary's Gazette*, September 10, 1857; on the death of Reliance, see October 7, 1858. On the economy of southern Maryland see Kevin Conley Ruffner, *Maryland's Blue and Gray: A Border State's Union and Confederate Junior Officer Corps* (Baton Rouge: Louisiana State University Press, 1997), 16; Barbara Fields, *Slavery and Freedom*, 11–12. On the slave revolt see, Junius P. Rodriguez, "Saint Mary's Plot," in Junius Rodriguez, ed., *Encyclopedia of Slave Resistance and Rebellion*, Vol. 2 (Westport, CT: Greenwood Press, 2007), 411–412.

12. John T. Willis and Herbert C. Smith, *Maryland Politics and Government: Democratic Dominance* (Lincoln: University of Nebraska Press, 2012), 26–30.

13. John T. Willis and Hebert C. Smith, *Maryland Politics and Government: Democratic Dominance*, 27–30; Frank Towers, *The Urban South and the Coming of the Civil War* (Charlottesville: University of Virginia Press, 2004), 55–59.

14. Kevin Conley Ruffner, *Maryland's Blue and Gray: A Border State's Union and Confederate Junior Officer Corps*, 26–27.

15. Lanman interviewed Harris twice, once in 1882 and once in 1864. In 1864 he published a short biographical sketch of Harris. See Charles Lanman, *Dictionary of the United States Congress: Compiled as a Manual of Reference* (Washington, D.C.: GPO, 1864), 171.

16. Jean Butenhoff Lee, *The Price of Nationhood: The American Revolution in Charles County* (New York: W.W. Norton, 1994), 250–251; Laws of the State of Maryland (Baltimore, 1832), 27.

17. Obituary, *Port Tobacco Times*, May 11, 1894, Vol. L No. 49; *Obituary Record of the Graduates of Yale University, Deceased from June 1890 to June 1900* (New Haven: Tuttle and Co., 1900), 214–215.

18. William Russell Cone, *Memorial of the Class of 1830 of Yale College* (Hartford, CT: Case, Lockwood, and Brainard, 1871).

19. *A Catalogue of the Students of Law in Harvard University Law School, to the end of the First Term in the Year 1842* (Cambridge: Metcalfe, Keith and Nichols, 1842), 21.

20. John W. Mitchell Papers, Contract at Port Tobacco, Sept. 1848 [JWM / MDHS MS 1782]; Probate contest notification at Port Tobacco, February 1, 1860 [JWM / MDHS MS 1782]; J.G. Chapman, Report of the Weverton Manufacturing Company, 1849 [Chapman Family Papers—SMH / 5]; MGH, diary entry for May 5, 1851 [MEH / 1]; Eugenia Calvert, "Miniatures in the Collection of the Maryland Historical Society," *Maryland Historical Magazine* 4 (December 1956), 341–355.

21. On Harris serving as a campaign manager, see "Whig Barbeque," *Saint Mary's Gazette*, October 28, 1852. On Harris' transition to the Democrat Party, see "Democrats Attention," *Saint Mary's Gazette*, January 27, 1853. For general information on the area, see William J. Evitts, *A Matter of Allegiences: Maryland from 1850 to 1861* (Baltimore: Johns Hopkins University Press, 1974), 14.

22. On the anti-Catholic ideology of the Know-Nothing Party and their impact see Ira Leonard and Robert Parmet, *American Nativism, 1830–1860* (New York: Van Nostrand Reinhold, 1971), 50–73. Benjamin Gwinn Harris, *Speech of Benjamin G. Harris, ESQ of St. Mary's County upon the Reports of the Committee on Secret Societies in the House of Delegates of Maryland* (1855?).

23. Lanman, interview notes. On the internal fracture over slavery in the Whig Party, see Michael F. Holt, *The Rise and Fall of the American Whig Party: Jacksonian Politics and the Onset of the Civil War* (New York: Oxford University Press, 1999), 238; Michael F. Holt, *The Fate of Their Country: Politicians, Slavery Extension, and the Coming of the Civil War* (New York: Hill and Wang, 2005), 20–77. On the Whig Party's anti-Jackson origins, see E. Malcom Carroll, *Origins of the Whig Party* (Durham: Duke University Press, 1925), 70–169.

24. MEH, diary entry September 4, 1851; on the Whig view of social stability, see Kinley J. Brauer, *Cotton versus Conscience: Massachusetts Whig Politics and Southwestern Expansion* (Lexington: University of Kentucky Press, 1967), 24.

25. On nativism in Maryland, see William Evitts, *A Mater of Allegiances*, 90–91. See also Jean M. Baker, *Ambivalent Americans: The Know Nothing Party in Maryland* (Baltimore: Johns Hopkins University Press, 1977); Mary St. Patrick McConville, *Political Nativism in the State of Maryland, 1830–1860* (Washington, D.C.: Catholic University of America, 1928), 1–101.

26. See, e.g., Douglas Bowers, "Ideology and Political Parties, 1851–1856," *Maryland Historical Magazine* (Fall 1969), 197–217.

27. Ibid.

28. Idbi.

29. Benjamin G. Harris, *Speech of Benjamin G. Harris, ESQ of St. Mary's County upon the Reports of the Committee on Secret Societies in the House of Delegates of Maryland* (1856?).

30. Ibid., 6–7.

31. Ibid.

32. Ibid.

33. Ibid.

34. See, e.g., *Jason v. Henderson*, 7 Md. 430 (Md. 1855). On the training of lawyers, see John H. Langbein, "Blackstone, Litchfield, and Yale: The Founding of Yale's Law School," in Anthony T. Kronman, ed., *History of the Yale Law School: The Tercentennial Lectures* (New Haven: Yale University Press, 2004), 17–52.

35. Thomas D. Morris, *Free Men All: Personal Liberty Laws of the North, 1780–1860* (Baltimore: Johns Hopkins University Press, 1974), 91–102; Paul Finkelman, "Prigg v. Pennsylvania and Northern State Courts: Anti-Slavery Use of a Pro-Slavery Decision," in John R. McKivigan, *Abolitionism and American Law* (New York: Garland, 1999), 199–203.

36. Thomas D. Morris, *Free Men All: Personal Liberty Laws of the North, 1780–1860* (Baltimore: Johns Hopkins University Press, 1974), 91–102.

37. *Prigg v. Pennsylvania*, 41 U.S. 539 (1842).

38. Paul Finkelman, "State Constitutional Protections of Liberty and the Antebellum New Jersey Supreme Court: Chief Justice Hornblower and the Fugitive Slave Law," *Rutgers Law Review* 23 (1992), 753–759.

39. Wilentz, *The Rise of American Democracy: Jefferson to Lincoln*, 708–711.

40. On Taney, see R. Kent Newmeyer, *The Supreme Court under Marshall and Taney* (New York: Crowell Press, 1968); James F. Simon, *Lincoln and Chief Justice Taney: Slavery, Secession, and the President's War Powers* (New York: Simon & Schuster, 2007), 5–44.

41. *Fenwick v. Chapman*, 34 U.S. 461 (1835); See also *Charles v. Sheriff*, 12 Md 274 (Md. 1858).

42. *Lowe v. Gist* (Md. 1789); *Davis v. Jacquin & Pomerait*, 5 H. & J. 100 (Md. 1820); *Negro David v. Porter*, 4 H. & McH 418 (Md. 1799).

43. *Scaggs v. Baltimore and Western Maryland Railroad*, 10 Md. 628 (Md. 1856).

44. *State v. Nutwell*, 1 Gil. 54 (Md. 1843); *Franklin v. State*, 12 Md. 236 (Md. 1858).

45. *Gough v. Edelen*, 5 Gil 101 (Md. 1847).
46. *Abell v Harris*, 11 Gill 367 (Md. 1841); See Equity papers, MS Index, 94 [MD State Archives].
47. *Hughes v. Jackson*, 12 Md. 450 (1858).
48. "Congressional," *Saint Mary's Gazette*, May 5, 1859; "Public Meeting," *Saint Mary's Gazette im* April 4, 1859.
49. See, e.g., Nicole Etchison, *Bleeding Kansas: Contested Liberty in the Civil War Era* (Lawrence: University of Kansas Press, 2004), 1–27.
50. Harris to Stephen A. Douglas [U-Chi / 36–8].
51. Resolution of Saint Mary's Democrats, September 1, 1860 [U-Chi / 36–8].
52. "Political Miscellany," *New York Times*, September 11, 1860.
53. Sean Wilentz, *The Rise of American Democracy: Jefferson to Lincoln*, 755–762; Eric Foner, *The Fiery Trial: Abraham Lincoln and American Slavery* (New York: W.W. Norton, 2010), 140–144; MEH, diary entry for November 3, 18.
54. MEH, diary entry for November 6, 1860; MEH, diary entry for November 8, 1860.

Chapter 2

1. MEH, diary entries for April 13 and 14, 1861.
2. MEH, diary entry for April 21, 1861; William Marvel, *Mr. Lincoln Goes to War*, 28–29; William H. Rehnquist, *All The Laws But One: Civil Liberties in Wartime* (New York: Alfred A. Knopf, 1998), 24–25.
3. Lincoln to Scott, April 25, 1861 [PAL-LOC]; Scott to Butler, April 26, 1861, OR Ser. II, Vol. 1, 657.
4. Miles to Hicks, April 27, 1861, in *Journal of Senate Proceedings of the Senate of Maryland in Extra Session* (Annapolis: Beale H. Richardson Printer, 1861), 11; "Release of State Prisoners," *New York Times*, April 9, 1862; "From General Banks' Army: Affairs in Frederick, MD," *New York Times*, September 27, 1861.
5. For the Supreme Court's determination as to judicial authority see, *Marbury v. Madison*, 5 U.S. 137 (1803). *United States v. Hamilton*, 3 U.S. 17 (1795). One of other the earliest habeas cases is *Ex Parte Bollman*, 8 U.S. (4 Cranch) 75 (1807). For an interesting explanation see, Anthony Gregory, *The Power of Habeas Corpus in America: From the King's Prerogative to the War on Terror* (New York: Cambridge University Press, 2013), 69–74; George C. Thomas, *The Supreme Court on Trial: How the American Justice System Sacrifices Innocent Defendants* (Ann Arbor: University of Michigan Press, 2008), 103–104.
6. On this episode see, Louis Fisher, *The War Power: Original and Contemporary* (Washington, D.C.: American Historical Association, 2009), 12; Thomas P. Slaughter, *The Whiskey Rebellion: Frontier Epilogue to the American Revolution* (New York: Oxford University Press, 1986), 192.
7. See, e.g., William Howard Taft, *Our Chief Magistrate and His Powers* (New York: Columbia University Press, 1925); *Ex Parte Grossman*, 267 U.S. 87, 107 (1925); *Tumey v. Ohio*, 273 U.S. 510 (1927).
8. Winthrop, *Military Law and Precedents*, 777; Mark Neeley, *The Fate of Liberty*, 162; William Birkhimer, *Military Government and Martial Law*, 222.
9. Lynn Hudson Parsons, *The Birth of Modern Politics: Andrew Jackson, John Quincy Adams, and the Election of 1828* (New York: Oxford University Press, 2009), 36–40; Jonathan Lurie, *Arming Military Justice: The Origins of the United States Court of Military Appeals, 1775–1950* (Princeton: Princeton University Press, 1992), 11–19.
10. John Simon, *Lincoln and Chief Justice Taney, Slavery, Secession, and the President's War Powers* (New York: Simon & Schuster, 2006), 186–188; G. Edward White, *Law in American History: Vol. I, the Colonial Years through the Civil War* (New York: Oxford University Press, 2012), 444.
11. Bryan McGinty, *The Body of John Merryman: Abraham Lincoln and the Suspension of Habeas Corpus* (Cambridge: Harvard University Press, 2011), 6–8. See also David Silver, *Lincoln's Supreme Court* (Urbana: University of Illinois Press, 1956), 28–32.
12. "United States Court: Important Proceedings, the Case of John Merryman," *Baltimore Sun*, May 28, 1861; "The Suspension of the Writ of Habeas Corpus," *Baltimore Sun*, May 29, 1861; "The Merryman Case: The Opinion of Chief Justice Taney," *Baltimore Sun*, June 3, 1861.
13. Adam Arenson, "Dred Scott versus the Dred Scott Case: The History and Memory of a Signal Moment in American History," in David Thomas Konig, Paul Finkelman, and Christopher Alan Bracey, ed,. *The Dred Scott Case: Historical and Contemporary Perspectives on Race and Law* (Athens: Ohio University Press, 2010), 25–48; Paul Finkelman, "The Strange Career of Dred Scott," in *The Dred Scott Case: Historical and Contemporary Perspectives on Race and Law*, 227–249. See also Donald Fehrenbacher, *The Dred Scott Case: Its Significance in American Law and Politics* (New York: Oxford University

Press, 1978); Philip Auchampaugh, "James Buchanan, the Court, and the Dred Scott Case," *Tennessee Historical Magazine* 9 (1929). See also *Kentucky v. Dennison*, 65 M.J. 24 (1861).

14. On Kane, see Jonathan W. White, *Abraham Lincoln and Treason in the Civil War: The Trials of John Merryman* (Baton Rouge: Louisiana State University Press, 2011), 51; Frank Towers, *The Urban South and the Coming of the Civil War* (Charlottesville: University of Virginia Press, 2004), 115–153.

15. Jonathan W. White, *Abraham Lincoln and Treason in the Civil War*, 51.

16. Banks to Third Wisconsin Regiment, September 16, 1861 in Charles W. Mitchell, ed., *Maryland Voices of the Civil War* (Baltimore: Johns Hopkins University Press, 2007), 238. See also Cameron to Banks, September 11, 1861, OR Ser. I, vol. 5, 193; McClellan to Dix, September 10, 1861 [MP, A25 R12]; David Work, *Lincoln's Political Generals* (Urbana: University of Illinois Press, 2007), 161–162; Ethan S. Rafuse, *McClellan's War* (Bloomington: Indiana University Press, 2005), 132–133; Thomas G. Mitchell, *Anti-Slavery Politics in Antebellum and Civil War America* (Westport, CT: Praeger, 2007), 183; Mark Neeley, *The Fate of Liberty: Abraham Lincoln and Civil Liberties*, 14–18. See also "Memoranda concerning the Arrest of Certain Members of the Maryland Legislature," OR Ser. 2, Vol. I, 668.

17. Mark E. Neely, *The Fate of Liberty: Abraham Lincoln and Civil Liberties*, 27; The title of the decision is *United States ex rel Murphy v. Porter*, 27 F. Cas, 599 (1861).

18. Jonathan W. White, "Sweltering with Treason: The Civil War Trials of William Matthew Merrick," *Prologue* 39 (Summer 2007), 26–36; Jeffrey Brandon Morris, *Calmly to Pose the Scales of Justice: A History of the Courts of the District of Columbia Circuit* (Durham: Carolina Academic Press, 2001), 35.

19. For an account of Johnson's life, see Bernard Christian Steiner, *Life of Reverdy Johnson* (New York: Russell & Russell, 1970), 1–22; Glenda R. Schroeder-Lein and Richard Zuczek, *Andrew Johnson: A Biographical Companion* (Santa-Barbara: ABA-CLIO, 2001), 167; Cong. Globe. (1864), 1419–1424.

20. Speech of the Honorable Reverdy Johnson of Maryland Delivered Before the Political Friends of Stephen A. Douglas, at a Meeting in Fanueil Hall in Boston, on Thursday, June 7, 1860 (Baltimore: John Murphy & Co, 1860), 10.

21. Bernard Steiner, *Life of Reverdy Johnson*, 37;

22. E.A. Townsend to George McClellan, August 22, 1861, in OR Ser. I, Vol. 5, 578; George McClellan to Edwin Stanton, March 22, 1862, in OR Ser. I, Vol. 5, 758–759; "Guano," *Saint Mary's Beacon*, October 2, 1862.

23. Thomas Hicks to Winfield Scott, January 11, 1861; Hicks to John J. Crittenden, December 18, 1860; Hicks to Major General John A. Dix, August 20, 1918 [MDHS / MS 2104]. See also George L. P. Radcliffe, *Governor Thomas H. Hicks of Maryland and the Civil War* (Baltimore: Johns Hopkins University Press, 1901), 30–73.

24. Augustus W. Bradford, *Inaugural Address of Hon. Augustus W. Bradford, Governor of Maryland: Delivered in the Senate Chamber, in Annapolis, January 8, 1862* (Annapolis: Thos J. Wilson, 1862), 5–15.

25. Bradford, journal entry for June 18, 1862 [MDHS / MS 90].

26. Bradford, journal entry, September 8, 1862 [MDHS / MS 90]. On Lee's campaigns in Virginia and Maryland, see James McPherson, *Battle Cry of Freedom: The Civil War Era* (New York: Oxford University Press, 1988), 524–545.

27. Roger Combs Hammett, *History of Saint Mary's County, MD: 1834–1900* (Baltimore: Ridge Press, 2000), 123–124.

28. On the "Resolutions," see Gordon S. Wood, *Empire of Liberty: A History of the Early American Republic* (New York: Oxford University Press, 2009), 269–273; Brian Steel, *Thomas Jefferson and American Nationhood* (New York: Cambridge University Press, 2012); 243–244; Richard Beeman, *The Old Dominion and the New Nation* (Lexington: University Press of Kentucky, 1972), 188–193; Stanley Elkins and Erick McKittrick, *The Age of Federalism: The Early American Republic, 1788–1800*, 719–726; Harris G. Mirkin, "Rebellion, Revolution, and the Constitution: Thomas Jefferson's Theory of Civil Disobedience," *American Studies* 13 (1972).

29. Sanford W. Higginbotham, *The Keystone in the Democratic Arch: Pennsylvania Politics, 1800–1816* (Harrisburg: Pennsylvania Historical and Museum Commission, 1956), 183–198.

30. On the "Gag Rule," see Patricia Roberts-Miller, *Fanatical Schemes: Proslavery Rhetoric and the Tragedy of Consensus* (Tuscaloosa: University of Alabama Press, 2009), 187–191; Edward B. Rugemer, "Caribbean Slave Revolts and the Origin of the Gag Rule," in John Craig Hammond and Matthew Mason, *The Politics of Bondage and Freedom in the New American Nation: Contesting Slavery* (Charlottesville: University of Virginia Press, 2011), 93–109.

31. Harris G. Mirkin, "Rebellion, Revolu-

tion, and the Constitution: Thomas Jefferson's Theory of Civil Disobedience," *American Studies* 13 (1972).
32. *Entick v. Carrington* (1765) 19 St. Tr. 1030. For an exposition on this decision see K.D. Ewing and C.A. Gearty, *The Struggle for Civil Liberties: Political Freedom and the Rule of Law in Britain* (Oxford: Oxford University Press, 2000), 29–31. *Entick* continues to be cited today, including by the Supreme Court. See, e.g., *United States v. Jones*, 132 S.Ct 945 (2012).
33. T.R.S. Allen, *Constitutional Justice: A Liberal Theory on the Rule of Law* (New York: Oxford University Press, 2003), 39–43; David Feldman, "The Politics and People of Entick v. Carrington," in Adam Tomkins and Paul Scott, *Entick v. Carrington: 250 Years of the Rule of Law* (London: Hart Publishing, 2015), 5–42.
34. "Public Meeting," *Saint Mary's Beacon*, April 25, 1861.
35. Aleck Loker, *A Most Convenient Place: Leonardtown, Maryland, 1650–1950* (Leonardtown, MD: Solitude Press, 2001), 60–65.
36. Charles Lewis Wagandt, *The Mighty Revolution: Negro Emancipation in Maryland, 1862–1864* (Baltimore: Johns Hopkins University Press, 1964), 20.
37. Charles Benedict Calvert, Slave account book of Charles Benedict Calvert, listing names, ages, value, and sale price of 330 slaves residing at several of Calvert's farms (University Maryland, Special Collections); Nathan A. Branch Miles, Monday M. Miles, and Ryan J. Quick, *Prince George's County and the Civil War: Life on the Border* (Charleston, SC: The History Press, 2013), 69.
38. "Maryland Congressional Elections," *The National Republican*, June 15, 1861, pp 2.
39. Alan G. Bogue, *The Congressman's Civil War* (New York: Cambridge University Press, 1989), 65–66; Eugene M. Wait, *The Opening of the Civil War* (Commack, NY: Nova Science Publishers, 1999), 275.
40. Baker to Montgomery Blair, January 14, 1862 in Lafayette C. Baker, *History of the U.S. Secret Service* (New York: AMS, 1973), 108–109.
41. Buchanan to Pearce, June 26, 1861 [MDHS / MS 1384].
42. See *Saint Mary's Beacon*, June 27, 1861; Unittited, *Saint Mary's Beacon*, September 5, 1861; "Notice," *Saint Mary's Beacon*, September 12, 1861.
43. "County Convention," *Saint Mary's Beacon*, September 5, 1861; "Maryland Election," *Cumberland Civilian and Telegraph*, November 19, 1863; Harry Wright Newman, *Maryland and the Confederacy* (Annapolis: Harry Wright Newman, 1976).
44. James Oakes, *Freedom National: The Destruction of Slavery in the United States, 1861–1865* (New York: W.W. Norton, 2013), 90–148.
45. Benjamin G. Harris Dead," *Saint Mary's Gazette*, April 11, 1895.
46. Carl Everstine, *The General Assembly of Maryland, 1850–1920* (New York: Michie, 1980), 162.
47. Alexander Randall, entry for July 25, 1863 [MDHS / 652]. Randall, like Harris, was a slave owner and made formal claims to the War Department during the war for reimbursement after two of his slaves enlisted into the Army. See Randall, Provost Marshal Claim, May 28, 1864 [MDHS / MS 2816].

Chapter 3

1. William A. Blair, *With Malice Toward Some: Treason and Loyalty in the Civil War Era* (Chapel Hill: University of North Carolina Press, 2014), 20–30. Interestingly, Professor Blair is one of the few historians to mention Harris in his book, although he does so in a paragraph, his use of Harris to show the extent of how the Lincoln administration treated political dissent is noteworthy.
2. Charles A. Stevenson, *Warriors and Politicians: U.S. Civil-Military Relations Under Stress* (New York: Routledge, 2006), 21–49; William A. Blair, *With Malice Toward Some: Treason and Loyalty in the Civil War Era*, 80–82; Robert Remini, *Daniel Webster, The Man and His Times* (New York: W.W. Norton, 1997), 243–246.
3. Robert Remini, *The House: A History of the House of Representatives* (New York: Harper, 2007), 1–9.
4. See, e.g., Robert Forbes, *The Missouri Compromise and its Aftermath: Slavery and the Meaning of America* (Chapel Hill: University of North Carolina Press, 2007), 30–41; Stephanie Kermes, *Creating an American Identity* (New York: Palgrave Macmillan, 2008),145–168.
5. Michael S. Green, *Politics and America in Crisis: The Coming of the Civil War* (Santa Barbara: ABC-CLIO, 2010), X; Sean Wilentz, *The Rise of American Democracy: Jefferson to Lincoln*, 602.
6. Karl Jack Bauer, *The Mexican War, 1846–1848* (Lincoln: University of Nebraska Press, 1976), 10–22.
7. Amy S. Greenberg, *A Wicked War: Polk, Clay, Lincoln and the 1846 U.S. Invasion of Mexico* (New York: Vintage, 2012), 10.
8. Brien Hallett, *Declaring War: Con-*

gress, the President, and What the Constitution Does Not Say (New York: Cambridge University Press, 2012), 131.

9. Michael S. Green, Politics and America in Crisis: The Coming of the Civil War (Santa Barbara: ABC-CLIO, 2010), 6–10; Sam W. Haynes, James K. Polk and the Expansionist Impulse (New York: Longmans Press, 1997), 147–159.

10. Roger L. Ransom, Conflict and Compromise: The Political Economy of Slavery, Emancipation, and the American Civil War (New York: Cambridge University Press, 1989), 97; Keith T. Poole and Howard Rosenthal, A Political-Economic History of Roll Call Voting (New York: Oxford University Press, 1997), 160–161; Stephen W. Stathis, Landmark Debates in Congress: From the Declaration of Independence to the War in Iraq (Washington, D.C.: CQ Press, 2009), 119–123.

11. See, e.g., Donald J. Ratcliffe, One Party Presidential Contest: Adams, Jackson, and 1824's Five-Horse Race (Lawrence: University Press of Kansas, 2015); Sean Wilentz, The Rise of American Democracy: Jefferson to Lincoln, 240–253; Robert Remini, Daniel Webster, The Man and His Times, 243–246.

12. Stephen W. Stathis, Landmark Debates in Congress: From the Declaration of Independence to the War in Iraq, 127–129.

13. William James Hoffer, The Caning of Charles Sumner: Honor, Idealism, and the Origins of the Civil War (Baltimore: Johns Hopkins University Press, 2010), 1–31; Joshua Kastenberg, Law in War, Law as War, 128.

14. David M. Potter, The Impending Crisis, 1848–1861 (New York: Harper-Perennial, 1976), 140–145.

15. Sean Wilentz, The Rise of American Democracy: Jefferson to Lincoln, 713–715.

16. Benton Rain Patterson, Ending the Civil War: The Bloody Year from Grant's Promotion to Lincoln's Assassination (Jefferson, NC: McFarland, 2012), 190; Joanna Cowden, "Heaven Will Frown on Such a Cause as This": Six Democrats who Opposed Lincoln's War, xv-xvi.

17. Forrest G. Wood, Black Scare: The Racist Response to Emancipation and Reconstruction (Los Angeles: University of California Press, 1968), 78; Frank Klement, Lincoln's Critics: The Copperheads of the North, 112–113.

18. Frank Klement, The Limits of Dissent: Clement L. Vallandigham and the Civil War, 122–130 (Lexington: University of Kentucky Press, 1970); James B. Conroy, Our One Common Country: Abraham Lincoln and the Hampton Roads Peace Conference on 1865 (Guilford, CT: Lyons Press, 2014), 50–51.

19. On Pendleton, see Thomas Mach, "Gentleman George" Hunt Pendleton: Party Politics and Ideological Identity in Late Nineteenth Century America (Kent, OH: Kent State University Press, 2007), 1–36; Samuel S. Cox, Three Decades of Federal Legislation, 1855–1885 (New York: Ayer and Co., 1885); Michael Vorenberg, The Final Freedom: The Civil War and the Abolition of Slavery and the Fifteenth Amendment (New York: Cambridge University Press, 2001), 196.

20. George Pendleton, Speech of Hon Geo. Pendleton of Ohio (Washington, D.C,: GPO, 1861).

21. Dan Monroe and Bruce Tap, Shapers of the Great Debate on the Civil War: A Biographical Dictionary (Westport, CT: Greenwood Press, 2005), 300–322; Frank Klement, The Limits of Dissent: Clement L. Vallandigham and the Civil War (New York: Fordham University Press, 1998), 38–63.

22. On Wood, see Jerome Mushkat, Fernando Wood: A Political Biography (Kent, OH: Kent State University Press, 1990), 1–34.

23. See, e.g., Sean Wilentz, The Rise of American Democracy: Jefferson to Lincoln, 679–694; Lewis L. Gould, The Republicans: A History of the Grand Old Party (New York: Oxford University Press, 2014), 1–21.

24. Robert D. Ilsevich, Galusha A. Grow: The Peoples' Candidate (Pittsburgh: University of Pittsburgh Press, 1988), 201–202.

25. Bruce Tap, Over Lincoln's Shoulder: The Committee of the Conduct of the War (Lawrence: Kansas University Press, 1998), 1–54; Charles A. Stevenson, Warriors and Politicians: U.S. Civil-Military Relations Under Stress, 40; William Marvel, Mr Lincoln Goes to War, 268–272; on the Word War I experience, on proposals to resurrect the Committee on the Conduct of the War, see David Kennedy, Over Here: The First World War and American Society (New York: Oxford University Press, 1980), 123; Clinton Rossiter, Constitutional Dictatorship: Crisis Government in Modern Democracies (New York: Harcourt Brace, 1963), 246–248.

26. See Willard H. Smith, Schuyler Colfax: The Changing Fortunes of a Political Idol (Indianapolis: Indiana Historical Bureau, 1952), 1–192.

27. Thaddeus Stevens, "Speech of June 10, 1850," in Beverly Wilson Palmer, ed., The Selected Papers of Thaddeus Stevens, Vol. I, January 1814–March 1865 (Pittsburgh: University of Pittsburgh Press, 1997), 110–116; Thaddeus Stevens, "Speech of December 16, 1861," Ibid., at 234. See also Victor B. Howard, Religion and the Radical Republican Movement (Lexington: University Press

of Kentucky, 1990), 110; Sean Wilentz, *The Rise of American Democracy: Jefferson to Lincoln*, 486–487.
28. On Stevens, see Hans Treffouse, *Thaddeus Stevens: Nineteenth Century Egalitarian* (Chapel Hill: University of North Carolina Press, 1997), 1–127.
29. Gerard N. Magliocca, *American Founding Son: John Bingham and the Invention of the Fourteenth Amendment* (New York: New York University Press, 2013), 73–82; Leonard L. Richards, *Who Freed the Slaves: The Fight Over the Thirteenth Amendment* (Chicago: University of Chicago Press, 2015).
30. Daniel W. Crofts, *Lincoln and the Politics of Slavery: The Thirteenth Amendment and the Struggle to Save the Union* (Chapel Hill: University of North Carolina Press, 2015), 177; David Montgomery, *Beyond Equality: Labor and the Radical Republicans, 1862–1872* (Urbana: University of Illinois Press, 1967) 75.
31. William A. Blair, *With Malice Toward Some: Treason and Loyalty in the Civil War Era*, 83–85.
32. On Lincoln's independent actions in issuing the Emancipation Proclamation see Burrus M. Carnahan, *Act of Justice: Lincoln's Emancipation Proclamation and the Law of War* (Lexington: University of Kentucky Press, 2007), 99–131; John Fabian Witt, *Lincoln's Code: The Laws of War in American History* (New York: The Free Press, 2012), 146–147.

Chapter 4

1. "The War Upon Women," *Saint Mary's Beacon*, April 2, 1863; also see, e.g., Edwin Beitzell, "Hon Benjamin Gwinn Harris," *Chronicles of Saint Mary's*, April 1956, Vol. 4, pp. 16–23.
2. Bradford, Journal entry for November 2, 1863 [MDHS / MS 90]; "The Military Election in Maryland," *Saint Mary's Gazette*, December 3, 1863.
3. Margaret Law Callcott, *The Negro in American Politics* (Baltimore: Johns Hopkins, 1969), 8; Text of speech from Saulsbury, December 28, 1862 [WS U-Del / 63]; Speech of Hon Willard Saulsbury of Delaware, Delivered in the Senate of the United States, March 24 and 25, 1864.
4. Richard F. Miller, *States at War, Vol. IV: A Reference Guide for Maryland, Delaware, and New Jersey* (Hanover, NH: University Press of New England, 2015), 419; John Thomas Scharf, *History of Western Maryland, Volume I*, 352; Louis Wagandt, *The Mighty Revolution*, 179; "The Election," *Saint Mary's Gazette*, November 5, 1863.

5. "Late Sheriff's Sale of Young Negroes," *Saint Mary's Gazette*, December 10, 1863.
6. Christopher Phillips, *The Civil War in the Border South* (Santa Barbara: ABC-CLIO 2013), 68–71.
7. James M. McPherson, *Battle Cry of Freedom* (New York: Oxford University Press, 1988), 561–562.
8. MEH, diary entry for July 25, 1861; dairy entry for July 4, 1862; Barbara J. Fields, *Slavery and the Middle Ground, Maryland During the Nineteenth Century*, 116–117.
9. Harris to Sothoron, October 14, 1863; see, e.g., Douglas R. Egerton, *The Wars of Reconstruction: The Brief, Violent History of America's Most Progressive Era* (New York: Bloomsbury Press, 2014), 52–136.
10. On Schenck in Maryland, see Robert Brugger, *Maryland, A Middle Temperament: 1634–1980*, 293; Dan Friedman, *The Maryland State Constitution* (New York: Oxford University Press, 20122), 12.
11. The recent study referenced is Brian McGinty, *Lincoln and the Court*, 183–184. Melvin Urofsky, *March of Liberty*, Vol. I, 416.
12. Mary B. Allen, *Joseph Holt: Judge Advocate General (1862–1875): A Study in the Treatment of Political Prisoners by the United States Government During the Civil War*, 117; Joanna D. Cowden, "Heaven Will Frown on Such a cause as This": Six Democrats Who Opposed Lincoln's War, 6.
13. General Orders No. 38, Department of the Ohio, dated April 13, 1863; Phillip Paludan, *A People's Contest*, 240–241; Brian McGinty, *Lincoln and the Court*, 185; William Rehnquist, *All the Laws But One*, 63–64; Richard P.L. Baber to Francis P. Blair (forwarded to Lincoln), April 12, 1862. According to the letter Holt urged Ohio Unionists the importance of defending the war's progression as a counter to Vallandigham.
14. 28 F. Cas. 874 (1863); Carl Brent Swisher, Biographical Sketch: Humphrey Howe Leavitt n.d. [Carl Brent Swisher Collection, Box 16, LOC]; Edwin Stanton, draft order May 13, 1863 [PAL-LOC]; *The Trial of Hon. Clement L. Vallandigham by a Military Commission and the Proceedings Under his Application For a Writ of Habeas Corpus In the Circuit Court of the United States For the Southern District of Ohio* (Cincinnati: Rickey & Carroll, 1863), 11–12 [hereafter *Trial of Hon. Clement L. Vallandigham*].
15. *New York World*, May 20, 1863; Brian McGinty, *Lincoln and the Court*, 188; James Ely jr, *The Chief Justiceship of Melville W. Fuller, 1888–1910* (Columbia: University of South Carolina Press, 1995), 50.
16. "Maryland Elections," *Daily National Republican*, October 3, 1863, p. 2; *New York*

Tribune, November 28, 1863, p. 6; John Frazier to Cresswell, November 28, 1863 [MDHS / MS 1247].

17. See Thomas R. March, *"Gentleman George" Hunt Pendleton: Party Politics and Ideological Identity in Nineteenth Century America* (Kent, OH: Kent State University Press, 2007); Alan C. Guezlo, *Fateful Lightning: A New History of the Civil War and Reconstruction* (New York: Oxford University Press, 2012), 228.

18. Harris to Dent, February 5, 1864 [SMH].

19. Vote on McPherson [JHR Dec. 8, 1863].

20. MEH, diary entry for January 21 1864; "Benjamin Harris, Copperhead Representative," *Gallipolis Journal*, February 4, 1864; "Persons Ordered South," *Saint Mary's Gazette*, January 28, 1864.

21. Resolution of Schenck [JHR, February 16, 1863]. On historic opposition to the draft see, Reginald C. Stuart, *Civil Military Relations During the War of 1812* (Santa Barbara: Greenwood Press, 2009), 87–110; Donald P. Cole, *Martin van Buren and the American Political System* (Princeton: Princeton University, 1984), 37–40.

22. The Freedmen's Bureau vote arose from House Resolution (hereafter HR) 51 [JHR, February 9, 1864]. On the Freedmen's Bureau see, James McPherson, *Battle Cry of Freedom: The Civil War Era*, 710.

23. HR 333 [JHR, February 5, 1864].

24. "Hon Benj. G. Harris," *Saint Mary's Gazette*, February 11, 1864; "Late Sheriff's Sale of Personal and Valuable Real Estate," *Saint Mary's Gazette*, March 3, 1864.

25. Judge Advocate Report for September 3, 1864; L.C. Turner to General James Barnes, November 11, 1864 [NA RG 393, Pt. II, S 6834].

26. Captain Jo. Mix to Headquarters, St Mary's District, March 27, 1864; Jo. Mix to Turner, March 28, 1864 [NA RG 393, Pt II, S 6834].

27. Frank L. Klement, *Dark Lanterns: Secret Societies, Conspiracies, and Treason Trials in the Civil War*, 136–138.

28. William Norwood Brigance, *Jeremiah Sullivan Black: Defender of the Constitution and the Ten Commandments* (Philadelphia: University of Pennsylvania Press, 1934), 82; Jeremiah Black to Charles R. Buckalew, January 28, 1861 [Jeremiah S. Black papers, LOC, R-18].

29. *Trop v. Dulles*, 356 U.S. 86 (1958).

30. Id., See also Mary Bernard Allen, *Joseph Holt: Judge Advocate General (1862–1875): A Study in the Treatment of Political Prisoners by the United States Government During the Civil War*, Ph.D, diss., University of Chicago, 1927, 47–50; Joan E. Kleber, *The Kentucky Encyclopedia* (Lexington: University Of Kentucky Press, 1992), 438; L.D. Ingersoll, *A History of the War Department of the United States, with Biographical Sketches of the Secretaries* (Washington, D.C.: Francis B. Mohun, 1880), 520. Holt's Autobiographical Sketch [Box 117 PJH LOC] [also in Carl Brent Swisher Collection, LOC].

31. William Henry Smith, *History of the Cabinet of the United States of America, from President Washington to President Coolidge* (New York: Gale Learning, 1925), 381; Lucius P. Little, *Ben Hardin, His Times and his Contemporaries* (Louisville: Courrier-Journal, 1887), 587.

32. Holt to James O. Harrison, June 8, 1849 [James O. Harrison papers, LOC, misc.]; Allen, Joseph Holt, 50;, Robert N. Rosen, *The Jewish Confederates* (Columbia: University of South Carolina Press, 2000), 330; Moore, ed, *The Works of James Buchanan*, Vol. XII, 94; Robert Remini, *Henry Clay, Statesman for the Union* (New York: Norton, 1991), 507. On Holt's background as a beneficiary of slavery, see William Marvel, *Lincoln's Autocrat*, 250–251.

33. Edward Bates, *The Diary of Edward Bates, 1859–1866*, ed. Howard Beale (New York: Da Capo, 1971), 95 [entry for February 2, 1859].

34. Joseph Holt, *Fallacy of Neutrality*, 7; Holt's Autobiographical Sketch, Box 117 [PJH]; James Buchanan, First Annual Message, delivered December 8, 1857, in Moore, *The Works of James Buchanan* Vol. X 1856–1860, 129. For the composition and ideology of Buchanan's cabinet, see William W. Freehling, *The Road to Disunion, Vol. II, Secessionists Triumphant, 1854–1861*, 105–108; James G. Blaine, *Twenty Years of Congress: From Lincoln to Garfield With a Review of the Events Which Led to the Political Revolution of 1860*, Vol. I (Norwich, CT: Henry Bill Publishers, 1884), 235.

35. See William McKee Dunn, *A Sketch of the History and Duties of the Judge Advocate General's Department*, 4; Ingersoll, *History of the War Department of the United States*, 148.

36. *Congressional Globe*, 37th Congress, U.S. Senate, 1st Session, January 19, 1863, 33; Joseph Holt to James Speed, September 12, 1862, in Frank Moore, *The Rebellion Record, A Diary of Events, Vol. III* (New York: G.P. Putnam, 1862), 126.

37. Joshua E. Kastenberg, "A Sesquicentennial Historic Analysis of Dynes v. Hoover and the Supreme Court's Bow to Military Necessity: From its Relationship *Dred Scott v.*

Sandford to its Contemporary Influence," *University of Memphis Law Review* 39, no. 3, 659–701.

38. Alexander Long, "The Present Condition and Future Prospects of the Country: Speech of Alexander Long of Ohio," delivered in the House of Representatives, April 8, 1864. On Long, see Joanna Cowden, *"Heaven Will Frown on Such a Cause as This,"* 161.

39. Ibid.

40. Ibid.

41. Allan Peskin, *Garfield* (Kent, OH: Kent State University Press, 1968), 183.

42. See "Alexander Long, Resolution," *Washington Star*, April 9, 1864. On fears of foreign governments recognizing the Confederacy, see Mark A. Weitz, *The Confederacy on Trial: The Piracy and Sequestration Cases of 1861* (Lawrence: Kansas University Press, 2005), 50, 151; Burrus Carnahan, *Act of Justice: Lincoln's Emancipation Proclamation and the Law of War* (Lexington: University of Kentucky Press, 2007), 41–61; Brian McGinty, Lincoln and the Court, 119–143. On the other expulsions, see Ezra J. Warner, *Biographical Register of the Confederate Congress*; Steven A. Channing, *Encyclopedia of Kentucky, 3d Ed, Vol. I* (Somerset Publishers, 1999), 9.

43. On Gravel's conduct, see *Gravel v. United States*, 404 U.S. 606 (1972); Joshua Kastenberg, *Shaping U.S. Military Law: Governing a Constitutional Military* (Farnham: Ashgate Press, 2014), 132.

44. Harris' speech is found in a number of sources including the *Congressional Globe*. However, the following is used: *On the Resolution to Expel Mr. Long: Speech of Hon. Benjamin G. Harris of Maryland, in the House of Representatives of the United States, April 9, 1864* (Washington, D.C.: Constitutional Union Office, 1864), 3.

45. Ibid.

46. Ibid. On Butler's view of war, see B.F. Butler, *Character and results of the War: How to Prosecute it, and How to End It* (Philadelphia, 1863).

47. *On the Resolution to Expel Mr. Long: Speech of Hon. Benjamin G. Harris of Maryland* Harris also argued, "I do not believe the Puritans would sanction any such doctrine as [emancipation]. They were honest and straight-forward and I am sorry to see that their sons are so thoroughly degenerate." For other southerners espousing the same view, see, e.g., Howell Cobb, *A Scriptural Examination of the Institution of Slavery, with its objects and purposes* (Georgia, 1856), 1–2. A prominent congressman in the 1850s who rose to House speaker and was elected Georgia governor, Howell Cobb also served as treasury secretary in Buchanan's administration.

48. Ibid.

49. "A Proposition to Expel Mr. Long, of Ohio, for Treasonable, Sentiments. Bold Avowal of Disloyalty by Mr. Harris, of Maryland," *New York Times*, April 10, 1864; "Freedom of Debate in Congress," *New York Times*, April 12, 1864; "Benjamin G. Harris Dead," *Saint Mary's Gazette*, April 11, 1895.

50. "Excitement in Congress," *Saint Mary's Gazette*, April 21, 1864; "A Maryland Representative in Congress," *Annapolis Gazette*, April 14, 1864.

51. *House of Representatives Journal* for April 9, 1864.

52. *Ibid.*; Benjamin Wood to Manton Marble, April 12, 1864 [LOC-MM / 7]; Vorhees to Marble, April 13, 1864 [Manton marble, Box 7]; Saulsbury to Gove Saulsbury, April 19, 1864 [WS U-Del / 63].

53. A.J. Mattson to Elihus Washburne, April 13, 1865 [LOC-EBW / 37].

54. Lieber to McPherson, April 14, 1864 [LOC-EM / 49].

55. Lamon to Lincoln, April 10, 1864 [PAL].

Chapter 5

1. Jonathan W. White, *Emancipation, the Union Army, and the Reelection of Abraham Lincoln* (Baton Rouge: Louisiana State University Press, 2014), 98–99; Frank Luther Mott, *American Journalism: A History, 1690–1960* (New York: Macmillan, 1962), 347–358.

2. On the Knights of the Golden Circle, see David C. Keehn, *Knights of the Golden Circle: Secret Empire, Southern Secession, Civil War* (Baton Rouge: Louisiana State University Press, 2013), 1–31; Frank L. Klement, *Dark Lanterns: Secret Political Societies, Conspiracies, and Treason Trials in the Civil War*, 7–10; David M. Potter, *The Impending Crisis*, 1848–1861 (New York: HarperCollins, 1976), 466.

3. Wood Gray, *The Hidden Civil War: The Story of the Copperheads* (New York: Viking, 1942); Frank Klement, *Lincoln's Critics: The Copperheads of the North* (New York: White Mane Publishing, 1998), 4; Jessica Weber, *Copperheads*, 9–12.

4. Adam I.P. Smith, *No Party Now: Politics in the Civil War North* (New York: Oxford University Press, 2006) 160–162; Jean H. Baker, *Affairs of Party: The Political Culture of Northern Democrats in the Mid Nineteenth Century* (New York: Fordham University Press, 1998), 281–288.

5. For information on Pratt's arrest in 1861, see Colonel F.J. Porter to Levi Woodhouse, July 25, 1861 in OR Ser. I, Vol. 2, 174; Phillip St. George Cooke to Robert E. Lee, April 25, 1861, in OR Ser. I, Vol. 2, 780; on Pratt's arrest in 1863, see Donn Piatt to Edwin Stanton, November 23, 1863, in OR Ser. II, Vol. 6, 607; for a dated and partisan view of Pratt's life, see Caleb Clarke Magruder, Jr., *Thomas George Pratt, Governor of Maryland, 1845–1848; United States Senator, 1850–1857* (Baltimore: Waverley Press, 1913).

6. Montgomery Blair to Lincoln December 18, 1862 [PAL]; Pratt to Stanton, November 28, 1863 [PAL]; Clayton Coleman Hall, *Baltimore: Its History and Its People, Vol. I* (New York: Lewis Historical Publishing Co. 1912), 195; Wagandt, *The Mighty Revolution*, 177; on Butler's plan, see Stanton to Benjamin Butler, December 1, 1863, in OR Ser. II, Vol. 6, 607 and 626.

7. Richard Carmichael, June 23, 1861 [JPP-MDHS / MS1334]; on Pierce, see Steven A. Channing, *Crisis of Fear: Secession in South Carolina* (New York: W.W. Norton, 1974), 32.

8. William Henry Seward to John Adams Dix, October 3, 1861, in OR Ser. II, Vol. 2, 85; John A. Dix to Augustus Bradford, February 2, 1862, in OR Ser. II, Vol. 2, 313; George Dodge to Dix, November 27, 1861 in OR Ser. II, Vol. 1, 712; Dix to Brigadier General Lorenzo Thomas, Adjutant General U.S. Army, June 19, 1864, in OR Ser. 2, Vol. 4 39–40.

9. Col. Samuel Hambleton and James Lloyd to James A. Pearce providing a detailed account of Carmichael's arrest [Maryland State Archives (hereafter MSA) C1892, 1–43-4–6]. (Taken from http://teachingamericanhistorymd.net); Dix to H.H. Goldsborough, May 23, 1862 in, OR Ser. II, Vol. 3, 576–577; Dix to Stanton, June 25, 1862, Ser. II, Vol. 4, 63–64.

10. Dix to Stanton, June 25, 1862, Ser. II, Vol. 4, 63–64; John E. Wool to Edwin Stanton, June 30, 1862 in OR Ser. II, Vol. 4, 104; Carmichael to Lincoln, July 22, 1862 [PAL].

11. Lincoln to John W. Crisfield, June 26, 1862 [PAL]; Lieutenant Colonel Martin Burke to E.D. Townsend, in OR Ser. II, Vol. 4, 548; E.D. Thomas Hicks to Lincoln, May 30, 1862 [PAL] Townsend to Commanding Officer, Fort Delaware, December 2, 1862, in OR Ser. II, Vol. 5, 9.

12. Richard P. Fuke, *Imperfect Equality: African Americans and the Confines of White Racial* (New York: Fordham University Press, 1999), 219.

13. William H. Barnes, *The Fortieth Congress of the United States: Historical and Biographical*, Vol. II (New York: George Perrine, 1870), 320.

14. *Official Proceeding to the Democratic National Convention Held in 1864 at Chicago* (Times Steam Book and Job Printing House, 1864), 1.

15. Ibid., 2–6; Joseph Holt to James Glynn, W.S. Walker, Adam J. Slemmer, January 29, 1861, in OR Ser. I, Vol. 1, 355–356; Weber, *Copperheads*, 169.

16. David Hunter to Edwin Stanton, June 23, 1862, in OR Ser. II, Vol. 1, 821–822.

17. Lowell Hayes Harrison, *Kentucky's Governors* (Lexington: University of Kentucky Press, 2004), 75–77; *Official Proceeding to the Democratic National Convention*, 7.

18. Convention, 16–20.

19. Convention, 27–28.

20. Ibid.

21. Convention, 29; on Powell's position on slavery, see Speech of Hon. Lazarus W. Powell, of Kentucky, on the state of the Union, delivered in the Senate of the United States, January 22, 1861 (Congressional Globe Office, 1861). On Grant's order expelling Jews from the area of his command, see Lloyd P. Garner, *History of the Jews in Modern Times* (New York: Oxford University Press, 2012).

22. Convention, 30.

23. Ibid.; Stewart Mitchell, *Horatio Seymour of New York* (Boston: Harvard, 1938), 360.

24. Convention, 32.

25. ibid.; Jack Waugh, *Reelecting Lincoln: The Battle for the 1864 Presidency* (New York: Crown, 1997), 287.

26. Convention, 37.

27. Jack Waugh, *Reelecting Lincoln*, 289.

28. Convention, 45.

29. Ibid; Jennifer Weber, *Copperheads*, 172. On Pendleton's selection see, Jerome Mushkat, *Fernando Wood: A Political Biography* (Kent, OH: Kent State University Press, 1990), 149–150.

30. Joshua Kastenberg, *Law in War, Law as War*, 345–351; Joseph Holt, *Report of the Judge Advocate General on the Order of American Knights of Sons of Liberty: An American Conspiracy in Aid of the Southern Rebellion* (Washington, D.C.: GPO, 1864); Charles Fairman, *Mr. Justice Miller*, 92; McPherson, *Battle Cry of Freedom*, 782–783; Mark Neely, *The Union Divided: Party Conflict in the Civil War North*, 164–165; Jonathan W. White, *Emancipation, the Union Army, and the Reelection of Abraham Lincoln*, 98–128.

31. *Cincinnati Convention Proceedings*, October 20, 1864, printed in the *New York Daily News*, October 24, 1864.

32. Ibid.

33. "The Chicago Convention," *Saint Mary's Gazette*, September 1, 1864; "News Items," *Easton Gazette*, September 3, 1864.
34. McClellan to Manton Marble, September 16, 1864, in Stephen Sears, ed., *The Civil War Papers of George B. McClellan* (New York: Da Capo Press, 1989), 599.
35. Noah Brooks to Lincoln, September 2, 1864 [PAL]; James G. Blaine, *Twenty Years of Congress from Lincoln to Garfield with a review of the Events which led to the Political Revolution of 1860*, Vol. I (Norwich, CT: Henry Bill Publishing, 1884), 528–538.
36. Alan Nevins, *Ordeal of the Union: The Organized War for Victory*, Vol. IV (New York: Charles Scribner's Sons, 1971), 116; *Proceedings of the State Convention of Maryland to Frame a New Constitution, Commenced at Annapolis, April 27, 1864* (Annapolis: Richard P. Bayly, printer,1864); Michael Burlingame, *Abraham Lincoln, A Life Vol. II* (Baltimore: Johns Hopkins University Press, 2008), 714–716.
37. William Starr Myers, *The Self Reconstruction of Maryland, 1864–1867* (Baltimore: Johns Hopkins University Press, 1909), 21–22. See also Ira Berlin and Stephen F. Miller, eds., *The Wartime Genesis of Free Labor: The Upper South, A Documentary History of Emancipation*, Vol. 2 (New York: Cambridge University Press, 1999), 497–499.
38. See, e.g., Stewart Mitchell, *Horatio Seymour of New York* (Boston: Harvard University Press, 1938), 379; Josiah Henry Benton, *Voting in the Field* (Norwood, MA: Plimpton, 1915), 161–165.
39. Donald S. Inbody, *The Soldier Vote: War, Politics, and the Ballot in America* (New York: Palgrave Macmillan, 2014), 166.
40. Michael Burlingame, *Abraham Lincoln, A Life Vol. II*, 440–445.
41. On the passage of the Thirteenth Amendment, see Rebecca E. Zietlow, "James Ashley's Thirteenth Amendment," *Columbia Law Review* 112 (2012): 1697–1731.
42. MEH diary entry for April 11, 1865 [MDHS].
43. *Speech of Hon. Henry Winter Davis, of Maryland, and the debate on his amendment to the miscellaneous bill, prohibiting the trial of citizens by military commissions: in the House of Representatives, March 2 and 3, 1865* (Washington, D.C.: GPO, 1865).
44. Edward Steers, *Blood on the Moon: The Assassination of Abraham Lincoln* (Lexington: University of Kentucky Press, 2001), 153; Kate Clifford Larson, *The Assassin's Accomplice: Mary Surratt and the Plot to Kill Abraham Lincoln* (New York: Basic Books, 2008); Ronald D. Smith, *Thomas Ewing Jr, Frontier Lawyer and Civil War General* (Columbia: University of Missouri Press, 2006), 268.

Chapter 6

1. On Johnson and Wade, see Jonathan T. Dorris, *Pardon and Amnesty Under Lincoln and Johnston: The Restoration of the Confederates to their Rights and Privileges* (Chapel Hill: University of North Carolina Press, 1954), 95.
2. MEH, diary entry, April 24, 1865. She wrote, "Pres Johnson is taking very opposite ground from Lincoln, has refused to accept any terms with the south but commands their subjugation."
3. Bradford, journal entry for May 21, 1862 [MDHS / MS 90] Barnes to Waite, April 22, 1865 [RG 393, S 6844 V4].
4. "News Items," *Easton Gazette*, May 13, 1865; Order of General Ulysses S. Grant, April 18, 1865; Order of Ulysses S. Grant, April 19, 1865.
5. See, e.g., Testimony of A.V. Roby, June 2, 1865 in 142; Testimony of Dorley B. Roby, June 5, 1865 in Edward Steers, *"General Conspiracy,"* in *The Trial: The Assassination of President Lincoln and the Trial of the Conspirators* (Lexington: University of Kentucky Press, 2003).
6. Roll of Prisoners of War, May 1, 1865, and associated documents [NA RG 393, Records of the Old Capitol Prison, file 2130, pt. IV].
7. Roll of Prisoners of War, May 1, 1865, and associated documents [NA RG 393, Records of the Old Capitol Prison, file 2130, pt. IV]. MEH, dairy entry for April 29, 1865.
8. Charles A. Dana to General C.C. Augur, April 29, 1865 [NA RG 94–797].
9. Joshua Kastenberg, *The Blackstone of Military Law, Colonel William Winthrop* (Lanham, MD: Scarecrow Press, 2009), 85–101; *Ex Parte Mason*, 105 U.S. 696 (1881). However, the facts of Mason are found in *Ex parte Mason*, 256 F 2 (DC 1882).
10. Holt to Stanton, September 28, 1863 [NA RG 153.1, Vol. V].
11. Winthrop to Stanton, June 20, 1865 [NA RG 153.1, Vol. XII]; Winthrop to Stanton, June 30, 1865 [NA RG 153.1, Vol. XII]; Winthrop to O. O. Howard, February 1, 1866 [NA RG, 153.1, Vol. XV].
12. See, e.g., William Chetwood De Hart, *Observation on Military Law: And the Constitution and Practice of Courts-Martial* (New York: John Wiley and Sons, 1859), 84–86. De Hart's treatise was the standard text for courts-martial prior to 1885. However,

this construct was also adopted into the Confederate Armies during the Civil War, see Robert C. Gilchrist, *The duties of a judge advocate, in a trial before a general court-martial, compiled from various works on military law* (Columbia, SC: Evans and Cogswell, 1864), 37–39; Ransom H. Gillet, *The Federal Government: Its Officers and Their Duties* (New York: Woolworth, Ainsworth, and Co, 1872), 306.

13. On courts-martial of the era, see, in addition to William Chetwood De Hart, John O'Brien, *A Treatise on American Military Laws and the Practice of Courts-Martial With Suggestions for Their Improvement* (Philadelphia: Lee & Blanchard, 1848). On Porter's claims, see Montgomery Blair, *Hon. Montgomery Blair: Postmaster General During Lincoln's Administration to Fitz John Porter*, written on January 26, 1874 (Washington, D.C., 1874). The classic work on the Fitz John Porter case is Otto Eisenschiml, *The Celebrated Case of Fitz John Porter: An Dreyfus Affair* (Indianapolis: Bobbs-Merrill, 1950). As the title suggests, Eisenschiml believed the case a travesty of justice. Donald Jermann published *Fitz-John Porter, Scapegoat of Second Manassas: The Rise, Fall and Rise of the General Accused of Disobedience* (Jefferson, NC: McFarland, 2009).

14. On Willcox, see Robert Garth Scott, *Forgotten Valor, The Memoirs, Journals, and Civil War Letters of Orlando B. Willcox* (Kent, OH: Kent State University Press, 1999) generally. For his own court-martial, see 62–90. Unfortunately Willcox did not leave to posterity his impressions of the Harris trial. On Parke's command over Willcox, see 615. On Parke, see John H. Eicher and David J Eicher, *Civil War High Commands* (Palo Alto: Stanford University Press, 2001), 850–856. On Parke's assumption of command see, Edward G. Longacre, *General Ulysses S. Grant: The Soldier and the Man* (New York: DaCapo Press, 2006), 250. Parke authored *Laws of the United States relating to public works for the improvement of rivers and harbors: from August 11, 1790, to August 14, 1876* (Washington, D.C.: GPO, 1877).

15. On Humphreys, see Stephen R. Taafe, *Commanding the Army of the Potomac* (Lawrence: University of Kansas Press, 2006), 111.

16. On Rawlins, see Steven Woodworth, "John Rawlins," in David T. Zebecki, ed., *Chief of Staff: The Principal Officers Behind Histories Great Commanders* (Annapolis MD: Naval Institute Press, 2006), 75–90.

17. William S. McFeeley, *Grant: A Biography* (New York: W.W. Norton, 2002), 245–246; Guy V. Henry, *Military Record of Civilian Appointments in the United States Army*, 13.

18. On Foster, see Eicher, *Civil War High Commands*, 101. On Haskin, see Eicher, *Civil War High Commands*, 191.

19. "Arrest of Benjamin G. Harris," *Freemont Journal*, May 5, 1865, p. 1; "News from Washington," *Houston Tri-Weekly*, May 29, 1865, p. 1. For a sampling of other newspapers, see,"The Latest News from Washington: The Case of Mr. Harris," *The Tri Weekly News*, Winsboro, South Carolina, June 15, 1865.

20. Transcript, 3.
21. Ibid., 4.
22. Ibid., 5–6.
23. Ibid., 6.
24. Ibid.
25. This information is contained on the muster rolls of the Thirty-Second Regiment, Virginia Infantry, see NA RG, M382 roll 10; NA RG M382 roll 46.
26. Transcript, 8.
27. Ibid., 9.
28. Ibid., 9–10.
29. Ibid., 11.
30. Ibid., 12.
31. Ibid., 14.
32. Ibid.
33. *New York Times*, May 3, 1865, p. 2; *Philadelphia Inquirer*, May 3, 1865, p.1; *Philadelphia Inquirer*, May 4, 1865, p. 1; *Baltimore Sun*, May 4, 1865, p. 1; *Chicago Tribune*, May 4, 1865, p. 1; "Trial of Hon B.J. Harris," *Cleveland Leader*, May 4, 1865, p. 1.
34. Transcript, 15.
35. Ibid., 17.
36. Ibid., 17–18; MEH, diary entry for August 4, 1851; MEH, diary entry for October 22, 1860.
37. Transcript, 20.
38. "Treason at Home," *New York Times*, May 7,1865, p. 1; "Trial Resumed," *New York Times*, May 9, 1865, p. 1; "Progress of the Harris Court Martial," *Philadelphia Inquirer*, May 8, 1865, p.1; *Chicago Tribune*, May 8, 1865, p. 1; *Saint Mary's Beacon*, May 11, 1865.
39. See, e.g., *Respublica v. Roberts*, 1 U.S. 39 (1788).
40. Transcript, 22.
41. Ibid.
42. Transcript, 25. See, Record of Chapman at M382 Roll 10 NARA; Record of Reed at M382 Roll 48 NARA.
43. Address of the Accused, May 11, 1865.
44. *Cramer v. United States*, 325 U.S. 1 (1945).
45. Judge Advocate Summation, May 11, 1865.
46. Holt, Official Review by the Judge

Advocate General of the Case of B.G. Harris, May 13, 1865.

47. BGH to AGH. May 22, 1865 [MHS / BGHP].

48. Roll of Prisoners of War, June 10, 1865, and associated documents [NA RG 393, Records of the Old Capitol Prison, file 2130, pt. IV].

Chapter 7

1. "News," *Annapolis Gazette*, October 12, 1865; "Who has Changed," *Annapolis Gazette*, November 30, 1865; Johnathan T. Dorris, *Pardon and Amnesty under Lincoln and Johnson: The Restoration of the Confederates to Their Rights and Privileges*, 111–112.

2. Vallandigham to Long, June 11, 1865 [AL-CHS / 5]; Bradford, Journal entry, May 9, 1865 [MDHS / MS90].

3. The affidavits are contained in Secretary of War Stanton's letter to the House of Representatives, delivered on January 5, 1866; on Blair's role, see Blair to J.F. Lee, June 21, 1865; *A Most Convenient Place: Leonardtown, MD, 1650–1950* (Leonardtown, 2001). On the Vietnam war crimes case, see Michal R. Belknap, *The Vietnam War on Trial: the My Lai Massacre and the Court Martial of Lieutenant Calley* (Lawrence: University Press of Kansas, 2002). On recent congressional interest in an Air Force general's conduct in overturning the fighter pilot's conviction, see e.g., Robert Draper, "The Military's Rough Justice on Sexual Assault," *New York Times*, November 26, 2014.

4. Winthrop, *Military Law and Precedents*, 631–633.

5. Montgomery Blair, *Proscription in Maryland: Speeches of the Honorable Montgomery Blair as President of the Anti-Registry Convention to the Convention and to the Legislature of Maryland* (Washington, D.C.: J. Pearson, 1868), 5.

6. J J.F. Lee to Montgomery Blair, August 28, 1866 [PMB, Reel 8, LOC]; F. Lee to Montgomery Blair March 6, 1867 [PMB, Reel 8, LOC]; J.F. Lee to Montgomery Blair, July 31, 1870; Papers of Montgomery Blair [PMB, Reel 8, LOC]. On Lee, see Joshua Kastenberg, *Law in War, Law as War*, 44.

7. "B.G. Harris," *Philadelphia Inquirer*, June 2, 1865, p. 1; "Harris Released," *Chicago Tribune*, June 3, 1865, p. 1; "Amnesty," *Baltimore Sun*, May 31, 1865, p. 2; "Welfare of Mr. Harris," *Baltimore Sun*, June 3, 1865, p. 2; "Suffrage," *Baltimore Sun* June 5, 1865, p. 2; "Military vs Civil Courts," *Baltimore Sun*, June 7, 1865, p. 2.

8. "The President's Release of Congressman Harris," *Indianapolis Daily Sentinel*, June 6, 1865; "Order from Johnson Releasing Harris," *Dayton Daily Empire*, June 5, 1865; "President's Order Releasing Benjamin Harris," *Daily Intelligencer*, June 6, 1865, pp 1.

9. Testimony of J.Z. Jenkins, 121–128, in Edward Steers, "General Conspiracy," in *The Trial: The Assassination of President Lincoln and the Trial of the Conspirators* (Lexington: University of Kentucky Press, 2003); Testimony of A.V. Roby, June 2, 1865, 142; Testimony of Dorley B. Roby, June 5, 1865, in Steers, *The Trial*.

10. "General News," *New York Times*, August 1, 1865; "The Draft," *Saint Mary's Gazette*, May 19, 1864.

11. 39th Congress, 1st Sess., Cong. Globe, Tuesday, December 19, 1865, p. 89.

12. "From Washington," *New York Times*, December 18, 1865, p. 1; "News," *Alexandria Gazette*, December 19, 1865.

13. Chase to Robert A. Hill, U.S. District Court Judge, Jacinto, MI, March 1, 1867 [Chase Letters Vol. 5, pp. 145–146]; 71 U.S. 333 (1866). *Garland* was decided alongside of a companion case, *Cummings v. Missouri*, 71 U.S. 277 (1867). Cummings was a Catholic Priest who was convicted for teaching and performing religious duties without having taken an oath of loyalty as required by the Missouri state constitution. The majority determined that Missouri's test oath an unconstitutional bill of attainder which legislatively punished an individual without a trial. See Brian McGinty, *Lincoln and the Court*, 252–61.

14. "Rights of the States," Speech of Benjamin Gwinn Harris of Maryland, in the House of Representatives, June 14, 1866 (Washington, D.C.: GPO, 1866).

15. "News," *Saint Mary's Gazette*, June 28, 1866; "B.G. Harris," *Saint Mary's Gazette*, July 29, 1866; "Views of Benjamin Gwinn Harris on the Test Oath," *New York Times*, September 16, 1866; "Another Letter from Hon. B.G. Harris from Maryland," *New York Times*, August 5, 1867.

16. "Accident to Harris," *Saint Mary's Gazette*, January 18, 1866; "Harris at Home," *Saint Mary's Gazette*, March 1, 1866; "Radicals After Harris," *Saint Mary's Gazette*, May 17, 1866; "News," *Saint Mary's Gazette*, June 7, 1866; "Hon Benjamin Gwinn Harris," *Chronicles of Saint Mary's*, 19.

17. "Views of a Maryland Democrat on the Situation," *New York Times*, July 29, 1867; "Letter from Benjamin Gwinn Harris: Our Late Representative," *Saint Mary's Gazette*, July 25, 1867.

18. "Letter," *Saint Mary's Gazette*, May 21, 1868; Curtis Jacobs to Creswell, January 15, 1866 [MDHS / MS1860].

19. "Political Affairs: Another Letter from B.G. Harris," *New York Times*, August 5, 1867; "Political Affairs: Hon Benj G. Harris on Constitution, he urges rejection," *New York Times*, September 12, 1867.

20. Proceedings of a State Convention to Frame a New Constitution Commenced at Annapolis, May 8, 1867; "B.G. Harris for Governor," *Saint Mary's Gazette*, September 26, 1867.

21. Johnathan Norris to "son," February 1, 1866 [MDHS / MS 1379].

22. Anon, *Industries of Maryland: A Descriptive Review of the Manufacturing and Mercantile Industries* (New York: Historical Publishing, 1892), 203; E.R. Hayden, ED., *The Annual Cyclopaedia of Insurance in the United States* (New York: Underwriter Printing, 1892), 193; *Neale v. Fowler*, 31 Md. 155 (Md 1869).

23. "Letter from Brick Pomeroy," *Saint Mary's Gazette*, March 12, 1868; Johnathan Norris to "son," February 1, 1866 [MDHS]; Annapolis Gazette, February 16, 1866. "Another Letter from B.G. Harris of Maryland," *New York Times*, August 5, 1867; Jonathan Norris to Henry CB Norris, his son, September 22, 1867 [JNP-MHS, MS 1379]; MEH diary entry, November 3, 1868.

24. Alexander Long to Salmon P. Chase, Oct 3, 1868 [PAL, NYHS]; Alexander Long to Salmon P. Chase, Oct 15, 1868 [PAL, NYHS].

25. MEH diary entry, June 7, 1871.

26. "Notes," *Washington Evening Star*, April 16, 1870; "Antiquity," *New York Herald*, April 19, 1870; Harris to Hamilton, May 4, 1871 [Hamiltons' of Port Tobacco Collection–SMSC / 4]; "Record of George Pendleton," *Hancock Jeffersonian*, September 17, 1969.

27. "Maryland: A Straight-Out Repudiationist of the Straightest Sect—Address by B.G. Harris, of St Mary's County," *New York Times*, October 26, 1872; MEH, diary entry for March 4, 1873.

28. "Personal Intelligencer," *New York Herald*, June 13, 1874; "Political Notes," *Omaha Daily Bee*, August 7, 1874.

29. "News from Washington," *Helena Weekly Herald*, July 2, 1874.

30. "Congress," *Catoctin* (MD) *Clarion*, November 19, 1875.

31. See Hans L. Trefousse, *Rutherford B Hayes* (New York: Times Books, 2002), 65–73; Xi Wang, *The Trial of Democracy: Black Suffrage and Northern Republicans, 1860–1910* (Athens: University of Georgia Press, 1997), 23–52.

32. "Democratic Congressional Convention," *Saint Mary's Gazette*, August ?, 1878.

33. "City and Suburban News," *New York Times*, March 24, 1892.

34. MEH, diary entry for June n.d. 1882; "Jefferson Davis and Benj G. Harris," *Saint Mary's Gazette*, December 12, 1889.

Conclusion

1. Harris to General Bradley T. Johnson, 4 June 1893 [MDHS].

2. Ibid.

3. "Benjamin G. Harris Dead," *Saint Mary's Gazette*, April 11, 1895; "Death of a Congressman," *San Fransisco Chronicle*, April 6, 1865; "Remarks of James W. Thomas," *Saint Mary's Gazette*, September 27, 1895.

4. See, e.g., *Proceedings, Findings and Opinions of the Court of Inquiry Convened Under the Act of Congress of February 13, 1874* (Washington, D.C.: GPO 1874); Jerome Mushkat, *Fernando Wood: A Political Biography*, 177–178.

5. Frank Klement, *The Limits of Dissent: Clement L. Vallandigham and the Civil War* (Lexington: University Press of Kentucky), 307–315.

6. Robert J. Brugger, *Maryland: A Middle Temperament*, 311–419; "Negroes Will Still Vote in Maryland," *Baltimore Sun*, October 24, 1909; "Amendment Is Full of Snakes," *Baltimore American*, October 25, 1909; "Bitter Opposition to Naming of Hill: Baltimore Attorneys Will Fight Taft Nominee for District Attorney," *Baltimore Chronicle*, March 25, 1910; "Bar Wires Protest Against Hill's Name," *Baltimore News*, March 26, 1910 [JPH / 1].

7. *Brown v. Board of Education*, 347 U.S. 483 (1954).

Bibliography

Primary Sources

Collections

Cincinnati Historical Society
Alexander Long
Library of Congress
Jeremiah Sullivan Black
James G. Blaine
Blair Family
Schuyler Colfax
Robert R. Hitt
Joseph Holt
Andrew Johnson
Abraham Lincoln
Manton Marble
Thaddeus Stevens
Lyman Trumbull
Elihu B. Washburne
Gideon Welles
Maryland Historical Society
Augustus Bradford
Benjamin Harris
Martha Elizabeth Harris
Thomas Hicks
Curtis Jacobs Diary
Reverdy Johnson
John W. Mitchell
Jonathan Norris

James Pearce
Alexander Randall
Thomas Swann
Taney-Merryman
National Archives and Records Administration
RG 153.2.1 (Records of the Judge Advocate General)
RG 393 (Records of the Old National Prison)
New York Historical Society
Salmon Chase Collection
Saint Mary's Historical Society
Harris Family
Southern Maryland Studies Center—College of Southern Maryland
Chapman Family Papers
Hamiltons of Port Tobacco Collection
University of Chicago
Stephen A. Douglas
University of Delaware
Willard Saulsbury
University of Maryland
Charles Lanman Collection

Other

Blair, Montgomery. *Hon. Montgomery Blair: Postmaster General During Lincoln's Administration to Fitz John Porter*, written on January 26, 1874. Washington, D.C., 1874.
Harris, Benjamin, G. *Speech of Benjamin G. Harris, ESQ of St. Mary's County upon the Reports of the Committee on Secret Societies in the House of Delegates of Maryland*, 1856.
Holt, Joseph. *Report of the Judge Advocate General on the Order of American Knights of*

Sons of Liberty: An American Conspiracy in Aid of the Southern Rebellion. Washington, D.C.: GPO, 1864.
Jacobs, Curtis. *The Free Negro Question in Maryland: Slavery and free negroism incompatible ... able letter of C.W. Jacobs on this all absorbing question*. Baltimore, 1859.
Proceedings of the State Convention of Maryland to Frame a New Constitution, Commenced at Annapolis, April 27, 1864. Annapolis: Richard P. Bayly, printer, 1864.
War Department. *The Trial of Hon. Clement L. Vallandigham by a Military Commission and the Proceedings Under his Application For a Writ of Habeas Corpus In the Circuit Court of the United States For the Southern District of Ohio*. Cincinnati: Rickey & Carroll, 1863.

Newspapers

Annapolis Gazette
Baltimore Sun
Catoctin (MD) *Clarion*
Chicago Tribune
Cleveland Leader
Easton Gazette
Gallipolis Journal
National Republican

New York Times
Philadelphia Inquirer
Port Tobacco Times
Saint Mary's Beacon / Gazette
The Tri Weekly News
Voice of Freedom
Washington Post
Washington Star

Primary Sources

Allen, Mary Bernard. *Joseph Holt, Judge Advocate General (1862–1875): A Study in the Treatment of Political Prisoners by the United States Government During the Civil War*. Ph.D. diss., University of Chicago, 1927.
Allen, T.R.S. *Constitutional Justice: A Liberal Theory on the Rule of Law* New York: Oxford University Press, 2003.
Arenson, Adam. "Dred Scott versus the Dred Scott Case: The History and Memory of a Signal Moment in American History." In David Thomas Konig, Paul Finkelman, and Christopher Alan Bracey, ed., *The Dred Scott Case: Historical and Contemporary Perspectives on Race and Law*. Athens: Ohio University Press, 2010.
Auchampaugh, Philip. "James Buchanan, the Court, and the Dred Scott Case." *Tennessee Historical Magazine* 231 (1929).
Baker, Jean M. *Affairs of Party: The Political Culture of Northern Democrats in the Mid Nineteenth Century*. New York: Fordham University Press, 1998.
_____. *Ambivalent Americans: The Know Nothing Party in Maryland*. Baltimore: Johns Hopkins University Press, 1977.
Barnes, Richard H. *The Fortieth Congress of the United States: Historical and Biographical, Vol. II*. New York: George Perrine, 1870.
Bauer, Karl J. *The Mexican War, 1846–1848*. Lincoln: University of Nebraska Press, 1976.
Beeman, Richard. *The Old Dominion and the New Nation*. Lexington: University Press of Kentucky, 1972.
Berlin, Ira, and Stephen F. Miller, eds. *The Wartime Genesis of Free Labor: The Upper South, a Documentary History of Emancipation, Vol. 2*. New York: Cambridge University Press, 1999.
Bierman, John. *Napoleon III and His Carnival Empire*. New York: St. Martin's Press, 1988.
Blaine, James G. *Twenty Years of Congress: From Lincoln to Garfield With a Review of the Events Which led to the Political Revolution of 1860, Vol. I*. Norwich, CT: Henry Bill Publishers, 1884.
Blair, William A. *With Malice Toward Some: Treason and Loyalty in the Civil War Era*. Chapel Hill: University of North Carolina Press, 2014.

Bogue, Allen. *The Congressman's Civil War.* New York: Cambridge University Press, 1989.
Bond, Carol T., ed. *Proceedings of the Maryland Court of Appeals.* Washington, D.C.: American Historical Society, 1933.
Bowers, Douglas. "Ideology and Political Parties, 1851–1856." *Maryland Historical Magazine* (Fall 1969).
Bracey, Christopher, ed. T*he Dred Scott Case: Historical and Contemporary Perspectives on Race and Law.* Athens: Ohio University Press, 2010.
Brigance, William Norwood. *Jeremiah Sullivan Black: Defender of the Constitution and the Ten Commandments.* Philadelphia: University of Pennsylvania Press, 1934.
Brauer, Kinley J. *Cotton versus Conscience: Massachusetts Whig Politics and Southwestern Expansion.* Lexington: University of Kentucky Press, 1967.
Burlingame, Michael F. *Abraham Lincoln, A Life Vol. II.* Baltimore: Johns Hopkins University Press, 2008.
Burton, Harold Hitz. "Two Significant Decisions: Ex Parte Milligan and Ex Parte McCardle." *American Bar Association Journal* 41 (February 1955).
Callcott, Margaret Law. *The Negro in American Politics.* Baltimore: Johns Hopkins University Press, 1969.
Calvert, Eugenia. "Miniatures in the Collection of the Maryland Historical Society." *Maryland Historical Magazine* 4 (December 1956).
Carnahan, Burris. *Act of Justice: Lincoln's Emancipation Proclamation and the Law of War.* Lexington: University of Kentucky Press, 2007.
Channing, Stephen A. *Crisis of Fear: Secession in South Carolina.* New York: W.W. Norton, 1974.
Chipman, Norton P. *The Tragedy of Andersonville: Trial of Captain Henry Wirz, the Prison Keeper.* San Francisco, 1911.
Cole, Donald P. *Martin van Buren and the American Political System*, Princeton: Princeton University, 1984.
Cone, William Russell. *Memorial of the Class of 1830 of Yale College.* Hartford, CT: Case, Lockwood, and Brainard, 1871.
Conroy, James B. *Our One Common Country: Abraham Lincoln and the Hampton Roads Peace Conference on 1865.* Guilford, CT: Lyons Press, 2014
Cowden, Joanna D. *"Heaven Will Frown on Such a Cause as This": Six Democrats Who Opposed Lincoln's War.* Lanham, MD: University Press of America, 2001.
Crofts, Daniel. *Lincoln and the Politics of Slavery: The Thirteenth Amendment and the Struggle to Save the Union.* Chapel Hill: University of North Carolina Press, 2015.
Dorris, Jonathan T. *Pardon and Amnesty Under Lincoln and Johnston: The Restoration of the Confederates to Their Rights and Privileges.* Chapel Hill: University of North Carolina Press, 1954.
Douglas, William O. *An Almanac of Liberty.* New York: Doubleday, 1954.
Eicher, John, and David J. Eicher. *Civil War High Commands.* Palo Alto: Stanford University Press, 2001.
The 1850 Census of Saint Mary's County, Maryland. Saint Mary's Country: Genealogical Committee of the St. Mary's Historical Society, 1978.
Elkins, Stanley, and Eric McKittrick. *The Age of Federalism: The Early American Republic, 1788–1800.* New York: Oxford University Press, 1993.
Ely, James, Jr. *The Chief Justiceship of Melville W. Fuller, 1888–1910.* Columbia: University of South Carolina Press, 1995.
Etchison, Nicole. *Bleeding Kansas: Contested Liberty in the Civil War Era.* Lawrence: University of Kansas Press, 2004.
Everstine, Carl. *The General Assembly of Maryland, 1850–1920.* New York: Michie, 1980.
Evitts, William J. *A Matter of Allegiences: Maryland from 1850 to 1861.* Baltimore: Johns Hopkins University Press, 1974.
Ewing, K.D., and C.A. Gearty. *The Struggle for Civil Liberties: Political Freedom and the Rule of Law in Britain.* Oxford: Oxford University Press, 2000.

Fehrenbacher, Donald. *The Dred Scott Case: Its Significance in American Law and Politics.* New York: Oxford University Press, 1978.
Fields, Barbara Jeanne. *Slavery and Freedom on the Middle Ground: Maryland During the Nineteenth Century.* New Haven: Yale University Press, 1972.
Finkelman Paul. "Prigg v. Pennsylvania and Northern State Courts: Anti-Slavery Use of a Pro-Slavery Decision." In John R. McKivigan, *Abolitionism and American Law.* New York: Garland, 1999.
_____. "State Constitutional Protections of Liberty and the Antebellum New Jersey Supreme Court: Chief Justice Hornblower and the Fugitive Slave Law." *Rutgers Law Review* 23 (1992).
Fisher, Louis. *The War Power: Original and Contemporary.* Washington, D.C.: American Historical Association, 2009.
Floyd, Claudia. *Maryland Women in the Civil War: Unionists, Rebels, and Spies.* Charleston, SC: The History Press, 2013.
Forbes, Robert. *The Missouri Compromise and its Aftermath: Slavery and the Meaning of America.* Chapel Hill: University of North Carolina Press, 2007.
Frankfurter, Felix. *The Case of Sacco and Vanzetti: A Critical Analysis for Lawyers and Laymen.* Boston: Little, Brown, 1927.
Freehling, William M. *The Road to Disunion: Vol. II, Secessionists Triumphant, 1854–1861.* New York: Oxford University Press, 2007.
Friedman, Lawrence. *Law in America, A Short History.* New York: Random House, 2002.
Fuke, Richard P. *Imperfect Equality: African Americans and the Confines of White Racial.* New York: Fordham University Press, 1999.
Futch, Ovid. *History of the Andersonville Prison.* Gainesville: University of Florida Press, 1968.
Garner, James Wilfred. *International Law and the World War, Vol. II.* London: Longman, Greens, 1920.
Gray, Wood. *The Hidden Civil War: The Story of the Copperheads.* New York: Viking, 1942.
Green, Michael S. *Politics and America in Crisis: The Coming of the Civil War.* Santa Barbara: ABC-CLIO, 2010.
Greenberg, Amy S. *A Wicked War: Polk, Clay, Lincoln and the 1846 U.S. Invasion of Mexico.* New York: Vintage, 2012.
Gregory, Anthony. *The Power of Habeas Corpus in America: From the King's Prerogative to the War on Terror.* New York: Cambridge University Press, 2013.
Guezlo, Alan. *Fateful Lightning: A New History of the Civil War and Reconstruction.* New York: Oxford University Press, 2012.
Hall, Clayton Coleman. *Baltimore: Its History and Its People, Vol. I.* New York: Lewis Historical Publishing Co., 1912.
Hallett, Briene. *Declaring War: Congress, the President, and What the Constitution Does Not Say.* New York: Cambridge University Press, 2012.
Hammett, Roger Combs. *History of Saint Mary's County, MD: 1834–1900.* Baltimore: Ridge Press, 2000.
Harrison, Lowell Hayes. *Kentucky's Governors.* Lexington: University of Kentucky Press, 2004.
Haynes, James, and Harvey Klehr. *Early Cold War Spies.* New York: Cambridge University Press, 2006.
Haynes, Sam W. *James K. Polk and the Expansionist Impulse.* New York: Longmans Press, 1997.
Higginbotham, Sanford W. *The Keystone in the Democratic Arch: Pennsylvania Politics, 1800–1816.* Harrisburg: Pennsylvania State University Press, 1956.
Hoffer, William James. *The Caning of Charles Sumner: Honor, Idealism, and the Origins of the Civil War.* Baltimore: Johns Hopkins University Press, 2010.

Holt, Michael F. *The Fate of Their Country: Politicians, Slavery Extension, and the Coming of the Civil War*. New York: Hill and Wang, 2005.
____. *The Rise and Fall of the American Whig Party: Jacksonian Politics and the Onset of the Civil War*. New York: Oxford University Press, 1999.
Hunt, Henry Thomas. *The Case of Thomas J. Mooney and Warren K. Billings*. New York: Da Capo Press, 1927, reprint, 1971.
Inbody, Donald S. *The Soldier Vote: War, Politics, and the Ballot in America*. New York: Palgrave Macmillan, 2014.
Jordan, David M. *Winfield Scott Hancock: A Soldier's Life*. Bloomington: Indiana University Press, 1988.
Kastenberg, Joshua E. *The Blackstone of Military Law, Colonel William Winthrop*. Lanham, MD: Scarecrow Press, 2009.
____. *Law in War, Law as War: Brigadier General Joseph Holt and the Judge Advocate General's Department in the Civil War and Reconstruction*. Durham: Carolina Academic Press, 2011.
____. "A Sesquicentennial Historic Analysis of Dynes v. Hoover and the Supreme Court's Bow to Military Necessity." *University of Memphis Law Review* 39 (2009).
____. *Shaping U.S. Military Law: Governing a Constitutional Military*. Farnham: Ashgate Press, 2014.
Keehn, David C. *Knights of the Golden Circle: Secret Empire, Southern Secession, Civil War*. Baton Rouge: Louisiana State University Press, 2013.
Kleber, Joan E. *The Kentucky Encyclopedia*. Lexington: University of Kentucky Press, 1992.
Klement, Frank. *Dark Lanterns: Secret Political Societies, Conspiracies, and Treason Trials in the Civil War*. Baton Rouge: Louisiana State University Press, 1984.
____. *Lincoln's Critics: The Copperheads of the North*. New York: White Mane Publishing, 1998.
____. *The Limits of Dissent: Clement L. Vallandigham and the Civil War*. Lexington: University of Kentucky Press, 1970.
Langbein, John H. "Blackstone, Litchfield, and Yale: The Founding of Yale's Law School." In Anthony T. Kronman, ed., *History of the Yale Law School: The Tercentennial Lectures*. New Haven: Yale University Press, 2004.
Lanman, Charles. *Dictionary of the United States Congress: Compiled as a Manual of Reference*. Washington, D.C.: GPO, 1864.
Larson, Kate Clifford. *The Assassin's Accomplice: Mary Surratt and the Plot to Kill Abraham Lincoln*. New York: Basic Books, 2008.
Lee, Jean Butenhoff. *The Price of Nationhood: The American Revolution in Charles County*. New York: W.W. Norton, 1994.
Leonard, Ira, and Robert Parmet. *American Nativism, 1830–1860*. New York: Van Nostrand Reinhold, 1971.
Loker, Adam. *A Most Convenient Place: Leonardtown, Maryland, 1650–1950*. Leonardtown, MD: Solitude Press, 2001.
Longacre, Edward G. *General Ulysses S. Grant: The Soldier and the Man*. New York: Da Capo Press, 2006.
Lurie, Jonathan. *Arming Military Justice: The Origins of the United States Court of Military Appeals, 1775–1950*. Princeton: Princeton University Press, 1992.
Mach, Thomas. *"Gentleman George" Hunt Pendleton: Party Politics and Ideological Identity in Late Nineteenth Century America*, Kent, OH: Kent State University Press, 2007.
Magliocca, Gerard. *American Founding Son: John Bingham and the Invention of the Fourteenth Amendment*. New York: New York University Press, 2013.
Magruder, Caleb Clarke, Jr. *Thomas George Pratt, Governor of Maryland, 1845–1848; United States Senator, 1850–1857*. Baltimore: Waverley Press, 1913.
March, Thomas R. *"Gentleman George" Hunt Pendleton: Party Politics and Ideological Identity in Nineteenth Century America*. Kent, OH: Kent State University Press, 2007.

Marshall, Thomas. *Recollections of Thomas R. Marshall*. Indianapolis: Bobbs-Merrill, 1925.
Marvel, William. *Lincoln's Autocrat: The Life of Edwin Stanton*. Chapel Hill: University of North Carolina Press, 2015.
_____. *Mr. Lincoln Goes to War*. Boston: Houghton Mifflin 2006.
McConville, Mary St. Patrick. *Political Nativism in the State of Maryland, 1830–1860*. Washington, D.C.: Catholic University of America, 1928.
McFeeley, William S. *Grant: A Biography*. New York: W.W. Norton, 2002.
McGinty, Brian. *The Body of John Merryman: Abraham Lincoln and the Suspension of Habeas Corpus*. Cambridge: Harvard University Press, 2011.
_____. *Lincoln and the Court*. Cambridge: Harvard University Press, 2008.
McPherson, James M. *Battle Cry of Freedom*. New York: Oxford University Press, 1988.
Miles, Nathan A., Miles M. Monday, and Ryan J. Quick. *Prince George's County and the Civil War: Life on the Border*. Charleston, SC: The History Press, 2013.
Miller, Richard F. *States at War, Vol. IV A Reference Guide for Maryland, Delaware, and New Jersey*. Hanover, NH: University Press of New England, 2015.
Millis, Walter. *Arms and Men: A Study in American Military History*. New York: G.P. Putnam and Sons, 1956.
Mitchell, Charles W., ed. *Maryland Voices of the Civil War*. Baltimore: Johns Hopkins University Press, 2007.
Mitchell, Stewart. *Horatio Seymour of New York*. Boston: Harvard University Press, 1938.
Mitchell, Thomas G, *Anti-Slavery Politics in Antebellum and Civil War America*. Westport CT: Praeger, 2007.
Monroe, Dan, and Bruce Tap. *Shapers of the Great Debate on the Civil War: A Biographical Dictionary*. Westport, CT: Greenwood Press, 2005.
Montgomery, Daniel. *Beyond Equality: Labor and the Radical Republicans, 1862–1872*. Urbana: University of Illinois Press, 1967.
Morris, Jeffrey Brandon. *Calmly to Pose the Scales of Justice: A History of the Courts of the District of Columbia Circuit*. Durham: Carolina Academic Press, 2001.
Morris, Thomas D. *Free Men All: Personal Liberty Laws of the North, 1780–1860*. Baltimore: Johns Hopkins University Press, 1974.
Mott, Frank Luther. *American Journalism: A History, 1690–1960*. New York: Macmillan, 1962.
Mushkat, Jerome. *Fernando Wood: A Political Biography*. Kent, OH: Kent State University Press, 1990.
Myers, William Starr. *The Self Reconstruction of Maryland, 1864–1867*. Baltimore: Johns Hopkins University Press, 1909.
Neeley, Mark. *The Fate of Liberty: Abraham Lincoln and Civil Liberties*. New York: Oxford University Press, 1992.
Nevins, Alan. *Ordeal of the Union: The Organized War for Victory, Vol. IV*. New York: Charles Scribner's Sons, 1971.
Newman, Harry White. *Maryland and the Confederacy*. Annapolis: Harry Wright Newman, 1976.
Newmeyer, R. Kent. *The Supreme Court under Marshall and Taney*. New York: Crowell Press, 1968.
Oakes, James. *Freedom National: The Destruction of Slavery in the United States, 1861–1865*. New York: W.W. Norton, 2013.
Paludan, Phillip Shaw. *A People's Contest: The Union and the Civil War, 1861–1865*. Lawrence: University Press of Kansas, 1996.
Parsons, Lynn Hudson. *The Birth of Modern Politics: Andrew Jackson, John Quincy Adams, and the Election of 1828*. New York: Oxford University Press, 2009.
Patterson, Benton Rain. *Ending the Civil War: The Bloody Year from Grant's Promotion to Lincoln's Assassination*. Jefferson, NC: McFarland, 2012.
Peskin, Alan. *Garfield*. Kent, OH: Kent State University Press, 1968.

Phillips, Christopher. *The Civil War in the Border South.* Santa Barbara: ABC-CLIO, 2013.
____. *Freedom's Port: The African American Community of Baltimore, 1790–1860.* Urbana: University of Illinois Press, 1997.
Poole, Keith T., and Howard Rosenthal. *A Political-Economic History of Roll Call Voting.* New York: Oxford University Press, 1997.
Potter, David M. *The Impending Crisis, 1848–1861* New York: HarperCollins, 1976.
Radcliffe, George L. P. *Governor Thomas H. Hicks of Maryland and the Civil War.* Baltimore: Johns Hopkins University Press, 1901.
Ransom, Roger. *Conflict and Compromise: The Political Economy of Slavery, Emancipation, and the American Civil War.* New York: Cambridge University Press, 1989.
Rehnquist, William Hubbs. *All the Laws But One.* New York: Alfred Knopf, 1998.
Remini, Robert. *Daniel Webster, The Man and His Times.* New York: W.W. Norton, 1997.
____. *Henry Clay, Statesman for the Union.* New York: W.W. Norton, 1991.
____. *The House: A History of the House of Representatives.* New York: Harper, 200.
Richardson, Henry D. *Sidelights on Maryland's History With Sketches of Early Maryland Families.* Baltimore: Williams and Wilkins Co., 1903.
Ridgely, Helen West. *Historic Graves of Maryland and the District of Columbia: With the Inscriptions Appearing on the Tombstones in Most of the Counties of the States and in Washington.* New York: Grafton, 1908.
Roberts-Miller, Patricia, *Fanatical Schemes: Proslavery Rhetoric and the Tragedy of Consensus,* Tuscaloosa: University of Alabama Press, 2009.
Rodriguez Junius, ed. *Encyclopedia of Slave Resistance and Rebellion.* Westport, CT: Greenwood Press, 2007.
Ruffner, Kevin Conley. *Maryland's Blue and Gray: A Border State's Union and Confederate Junior Officer Corps.* Baton Rouge: Louisiana State University Press, 1997.
Ruhlman, Fred. *Captain Henry Wirz and Andersonville: A Reappraisal.* Knoxville: University of Tennessee, 2006.
Schroeder-Lein, Glenda R., and Richard Zuczek. *Andrew Johnson: A Biographical Companion.* Santa-Barbara: ABA-CLIO, 2001.
Scott, Robert. *Forgotten Valor: The Memoirs, Journals, and Civil War Letters of Orlando B. Willcox.* Kent, OH: Kent State University Press, 1999.
Sears, Stephenn, ed.,*The Civil War Papers of George B. McClellan.* New York: Da Capo Press, 1989.
Sharlitt, Joseph. *Fatal Error: The Miscarriage of Justice that Sealed the Rosenberg's Fate.* New York: Scribner's, 1989.
Silver, David. *Lincoln's Supreme Court.* Urbana: University of Illinois Press, 1956.
Simon, James F. *Lincoln and Chief Justice Taney: Slavery, Secession, and the President's War Powers.* New York: Simon & Schuster, 2007.
Slaughter, Thomas P. *The Whiskey Rebellion: Frontier Epilogue to the American Revolution.* New York: Oxford University Press, 1986.
Smith, Adam I. P. *No Party Now: Politics in the Civil War North.* New York: Oxford University Press, 2006.
Smith, Ronald D. *Thomas Ewing, Jr., Frontier Lawyer and Civil War General.* Columbia: University of Missouri Press, 2006.
Smith, Willard H. *Schuyler Colfax: The Changing Fortunes of a Political Idol.* Indianapolis: Indiana Historical Bureau, 1952.
Smith, William Henry. *History of the Cabinet of the United States of America, from President Washington to President Coolidge.* New York: Gale Learning, 1925.
Stathis, Stephen W. *Landmark Debates in Congress: From the Declaration of Independence to the War in Iraq.* Washington, D.C.: CQ Press, 2009.
Steel, Brian. *Thomas Jefferson and American Nationhood.* New York: Cambridge University Press, 2012.

Steers, Edward. *Blood on the Moon: The Assassination of Abraham Lincoln.* Lexington: University of Kentucky Press, 2001.
_____. "General Conspiracy." In *The Trial: The Assassination of President Lincoln and the Trial of the Conspirators.* Lexington: University of Kentucky Press, 2003.
Steiner, Bernard C. *The Institutions and Civil Government of Maryland.* Boston: Ginn and Co, 1899.
_____. *Life of Reverdy Johnson.* New York: Russell & Russell, 1970.
Stevenson, Charles A. *Warriors and Politicians: U.S. Civil-Military Relations Under Stress.* New York: Routledge, 2006.
Stuart, Reginald C. *Civil Military Relations During the War of 1812.* Santa Barbara: Greenwood Press, 2009.
Taafe, Stephen R. *Commanding the Army of the Potomac.* Lawrence: University of Kansas Press, 2006.
Taft, William Howard. *Our Chief Magistrate and His Powers.* New York: Columbia University Press, 1925.
Thomas, George C. *The Supreme Court on Trial: How the American Justice System Sacrifices Innocent Defendants.* Ann Arbor: University of Michigan Press, 2008.
Towers, Frank. *The Urban South and the Coming of the Civil War.* Charlottesville: University of Virginia Press, 2004.
Treffouse, Hans. *Thaddeus Stevens: Nineteenth Century Egalitarian.* Chapel Hill: University of North Carolina Press, 1997.
Urofsky, Melvin. *Division and Discord: The Supreme Court Under Stone and Vinson.* Columbia: University of South Carolina Press, 1997.
Vorenberg, Michael. *The Final Freedom: The Civil War and the Abolition of Slavery and the Fifteenth Amendment.* New York: Cambridge University Press, 2001.
Wagandt, Charles Lewis. *The Mighty Revolution: Negro Emancipation in Maryland, 1862–1864.* Baltimore: Johns Hopkins University Press, 1964.
Wait, Eugene M. *The Opening of the Civil War.* Commack, NY: Nova Science Publishers, 1999.
Warner, Ezra. *Generals in Blue.* Baton Rouge: Louisiana State University Press, 1964.
Watson, Bruce. *Sacco and Vanzetti: The Men, the Murders, and the Judgement of Mankind.* New York: Viking, 2007.
Waugh, Jack. *Reelecting Lincoln: The Battle for the 1864 Presidency.* New York: Crown, 1997.
Weitz, Mark A. *The Confederacy on Trial: The Piracy and Sequestration Cases of 1861.* Lawrence: Kansas University Press, 2005.
White, G. Edward. *Law in American History: Vol. I, the Colonial Years through the Civil War.* New York: Oxford University Press, 2012.
White, Jonathan W. *Abraham Lincoln and Treason in the Civil War: The Trials of John Merryman.* Baton Rouge: Louisiana State University Press, 2011.
_____. *Emancipation, the Union Army, and the Reelection of Abraham Lincoln.* Baton Rouge: Louisiana State University Press, 2014.
_____. "Sweltering with Treason: The Civil War Trials of William Matthew Merrick." *Prologue* 39 (Summer 2007).
Wilentz, Sean. *The Rise of American Democracy: Jefferson to Lincoln.* New York: W.W. Norton, 2005.
Willis, John T., and Herbert C. Smith. *Maryland Politics and Government: Democratic Dominance.* Lincoln: University of Nebraska Press, 2012.
Witt, John Fabian. *Lincoln's Code: The Laws of War in American History.* New York: The Free Press, 2012.
Wood, Forrest G. *Black Scare: The Racist Response to Emancipation and Reconstruction.* Los Angeles: University of California Press, 1968.
Wood, Gordon S. *Empire of Liberty: A History of the Early American Republic.* New York: Oxford University Press, 2009.

Woodworth, Steven. "John Rawlins." In David T. Zebecki, ed., *Chief of Staff: The Principal Officers Behind Histories Great Commanders*. Annapolis: Naval Institute Press, 2006.
Work, David. *Lincoln's Political Generals*. Urbana: University of Illinois Press, 2007.
Zietlow, Rebecca E. "James Ashley's Thirteenth Amendment." *Columbia Law Review* 112 (2012).

Index

Adams, John 53–4, 119
Adams, John Quincy 23, 67–69, 81; Benjamin Harris' hatred of 79, 102
Articles of War 4, 48, 128, 131, 142, 144, 146, 170

Baker, Lafayette C. 59
Baltimore 7, 29, 36, 40–41, 44, 57, 85, 96, 122, 126, 141; Convention of 1852 70; "Pratt Street Riots" 41; and re-enslavement movement 18
Baltimore and Ohio Railroad 22, 46, 47, 56, 161
Baltimore Sun 13, 22–26, 45, 134, 139, 150, 157, 161
Bates, Edward 7, 24, 45, 97
Belmont, August 112–113
Bigler, William 112, 116
Blair, Montgomery 13, 15, 34, 46, 59–60, 95, 98, 109, 131, 151
Bond, Thomas 19–20
Bradford, Augustus 85, 90, 110, 126, 148, 159
Breckenridge, John C. 23, 38–39, 53, 58, 95
Buchanan, James 38, 40, 49, 52, 59, 70–72, 95–97, 112, 153, 157
Bull Run, Battle of 1861, 57, 60–61, 133
Butler, Benjamin 40–41, 61, 85, 87, 101, 109, 116

Camalier, John 148
Carmichael, Richard B 109–111
Causin, John M.S. 17
Charlotte Hall Academy 24–25
Chase, Salmon 27, 46, 74, 88, 95, 98, 103, 154, 160–161
Cleveland, Grover 48, 154, 165
Colfax, Schuyler 1, 63, 78–79, 91, 99–100, 152–154
Confiscation Acts 81, 86–87, 93, 98–99
Court of Appeals, Maryland 20, 41; and slavery 35–38

Crain, Peter W. 140–143
Creswell, John 90, 148, 158

Davis, Jefferson 9–11, 58, 109, 123, 127, 135, 165
Davis, Henry Winter 90, 123
Democratic Party 27, 37–38, 54, 65, 70, 76, 80, 82, 96, 103; and secession 72; and slavery 27, 65; election of 1864 105–112
Dent, John F. 60, 158
Dix, Gen. John Adams 40, 47, 50–51 109–110
Douglas, Stephen A. 23, 38–39, 49, 50, 58, 70–72, 75, 78, 89; and Harris' opinion of 158
Douglas, William O. 6, 10,
Douglass, Frederick 37,
Dynes v Hoover 8, 48, 90

Ellenborough, estate 21–25, 141
Emancipation Proclamation 55, 81, 89, 98; and Harris 91
Entick v. Carrington 55–56
Ex Parte Bollman 42
Ex Parte Merryman 8–9, 44–47
Ex Parte Milligan 143, 149, 153–154, 170
Ex Parte Vallandigham 11, 130, 144

Fillmore, Millard 26, 48, 58, 72
Frankfurter, Felix 6, 15

Garfield, James 15, 99, 131, 168; and Harris 101, 164; and Milligan 153–154

Habeas Corpus 7, 9, 41; suspended by Abraham Lincoln 41–48, 74, 81, 161; suspended by Andrew Jackson 43
Harris, Benjamin and Abraham Lincoln 1, 5, 14, 38, 40, 48–50, 59, 61, 84–86, 93, 101–102, 104; ancestry 19–22; education of 24–27; and George McClellan 116–117; and Joseph Holt 94, 167; Lincoln advised to arrest Harris 105, 111, 116

Index

Harris, Joseph 19–20
Harris, Martha Elizabeth 21, 25, 39, 40, 59, 94, 125–126, 128, 141, 162, 165
Harvard University 25, 95, 129
Hicks, Thomas 7, 41, 47, 51, -52, 57, 60, 110, 148
Holt, Joseph 8–11, 94–98, 105, 107, 112, 124, 127, 129–130, 146, 149, 151, 167
House of Delegates, Maryland 17, 19–20, 25–30, 41, 50, 60; and arrest after threatened secession vote 50–52

Jackson, Andrew 23, 27, 34, 43, 55, 67, 69–70, 118
Jefferson, Thomas 42, 53, 63, 69, 115; and Virginia Resolution 5, 53, 98
Johnson, Andrew 9, 13, 15, 78, 95, 124–125; and Harris 128
Johnson, Reverdy 29, 34, 47, 49–52, 109; and Harris 131

Kane, George P. 46–47, 94
Key, Francis 21
Key, Philip Barton 20
Knights of the Golden Circle 99, 107; formed by George Bickley 107; reformed as Order of the Sons of Liberty 112
Know Nothing Party 2, 23–24, 28–31, 41, 47, 51, 65, 76

Leonardtown, Maryland 56–57, 60–63-128
Ligon, Thomas Watson 28
Lincoln, Abraham 7–15, 37–40; assassination 5; and Harris 1, 5, 14, 38, 40, 48–50, 59, 61, 84–86, 93, 101–102, 104; and suspension of Habeas Corpus 41–47
Long, Alexander 15, 98, 112–115, 118, 147, 160, 167

Madison, James 5, 69; and Kentucky Resolution 53
Manassas, First Battle of 88
Manassas, Second Battle of 6, 52, 82, 129
Marble, Manton 15, 104, 107, 129
McClellan, George Brinton 5, 50, 61, 95, 162; arrest of Maryland legislators 47; presidential candidate 106–120
Merrick, William Matthew 47–49, 160; removal from judgeship 49
Merryman, John 7–8, 44–47
Miles, Oscar 40–41, 56, 60
Milligan, Lambdin 10, 107, 143
Mudd, Samuel 121, 124, 127

Old Capitol Prison 127–128, 146, 150

Pearce, James 18, 52, 59, 109
Pendleton, George 73–74, 90, 113, 118, 161
Pierce, Franklin 26, 30, 48, 58, 63, 71, 96, 98, 109, 112, 115
Plater, George 20
Plater, John Rousby 20
Prigg v Pennsylvania 31–35, 108

Re-enslavement Movement in Maryland 17–20

Saint Mary's Beacon 37, 59, 84, 90, 141; renamed *Saint Mary's Gazette* 84, 85, 92, 120, 134
Saulsbury, Willard 85, 104, 115
Schenck, Robert 84–88, 92, 106, 161; and Harris 88, 100; and Long 100
Seward, William Henry 27, 43, 70, 88, 102, 110, 113, 124, 160
slave rebellions 27, 36; Maryland 1845 17; Nat Turner 17–18
Sothoron, James 20, 56, 88, 93, 147
Stanton, Edwin 7–13, 46, 50, 74, 88, 94–98, 105–110, 122, 128–133, 146, 149, 153, 167
Stevens, Thaddeus 1, 63, 77, 79, 91, 103, 124–125
Sumner, Charles 70, 130
Supreme Court, United States 6–12, 31–35, 39, 42, 48 , 53, 89–90, 95, 100, 122, 129–130, 143–144, 153
Surratt, Mary 9, 80, 121, 155
Swann, Thomas 87, 159

Taney, Roger Baldwin 7, 24, 30, 33–34, 39, 155, 168; Harris' efforts for a Taney presidency 46; and Merryman 44; and secession 82
Taylor, Zachary 22, 49, 58, 70, 76
Turner, Levi 94, 127, 165

Unionist Party 57–59, 73, 87, 90, 101, 104, 109, 111–112, 121

Vallandigham, Clement 7–9, 73–75, 88–90, 92, 109, 113–114, 117, 145, 148, 160, 168

Washburne, Elihu 63, 102
Whig Party 23–28; in Maryland 28–33
Winthrop, William 128–137
Wirz, Henry 9–10
Wood, Fernando 1, 15, 73, 91, 104, 163, 168

Yale University 25, 31, 95, 129

www.ingramcontent.com/pod-product-compliance
Ingram Content Group UK Ltd.
Pitfield, Milton Keynes, MK11 3LW, UK
UKHW042007140426
5217IPUK00015B/1038